T0333136

THE
ART OF
ICONIC
LEADERSHIP

POWER SECRETS OF
FEMALE WORLD LEADERS

JUSTINA MUTALE

FOREWORD BY

Baroness Sandip K. Verma
Member of The House of Lords, UK

Senator Donzella J. James
U.S. State Senator, Georgia State, USA

The Art of Iconic Leadership

First published in 2020 by

Panoma Press Ltd
48 St Vincent Drive, St Albans, Herts, AL1 5SJ, UK
info@panomapress.com
www.panomapress.com

Book layout by Neil Coe.

978-1-784529-28-4

The right of Justina Mutale to be identified as the author of this work has been asserted in accordance with sections 77 and 78 of the Copyright, Designs and Patents Act 1988.

A CIP catalogue record for this book is available from the British Library.

This book is available online and in bookstores.

DEDICATION

To my parents, Beatrice Nakawala and John Mutale,

for their pure and unconditional love, and their unwavering belief

in my potential and capabilities as a female child.

TESTIMONIALS

"Justina Mutale has presence… Her book is a source of knowledge, wisdom and life experiences about women leadership, a wisdom bible to stay on the shelf of every home on this planet."

SABINE BALVE

WORLD LEADERS FORUM DUBAI

"The Art of Iconic Leadership – Power Secrets of Female World Leaders is a resilient inspirational journey to empower the women of the world."

BRENDA MORANT

INTERNATIONAL WOMEN'S THINK TANK, USA

"This book goes beyond the dimensions of 'a basic leadership book'. It is almost irresistible not to go back and read it again and again."

AHMET SHALA

JAMES MADISON UNIVERSITY

SCHOOL OF STRATEGIC LEADERSHIP STUDIES, USA

THE LEADERSHIP FOUNDATION, KOSOVO

"An impressive book on female leadership. A masterpiece that every schoolgirl, parent and teacher must read."

FATOUMATA DIALLO

THE FD MINUTE FACTOR

"Profound insights for future women leaders. Pulling together politics, gender, economy, strategy, leadership and geo-politics in one place."

ANNA MASLON-ORACZ

WARSAW SCHOOL OF ECONOMICS, POLAND

"This book promises growth with the turn of every page. Go grab a copy."

LAMINE KONKOBO

BBC AFRICA

"We need women who are so strong they can be gentle; so educated they can be humble; so fierce they can be compassionate; so passionate they can be rational, and so disciplined they can be free."

KAVITA RAMDAS

ACKNOWLEDGEMENTS

To the God that lives within me and makes all things possible and His magnificent grace in holding my hand throughout the process of not only just writing this book but graciously leading me up the path that has constituted the entire project that is my leadership journey.

I would like to open by expressing a profound word of gratitude to my parents − to my mother, Beatrice Nakawala, for the feminine strength and fearlessness that she instilled in me. To my father, John Mutale, for instilling in me the belief that even as a female child, I could achieve just about anything that any male child could.

I express a special love and gratitude to my children, Mwice and Namwila, who taught me to be a mother, and who have graciously and loyally shared their precious time with my work and the people in my sphere. I have a special word of thanks for my daughter, Mwice, who had to endure my constant nagging to read the draft over and again, and for Namwila and Ann Marie, who had to tiptoe around me while I worked on the book, and had to be ready to be summoned on the spur of the moment to assist with grammar and punctuation.

I would also like to thank my siblings, who have played an immense role in my transformation to the person that I am today: my older sister, Anna Mutale, who has always believed in me and kept me grounded; my younger sister, Eliza, who transitioned into the spiritual realm at an early age and whose memory I have always carried with me; and my youngest sister, Bridget, who taught me to take responsibility for the younger generation.

I thank all my brothers and sisters for the love, and the experiences incident to growing up in a large family, and for teaching me patience and kindness, and how to accommodate various behaviors, attitudes, characteristics and aspirations. I also thank all the women in my family, who have defied the gender dynamics with their sheer strength and assertiveness, thereby making me believe that women are natural-born leaders and the world's most potent force for good.

To be in the valued possession of the idea for a book is one thing. To turn that idea into a book is an entirely different proposition. This book might quite possibly not have seen the light of day without the gentle, yet firm and persistent nudging of His Royal Highness Prince Yomi Garnett MD, who, as far back as five years ago, had initially suggested, based on my rich antecedents in the domain of women empowerment and gender-related issues, that I write a book of this nature. Dr. Yomi Garnett has graciously held my hand throughout the process of writing this book, from the inception of the idea and its subject matter, to assisting with the extensive research, editing of the content, refinement of language, and the deployment of his creative genius to achieve the final outcome that is this book. I express my heartfelt and sincere gratitude for his encouragement and guidance.

I express a sincere word of gratitude to Baroness Sandip K. Verma and Senator Donzella J. James for inspiring me as female role models and great women leaders, and for providing the brilliant Forewords to this book. I also thank my good friend Ahmet Shala, together with Lamine Konkobo, who endured reading the full manuscript to provide reviews and the accompanying Letters of Influence.

I would like to acknowledge and thank Nancy Spence and Rawwida Baksh and others from the Gender Section of the Commonwealth Secretariat, who introduced me to the global fight on gender equality and the empowerment of women.

I would like to thank Zarin Hainsworth and everyone at the United Kingdom's National Alliance of Women's Organisations, United Kingdom Civil Society Women's Alliance, United Nations Commission on the Status of Women, Commonwealth Women's Forum, and African Union Meetings on gender equality and the empowerment of women and girls, for keeping me up to date with emerging issues, news, information and networks in the global feminist movement.

Special thanks to Brenda Morant and her team at the International Women's Think Tank, who provided me with further push into my journey in the gender fight as spokesperson and global envoy for gender equality.

My expertise on gender issues, politics and international relations would not be so professionally and intellectually honed without having crossed paths with Diana Stirbu, Brian Tutt and Andrew Moran, who were my able and erudite lecturers at the London Metropolitan University, to whom I owe a depth of gratitude for my intellectual acumen on the issues raised in this book and elsewhere.

I also thank Eva Hansson and other Political Science lecturers at Stockholm University; and not forgetting Professor Ian Finlayson, Diplomacy and International Relations lecturer at the European School of Economics; Professor Jeffrey Sachs, The Earth Institute at Columbia University for lessons in the Age of Sustainable Development; and William Wray, London School of Philosophy and Economic Science, for allowing me to realize the power of philosophical thought.

Without the experience and support from my peers and team at the Justina Mutale Foundation and POSITIVE RUNWAY, I would not have had the justification and motivation to write this book. My special thanks go to Fatoumata Diallo, Michelle Walusimo, Manda Moyo, Chilombo Samiselo, Zipho Ntlanganiso, Mervin Azeta, Epi Mabika, Meeta Joshi, Sherry Ann Dixon, Alex Goslar, Denise O'Brien, Patricia McClendon, Mambwe Kamanga, Dwight Eubanks, Mary Chibula, Davies and Grace Chirwa, Christine Sharpe, Elio D'Anna, Ray Jackson, Honore Dusabimana, Ann Maslon, Anna Maria Rozek, Daniel Mwamba, Henry Mumbi, Chibwe Henry, Nhlanhla Shabangu, Evelyn Okoto, Rex Idaminabo, David James Egwu, Robin Marsh, Margaret Ali, Alex Goslar, Sabine Balve, and to all our partners, supporters, funders, sponsors, associates and affiliates. I also raise a hand of salute to all the female models, beauty queens, celebrities, scholarship students, interns, universities and colleges who have tirelessly worked with us on our various projects around the world.

My thanks go to all the organizations which I serve as President, Chair, Board Director, Ambassador, Patron, Consultant and Mentor, including the World Leaders Forum Dubai, Intercontinental School of Economics, Nelisa Consultancy, African Advancement Forum, Young African Leaders Forum, Liverpool Commonwealth Association, British Award for African

Development, Asia-African Chambers of Commerce, National Alliance of Women's Organizations, Universal Peace Federation, International Women's Think Tank and all the others.

To everyone I have had the chance to lead, be led by or simply observe from a distance, I would like to thank you for being the overall inspiration for this book. To each and every one of the great women world leaders featured in this book, I thank you for inspiring my leadership journey and giving me the confidence that it is possible to be a leader.

To every critic out there, I thank you for highlighting the inadequacies and bumps in my personal journey. You made me refine my "game" as it were, and I will forever treasure your inputs.

To every young girl in Zambia, Africa and the rest of the world, I say, "*It Is Possible for you to Lead!*"

Justina Mutale
London, UK
September 2020

FOREWORD

BARONESS SANDIP K. VERMA

I sincerely feel privileged to have been asked by the author, Justina Mutale, to write the Foreword to this commendable and outstanding literary effort. This book on female leadership, *The Art Of Iconic Leadership – Power Secrets of Female World Leaders*, is both timely and apt at a time where issues of gender equality and empowerment are now threaded into every conversation in international discourse. It is equally a remarkable feat on the author's part that this book is probably the first of its kind in its bold attempt to present a compendium of women who have broken the glass ceiling of the "Great Hall of Leadership" that had hitherto been dominated by men from time immemorial. The author has succeeded in presenting us with an extraordinary compilation of great female leaders who continue to traverse our world confidently and with humility.

Justina Mutale has the unassailable credentials that give her the authority to produce a book of this quality and content. In both consistently advocating for gender equality and women's empowerment, and promoting women's political participation and their economic empowerment, the author has won global acclaim as one of the most influential women of African origin, having in 2012 been named African Woman of the Year, sharing a platform with various African heads of state. A winner of numerous other international honors, awards and accolades across the globe, she has been honored on various platforms for her strong and outstanding leadership. She received numerous accolades for the World Book of Greatness in 2020, a pivotal moment for Justina.

Founder and President of the Justina Mutale Foundation and its Scholarship Program for young women and girls from Africa to access higher education across the globe, Justina is co-author of the highly cerebral book *Women on Corporate Boards: An International Perspective* and several other publications on women's leadership. She serves as Global

Envoy for Gender Equality and Spokesperson of the International Women's Think Tank and is Vice-President of the United Kingdom's National Alliance of Women's Organisations.

Justina has been a dedicated delegate, speaker and parallel event convener at the United Nations Commission on the Status of Women, the African Union High Level Panel on Gender Equality and the Empowerment of Women and Girls, held in the wings of the African Union Heads of State Summit, and the Commonwealth Women's Forum held in the wings of the Commonwealth Heads of State Summit alongside numerous forums held around the world that address gender equality and the empowerment of women and girls.

The entry of this book into the global literary market is both welcome and necessary. As of March 2018, there were only 20 female world leaders serving as head of state or head of government, representing a mere 6.3% of the total number of global leaders out of a total of 193 member states of the United Nations. Despite widespread acknowledgement that women form half of the world's population, and despite accelerated effort at numerous initiatives and affirmative actions aimed at gender equality, the number of women in political participation lags well below 50% in most countries.

As the world proceeds with the United Nations Agenda 2030 Global Goals for Sustainable Development, which ambitiously aspires to the achievement of a 50/50 planet by the year 2030, the author employs this ambitious ground-breaking book to highlight core leadership lessons from past and current women world leaders. The book aims at encouraging women and girls across the world to draw pertinent lessons from the inspiring stories of these phenomenal women.

This book should form an integral part of intellectual research, critical thinking and innovative solutions on issues that shine a light as to the barriers and benefits of women's participation in political leadership roles. I believe that this book will provide everyone with inspiration to learn from the trajectories of those extraordinary women who have embarked on their leadership journey. It is my hope that the leadership accounts in the book will motivate more women into political leadership, to become instrumental players on the political landscape and be integral in driving the world's social, economic and political agenda.

I wish Justina Mutale huge success for this book as it plays its part in an enduring legacy to inspire women and girls this century and beyond. It will certainly support everyone seeking knowledge and wisdom in essential leadership skills, tools and information. I urge all aspiring female political and business leaders to use this book as a valuable resource, as a tool for intellectual enrichment by applying to their own lives the stories, lessons, experiences, best practices and wisdom of the women leaders featured in this book.

Happy reading!

Baroness Sandip K. Verma
Member of The House of Lords
Chair, UN Women, UK
London, United Kingdom

FOREWORD

SENATOR DONZELLA J. JAMES

The Art of Iconic Leadership – Power Secrets of Female World Leaders details the remarkable achievements of several women who have demonstrated transformation in themselves and in the lives of others through courage, compassion and committed leadership. One of the greatest barriers to female leadership is institutionalized gender discrimination, which is reflected in a chronic failure to adjust the male work model to include the needs of women. Over the years, women's potential contributions to politics and economic advancement have been marginalized by a system that discriminates against them, limiting their full potential.

This book is making a timely debut at a significant moment in world history. This is, without an iota of doubt, a time in which issues of gender parity, and the empowerment of women, are taking their pride of place in global discourse. At a time in which female leaders are emerging as a formidable force to reckon with on the global political landscape, it is also becoming patently obvious that women do have the power to lead the world and mold it for better outcomes in the affairs of mankind.

For instance, the year 2020 is easily one in which women have decisively proved that when it comes to governance and leadership, their efforts cannot be discounted or underestimated. We now know that those countries that are led by women are the ones that have proved the far greater mettle in their response to the scourge that is COVID-19, the devastating disease caused by the novel coronavirus that has resulted in what is arguably one of the worst pandemics in global history for an entire century.

Thus, the world needs to invest in creating more opportunities for females to achieve leadership positions. Studies have shown that countries that have a higher number of women participating in the labor market also enjoy a greater degree of poverty reduction. To invest in women leadership is to catalyze economic growth. Additionally, women need to become increasingly more involved in governance in our global community. Women need to rise up, and start utilizing their talents, strengths and wisdom to inspire change, and to lead humanity as a whole to a future of gender equality in order to attain human prosperity and progress for all. To achieve this feat, women will need to be more assertive, and contribute to social, economic and political activity on an equal footing with their male counterparts.

It is my sincere hope that this book will inspire and motivate new generations of women across the globe to make our world a kinder and fairer place. Additionally, I hope that it encourages more women to venture into political leadership, becoming an integral part of the world's social, economic and political agenda. I encourage readers to use this book as a valuable resource for research on issues related to the participation of women in political leadership. In praying that this book will constitute a significant part of the arsenal of information that will inspire women and girls in the 21st century and beyond, I urge aspiring female political leaders to genuinely explore all the possibilities in applying to their own lives the experiences and wisdom of the women leaders that grace the pages of this book.

Happy reading!

Senator Donzella J. James
Senate of the State of Georgia
Atlanta, Georgia, USA

LETTERS OF INFLUENCE

In this remarkable ground-breaking book on female leadership, the author intellectually celebrates the emerging power of female world leaders on the global political landscape.

Drawing richly from an early background of strong feminine influence that shaped her belief that women are the backbone of society and the world's most potent force, Justina Mutale submits that women also have the power to lead the world and mold it for better outcomes in the evolution of mankind. She drives home the valid point that women are such natural-born leaders because of a strong sense of community which they cultivate by engaging at a very emotional level with their community in all they are able to do within the narrow corridors of opportunity that are available to them in a male-dominated society. To that end, she chronicles the remarkable achievements of a few brilliant women leaders that have employed mostly soft leadership skills to unleash remarkable transformation in their own lives and those of others, using the instrumentality of sheer industry, uncommon courage, unrivaled compassion and indomitability of spirit.

Essentially, this book aims to inspire and motivate a new generation of women all over the world through the stories of these iconic leaders who have made the world a kinder and fairer place with their brilliant personalities, ideas, and achievements.

Prince Yomi Garnett
Royal Biographical Institute, USA

I met Justina Mutale a few years ago at an international conference in Europe. At the very first conversation with her, I noticed and observed some unique leadership traits, attributes and characteristics of her that are typical traits of a unique (woman) leader.

When I read her book, nothing surprised me. The book reflects her living leadership style and character. It is a very well-structured book, easy to read, and simple. But still, deep, refreshing and rich. This book goes beyond the dimensions of "a basic leadership book."

The structure and content of the book, with a light and well-synchronized language, with practical advice and suggestions, keeps you, until the very last letter, insatiable, thirsty and breathless to absorb and understand the art and the essence of leadership and its secrets.

At the end of reading, it is almost irresistible not to go back and read it again and again, at least some certain parts of it.

Therefore, I invite you not only to read it but also to adopt and practice the messages of this amazing book. I am confident that within a short period of time you will notice a significant change in your life and career!

Ahmet Shala
James Madison University
School of Strategic Leadership Studies, USA
& The Leadership Foundation, Kosovo

This is a book on women empowerment, written by an authority on the very subject matter. In a luminous prose, and with utter clarity of voice, Justina Mutale dutifully weaves a tribute to great women, who have blazed quite some trails and, all along the way, she sends this overriding message to female minds across the world: If they were able to break through the glass ceiling, you can too.

The book promises growth with the turn of every page. Go grab your copy.

Lamine Konkobo
Broadcaster, BBC Africa

PREFACE

WOMEN: THE BACKBONE OF HUMANITY

"Nothing, arguably, is as important today in
the political economy of development as an
adequate recognition of political, economic and
social participation and leadership of women."

AMARTYA SEN

Women constitute our planet's most potent force. No human being can live without a spinal column. That is why one of the most devastating consequences of an accident is for one's spine to be broken. It leads to instant paralysis. The spine functions to protect the spinal cord and the body's internal organs, and to provide structural support and balance for the maintenance of an upright posture. That is why the spine is also called the backbone of the human body.

Women are natural-born leaders of their communities, and that is why, based on any known or acknowledged empirical and intellectual indices, women will have to qualify as the backbone of society. That is also why to unleash the exceedingly powerful matriarchal potential of women is to provide the vital key to many of the critical issues facing the world and humanity today. Such issues include the tragically sustained degradation of our environment, rising poverty levels, escalating wars and violence, global terrorism, social and economic injustice and inequality.

I have always had a very special relationship with, and sustained an enduring vested interest in, the subject of women's empowerment on social, political and economic fronts. That is hardly surprising. I come from a background of strong, powerful and assertive women; women who have defied patriarchal norms for many centuries. On the maternal side of my family, a woman rules the kingdom, and although a man rules the kingdom on the paternal side, this did not deter a single woman from rising to start a movement some people simply called a church but which many others characterized as an army. Yet, a host of many others reverently dubbed it a political party. Nonetheless, this extraordinary woman singlehandedly managed to cultivate a massive following that shook the political foundations of my county of birth, Zambia.

To underscore my point, while it is only in recent years that women in other parts of the world started retaining their maiden names after marriage, as part of the dividends of acknowledged gender parity and fundamental rights, since time immemorial women on my matrilineal line have always retained their maiden names, and never ever assumed the name of their husbands. In fact, women on my matrilineal line, having been given their own feminine second names right from birth, never had to take up their father's name either! Even more empowering for women from my background is the fact that in some parts of Africa, although a man rules the kingdom, heirs to the throne are selected from the king's sister's children, and not from among the king's own children. The rationale for this peculiar practice is that the relationship of the children of the king's sister to the monarch can never be a subject for dispute, while there are often sufficient grounds to cast some measure of suspicion on the authenticity of the paternity of a male's supposed offspring. I have always found this primeval tradition a true demonstration of the potent power and irrefutable influence of a woman.

Despite the fact that I come from a background of women who have been sufficiently assertive in the context of gender dynamics, I have not allowed myself to be lulled into any degree of complacence. I am only too sensitive to the fact that women in every nook and cranny of the globe, including in my own country Zambia, have always found themselves embroiled in an interminable fight regarding their rightful place in society. Thankfully, we seemingly are now in an era in which attitudes and behavior toward women continue to witness tremendous changes for the commendable.

In recent years, gender dynamics have evolved to a defining point for the role and perception of women in society. Yet, while it is inspiring that the movement for women's equality has garnered many positive gains over the years, it is also evident that these gains are too few and far between. It is heartbreaking that 200 years since the women's suffrage movement, and despite all the various initiatives and affirmations aimed at gender equality and the rights of women and girls, we are still fighting for women's equality in the 21st century. Quite frankly, it begs the question that there remains a huge gap in gender parity, with only a few women around the globe so far having been privileged to hold very prominent and visible positions of political and economic power, both locally and on the global turf.

It then becomes merely a matter of logic to wonder what the most significant barrier to female leadership is. Without an iota of doubt, the huge gender gap in the world's leadership systems can only be explicable on the basis of an institutionalized form of gender discrimination that is embedded in a chronic failure to adjust the male work model to fit the needs of women. Expressed differently, the world still lives in a patriarchal society where the majority of women continue to endure discrimination in all its complexions.

An eloquent demonstration of this fact is that, over the years, women's potential contributions to politics, economic advancement, social progress and environmental protection have been so marginalized by a system that discriminates against women that it ultimately establishes perceived limits on their full potential. The official theme of the 2014 International Women's Day of the United Nations was *"Gender Equality Is Progress For All."* The long-standing fight for gender equality is one many are familiar with. It is a fight that has taken many forms, starting from the Women's Suffrage Movement of the 19th century.

The year 2020 presents itself as an epoch-making confluence of significant anniversaries in the global feminist movement. For one, it marked 100 years of the women's vote in the USA and 40 years since the declaration of the United Nations Convention on the Elimination of All Forms of Discrimination against Women (CEDAW) in 1979. For another, it marked 25 years since the Beijing Platform for Action was adopted at the Fourth United Nations World Conference in 1995. For yet another, it marked 20 years of the United Nations Security Council Resolution 1325 on Women, Peace and Security, 10 years since UN Women was formed and 10 years of the Equality Act 2010. Remarkably, it also marked 64 years of the United Nations Commission on the Status of Women, 75 years since the creation of the United Nations, and five years into the Sustainable Development Goals.

Additionally, the year 2020 is representative of a confluence of anniversaries for some of Africa's own continental initiatives and affirmative actions on gender equality and the empowerment of women and girls. It marked over 25 years since the Pre-Congress of the 7th Pan-African Congress held in Kampala in Uganda, 17 years since the adoption of the Maputo Protocol (African Charter on Human and People's Rights of Women in Africa), 15 years of the Gender is My Agenda Campaign, 10 years and conclusion of the Decade of African Woman, and five years since the African Union declared 2015 as the African Union Year of Women's Empowerment.

One is, however, constrained to note that gender equality remains one Millennium Development Goal (MDG) that was not fulfilled, because of which it has once again been highlighted as a priority in the subsequent United Nations Agenda 2030 Global Goals for Sustainable Development. While these initiatives and affirmative actions have made some visible strides, women still lag far behind their male counterparts in all areas, and in nearly all parts of the world, for the simple reason that leadership roles in the economic, social and political systems of the world are still modeled on the ambitions and perspectives of men.

In most African countries, and indeed many other developing countries across the globe, women are culturally required to seek the permission of their husbands or male relatives before engaging in any form of business, social or political activity. Yet, certain exigent circumstances in history provide sufficient evidence that women are quite capable of assuming the role of competent leadership when it is demanded of them. The story of Rwanda is quite instructive in this regard. In the aftermath of the 1994 genocide in Rwanda, many women were thrown into the uncertainty of widowhood. With thousands more males incarcerated for war crimes or living as refugees in neighboring countries, Rwanda was left with an imbalanced population ratio of 60% female to 40% male. As a consequence, many women found themselves thrust into the role of household breadwinners, while also having to assume leadership roles in society, business and politics.

Prior to the genocide, the women of Rwanda had weak property rights, while female entrepreneurship was almost unheard of. In the aftermath of the genocide, however, society having been left with a yawning male leadership vacuum, it became an inevitability for reforms to be passed that enabled women to inherit property. Additionally, Rwandan women suddenly became agriculturists and businesswomen since they largely had to take over their husband's, father's, brother's or uncle's farms or businesses.

If the story of the Rwandan woman's circumstantial emancipation from the clutches of subjugation does not sufficiently demonstrate the innate sense of responsibility of women, then nothing will. The Rwandan woman has risen from the conflict stronger than any other woman in the world, taking up positions of power in politics, business and other walks of life that were merely a remote, if not the faintest possibility in the past.

In the Rwandan parliamentary elections of 2014, women took an overwhelming majority in parliament with over 64% of the seats. Rwanda remains the only country in the world with a female-dominated parliament, having first achieved the feat in the 2008 polls when women took up 56% representation in the House of Representatives. The impressive performance of Rwandan women in the elections was largely attributed to a unanimous decision by the political parties to give both genders equal chances at the polls, in contrast to the past practice in which men were automatically guaranteed a greater number of slots on party electoral lists.

Rwanda is also one of the few countries committed to Resolution 1325 of the UN Security Council that was adopted in 2000 to enable a greater participation of women at all levels of institutional prevention, management and resolution of conflicts, and the special protection of girls and women from sexual and other forms of violence. Toward the conclusion of the Millennium Development Goals, a United Nations report had highlighted Rwanda as the only country in the world that was on a path to achieving almost all of the Millennium Development Goals.

Gender disparities in electoral contests are not peculiar to Africa. For instance, in the 2011 general elections in Ireland, only 15% of women were elected to parliament. The world must resolutely move away from this untenable state of affairs if only because, when the voices of women are stifled, not only are their interests underrepresented, but their valuable skills, ingenuity, resilience and knowledge are also underexploited for the greater good of all. Raising women's voices, increasing their influence, and making leadership and decision-making roles more accessible to women are all needed to overcome poverty and hunger all over the world.

Indeed, there is an abundance of wealth to be freed up when women become equal participants in the dialogue and decision-making process, and this will lead to diversified economies, increased family income, balanced leadership, more productive dialogue, more effective decision-making strategies, a safer world for all, better education for children, greater environmental protection, healthier families, healthier communities, greater freedom, enhanced social justice and human rights, and stronger and more coherent social sectors.

Naturally, all these will ensure sustainable development, progress for all and human prosperity. Renowned economist Amartya Sen put it succinctly when he said, *"Nothing, arguably, is as important today in the political economy of development as an adequate recognition of political, economic and social participation and leadership of women."* Yet, to deny that there are also obstacles to female leadership that are unique and peculiar to women themselves is to proverbially hide one's head in the sand like the ostrich.

To be relevant, respected and effective leaders, women need to be empowered with the appropriate education, training and knowledge that will not only enable them to individually and collectively improve themselves but also permit them to strenuously push the limits to which their full potential can be subjected.

A system that is riddled with rampant gender discrimination also manifests in lopsided educational systems around the globe, such that a lack of adequate education, training and knowledge transfer hinders the potential of women in leadership roles. A well-coordinated process of unlearning the traditional mindsets and social conditioning of men and women would help to provide an enabling environment for women to realize their full intellectual potential, and to contribute effectively in leadership roles. To fast-track skills development and knowledge transfer so as to incorporate women in all spheres of the global agenda would be to break down gender and economic inequalities all over the world.

The purpose of this book is to celebrate women who have taken the bull by the horns to activate remarkable changes in the so-called natural order of things. Not unnaturally, there is no way any single volume could exhaustively list and chronicle the achievements of all the women who have made their gender proud in this manner. Therefore, this book merely employs a few of them as examples of a brilliant, old and new generation of women who have employed, and are still employing, the formidable combination of captivating feminine beauty, strength of personality and outstanding leadership skills to transform their lives and those of others, using the instrumentality of sheer industry, uncommon courage, unrivaled compassion and indomitability of spirit.

Indeed, the season has come to celebrate the hundreds, if not thousands or even millions of women around the world who have made the world a kinder and fairer place with their brilliant personalities, ideas and achievements. This book seeks to celebrate that season and these women. Welcome to the world of the iconic female leader.

Justina Mutale
London, UK
September 2020

CONTENTS

PROLOGUE

AN INTELLECTUAL OVERVIEW OF FEMALE LEADERSHIP

The oft-touted claim that mothers are natural-born leaders not being a far-fetched one is valid to a considerable degree. While one is not necessarily discounting the obvious exemplary leadership traits of many men, we can now state with some categorical emphasis that women in leadership positions tend to execute those leadership roles with a certain disposition that is remarkably different from that seen in their male counterparts. Women not only possess an uncommonly strong sense of community but also identify in the strongest possible terms with their connection to their community in whatever they do. Women also possess both an inbuilt generosity of spirit and the high degree of emotional intelligence that allows them to demonstrate a high index of sensitivity to the needs of others.

One study after the other has discovered that gender inequalities have led to widening social inequality, environmental degradation and severe economic loss all over the world. All these have been attributed to the economic model of the day; one that is largely built on the ambitions and perspectives of men. Nowhere is this fact in greater evidence than in the management and boards of failed banks and financial institutions, all of which are nearly 100% male in composition. Not surprisingly, the global financial crisis of 2008, considered the worst economic crisis since the Great Depression of the 1930s, has given rise to heightened criticism of the capitalist model, in which growth is fueled more by self-serving considerations than by ethical business leadership.

Such self-serving considerations include men's quest for competition, instant gratification and the quest for profits at the expense of grave human and social consequences. Also, women do not indulge in a near-infantile predilection for competitiveness like their male counterparts, who seem to have a need to continually flex the muscles of military superiority that has led to many unnecessary wars, suffering and perpetual flash points of global conflict. Women, through the ages, have been more inclined to demonstrate a limitless strength that is founded on the values of compassion, humility and strength of character. Through inherent emotional strength and wisdom, women are more inclined to display a strength that is more enduring than the physical, using these traits to traverse everyday challenges, and to continue with the struggle where men's physical strength has failed the world.

Our world is replete with anecdotes that imply that women might possibly be far better leaders than men. For instance, I have heard it said that *"If the Lehman Brothers were Lehman Sisters, the world would have never suffered the economic crisis of 2008!"* Arguable as that assertion may prove, the fact remains that the global financial services firm Lehman Brothers was the most prominent player in the unfortunate events that culminated in the economic crisis of 2008. A famous quote that is not credited to anyone in particular, and therefore wears the cloak of anonymity is *"If women ruled the world, there would be no wars... just a bunch of countries not speaking to one another!"*

Africa seems to illustrate eloquently the failure of the male model of leadership. While most African countries had, prior to COVID-19, been enjoying a spate of high economic growth, which led to the term *"Africa Rising,"* those gains did not trickle down to the majority of its citizens, most of whom continued to wallow in abject poverty. This disparity has been attributed to the fact that the African economy is a mirror image of the global male economic model, which is focused on competition and profits without due regard to social and human consequences. As a result, the rise in economic growth in Africa appears really quite plastic and unreal, having been eclipsed by a rise in poverty and unemployment, widening social and gender inequalities, as well as falling levels of education and healthcare provision.

Unlike men, women are more disposed toward using money and authority to improve the quality of life in their communities by improving on their home conditions, combating poverty and financing the education of their children. Many leading experts say that in efforts to finance the reduction of poverty in the developing world, women simply make better investments.

A major study in Brazil has also shown that the effect of money managed by women in poor households was many times more likely to be spent on improving conditions in the home than money managed by men who squander it outside the home on drinking and gambling.

The year 2020 has marked a significant though quite unpleasant milestone in world history. It is also the year in which women have decisively proved that when it comes to governance and leadership, they unequivocally hold the aces over and above men. Indeed, it is worthy of remarkable note that it is those countries that are led by women that have proved the far greater mettle in their response to the scourge that is COVID-19, the devastating disease caused by the novel coronavirus that has resulted in what is arguably the worse pandemic in global history for an entire century, at least in terms of its combined fatality, morbidity and economic devastation.

From Iceland to Taiwan, and from Germany to New Zealand, women have stepped up the ante in exemplary leadership in the management of a truly despairing global public health dilemma. When we add Finland, Iceland and Denmark to the picture, the pandemic wholesomely reveals that women have what it takes when the heat rises, not only in the kitchen but also in the hallowed corridors of power.

Angela Merkel of Germany stood up early and calmly told her countrymen the truth, and then acted proactively on that truth. Tsai Ing-wen of Taiwan decisively managed the situation to put up what CNN called "among the world's best responses." Jacinda Ardern of New Zealand employed uncommon clarity and decisiveness to save her country from the storm. Katrín Jakobsdóttir of Iceland deployed the formidable power of technology to make her country a key case study in the true spread and fatality rates of COVID-19 by a massive and unrivaled testing and tracking program as key agent in battling the coronavirus crisis. Erna Solberg of Norway simply fell back on the power of love in coming up with the innovative idea of using television to talk directly to her country's children. Overall, the empathy and care which all these female leaders have communicated to their people reflects an alternative to the male-oriented narrative the world is more familiar with.

On a very fundamental level, there are compelling reasons why the world needs to invest more in female leadership, and why the quest for gender parity is more relevant than ever before. Investing in women transforms the trajectory for children and families. It always catalyzes economic growth for the entire community. Women also have a greater sense of corporate social responsibility than male entrepreneurs since their primary motivation is not necessarily to compete or outdo one another. They are also generally averse to taking ill-informed risks that might prove counterproductive to their business or the society.

Studies have demonstrated that women's improved economic status produces many positive economic and welfare outcomes for children, families and societies. Evidence also abounds that women deploy their limited ability to access income, technology and paid work far more effectively to their children's welfare than their male counterparts. Studies have also shown that increases in household income that are powered by women tend to bear a closer correlation with a boost in children's nutrition and survival. That is why, especially in the developing world, a mother's social and economic status is considered one of the best indicators of the potential of her children to complete their education and enjoy a poverty-free and healthy adult life.

It is globally acknowledged that children whose educated mothers enjoy higher earning potential attain a generally higher education status than their more disadvantaged peers. Because of their generosity of spirit, women's economic advancement promotes overall economic growth for the whole society, and this is evidenced by the fact that those countries that have a higher number of women participating in the labor market also enjoy greater degrees of poverty reduction.

Women need to inspire change in themselves and in one another. To achieve this, all they need do is simply uncover what they already have. Women need to change their behavior and attitudes by unlearning those traditional mindsets and social conditioning that are holding them back from achieving their full potential. They also need to exert renewed effort in empowering their fellow women to continually improve and exceed the limitations that have been placed on their full participation in the political, economic and social spheres of their world, so that women and girls can become effective and influential players in a future global agenda.

Women will need to become increasingly more creative and more proactive in their quest to attain the much desired and very elusive equality for women, an equality for which they have been fighting for over 200 years. To do this, women need to be equipped with the necessary leadership skills that are required for them to close the gender gap. Ours is now a borderless world in which each one of us can cross boundaries into and out of both emerging markets and the developed world with infinite ease, creating opportunities for women on social, economic and political turfs.

This is a unique age of globalization and technological revolution, bringing with it unprecedented ease of travel and ease of communication. We can even literally cross borders without leaving our homes! Women will need to seize the rare opportunities of this borderless world to create global networks of influencers across the length and breadth of the globe. Employing technology and the media, the possibilities are endless for leveraging women's groups around the world to challenge cultural norms with regards to the value of women and girls to mankind. Through the abundantly available information and communication channels, women can connect with each other around the world to continually create and raise awareness about their intrinsic powers of transformation. The same channels also provide women the opportunity to engage, celebrate, educate and empower other women all around the world.

The most critical tool for the positive portrayal of women is the media, and its role in shaping perceptions about attitudes to women and girls in society cannot be overemphasized. It is only through media reports that women's abilities to contribute to societal causes can be brought to the fore of global consciousness. Technology renders it easy to connect, engage and inspire women into action in local communities around the world, and to attract women's voices and talents to create a global coalition of women in leadership for the acceleration of the fight for gender equality and women's rights.

For centuries, women and their potential contributions to economic advancement and social progress have been marginalized. The resultant failure to leverage on the potential and talents of female population groups has merely translated to a global underinvestment in readily available human capital that would have spurred sustainable development. If a world runs on half its human potential, half its human capital and half its economic capacity, it can only be expected that it will yield a mere half or less of its potential in growth on all conceivable fronts.

A concerted effort to utilize women's potential can only result in increased economic growth, reduced poverty, enhanced social wellbeing and sustainable development. That is why it can only be considered wise and prudent to invest in the capacity of women to engineer the transformative change that can enable real progress within the context of tangible human prosperity and a sustainable future for our globe.

Jim Yong Kim served as the 12th President of the World Bank from 2012 to 2019. He once said that countries around the world, and in Africa in particular, pay a big price by failing to realize the potential of women. In fact, a recent study by the World Bank found that women account for only 38% of their country's human capital wealth, versus 62% for men. According to the study, if this gap were closed in 141 countries, the world would generate $160 trillion in additional human capital wealth. During his tenure, Mr Kim consistently reiterated that the World Bank encourages and supports investment in women's education, workforce, development and entrepreneurship to realize the rising aspirations of developing countries and to build the human capital needed for the economy of the future.

The pursuit of global economic sustainability should, therefore, start with giving women opportunities for advancement on all leadership fronts. The critical choices that face our world today should ideally have women at their center, a resolute intention that should continually demand policies of transformation and a radically different mindset. The world will need to break down the structural barriers that confront women and girls, including conscious and unconscious bias and institutional discrimination.

To take our planet to its levels of maximum actualization, we need to bring women on board to drive the agenda for global sustainability, not just because it is the right thing to do but because it is the smart thing to do. The world simply cannot achieve the critical United Nations Sustainable Development Goals without securing the full and equal rights of half of the world's population.

One of the reasons why this book is making its debut at a critical time in human history is the need to highlight those areas of personal strength that women leaders have largely exploited to be able to stamp their mark of excellence in their own micro and macro operating environments. That is why I have opted to define those areas of strength and influence in terms of their "*power.*" The book essentially opens with the *power of visionary leadership,* and takes us all the way to the *power of millennial leadership,* in which the significant point is made that millennials are most definitely changing our traditional ways of viewing leadership.

Certainly, it is estimated that in less than two years, millennials will become the largest employee group on Earth. Without question, they have already become the major influence shaping the future of leadership all over the world. The *powers of vision, creativity and competence* constitute the earliest chapters of the book. That is not surprising. Exemplary leadership rides on the vehicle of an enabling vision. For leadership itself to arrest the imagination and fascination of the led, it must be spiced with the flavor of creativity. Without competence, a leader is not worthy of that appellation.

The *powers of versatility, resilience, purpose, focus and courage* are all presented with examples of iconic women who are totally representative of the fact that these fundamental traits are core components of an accomplished leader. In fact, without those five key attributes, the vessel of leadership becomes an empty one. The book also reserves a special place for mention of the indefatigable women leaders who have been great *advocates* for the cause of the emancipation and empowerment of women and girls, while it does not leave out those women who have been powerful and influential *reformers* of obsolete systems of governance and politics that have remained relics of a less than useful past.

The book does not close without celebrating three of the most beautiful traits that great women leaders possess: the *powers of compassion, charisma and intellect.* Almost invariably, most women leaders possess these three attributes in a combination of healthy doses. Finally, I employ my own personal experience to discuss what I personally consider the most powerful component of effective leadership; one that is totally reflective of the intrinsic feminine generosity of spirit. Indeed, it is the *power of emotional intelligence* that makes women genuinely sensitive to the needs of others.

In my own leadership journey, I was to learn quickly how to utilize emotional intelligence, self-awareness and social awareness skills in my relationships with other people. Emotional intelligence is a very potent tool in effective leadership because it gives one the ability to understand the feelings of others at a deep level, and thereby relate with them on a very positive platform.

Having comprehensively provided a brief overview of the book you hold in your hands, I invite you to partake of the captivating experiences of female world leaders and their leadership power.

CHAPTER 1

WHAT IS LEADERSHIP?

"A leader takes people where they want to go.
A great leader takes people where they don't
necessarily want to go but ought to be."

ROSALYNN CARTER,
FIRST LADY OF THE UNITED STATES (1977-1980)

Everything rises and falls on leadership. There has always been an enduring mystery to leadership, and that mystery becomes even more complex as soon as an attempt is made to define a good leader. To be considered good leaders, we are expected to be a Barack Obama, Hillary Clinton, Tony Blair, Nelson Mandela and Mahatma Gandhi, all rolled into just one person. What is indisputable is that we all seem to recognize a good leader any time we encounter one.

Yet, no leader is capable of conforming to a single template of characterization. In fact, there would appear to be as many different definitions of leadership as there are people who have attempted to define it. Expressed differently, the word can have different meanings for different people. In the final analysis, most people are in agreement that they simply cannot arrive at a consensual definition of leadership.

Yet, it is also widely acknowledged that everyone is capable of being a leader, and that all outstanding leaders tend to do certain things uncommonly well, and while that may not necessarily guarantee success, it does render success a more likely possibility. More importantly, however, one can certainly be a leader in one's own style, since one merely has to be the best version of who one already is. Boiled down to its basics, one only has to awaken to one's own highest potential.

Despite the multiplicity of ways in which leadership has been conceptualized, certain components are knowledgeably identified as central to the phenomenon of leadership. Leadership is a process. Leadership also involves influence. Leadership is not isolated to individual considerations. Leadership involves the sharing of common goals for the greater good. Based on these components, leadership may be conveniently defined as *"a process through which an individual rides on the vehicle of a vision to influence a group of individuals to transform that vision into action, with the ultimate aim of achieving a common goal."*

Leadership does not necessarily derive credibility from seniority in any known parameter. In real terms, leadership is not about position. Leadership is more about "what one does" and "how one conducts oneself while doing that thing." For these reasons, a person at the top of a government agency may be in a leadership position but may not be actually leading. That means leaders can exist at all levels of the hierarchy. Perhaps of the greatest significance, a leader needs followers. You may surpass the eclectic combination of Barack Obama, Hillary Clinton, Tony Blair, Nelson Mandela and Mahatma Gandhi, but if no one is following you, you are definitely not a leader.

The key characteristics of iconic leadership are an ability to motivate others, an enduring vision, the combination of honesty and integrity, a certain decisiveness and the ability to manage crisis situations effectively. A leader must also possess some disdain for the status quo, especially when that status quo translates to complacency in thought and in deed; perceived, yet irrational boundaries and barriers, and a pervasive fear of failure. A leader must possess not only deep-seated compassion for others but also an equal compassion for the changes that will compel a search for, or the creation of, viable paths to solutions.

Compassion is a particularly important trait for aspiring leadership. Its expression is a veritable reflection of the potential "bigness" of the human heart. In a leader, compassion finds expression in a profoundly silent and tender feeling that manifests itself as a constantly self-relinquishing disposition that is truly a hallmark of outstanding leadership. A leader must rise above a self-centered existence, and only genuine compassion can allow one to come out of oneself to feel the pains of the led. In fact, the one common denominator among the world's greatest political leaders, especially those of the feminine gender, is their selflessness, and their compassion for the powerless, the needy, the defenseless, the downtrodden, and those existing within a very narrow corridor of opportunities in a world that can, at times, be harsh, brittle and brutal.

A leader must have a crisp vision of desired objectives indelibly etched on her heart, and which provides her with the impetus to drive herself and her team. As mentioned in a later chapter in this book, vision is the fundamental emotive force that drives everything else in a leader's life, and it is the most potent motive for her actions. Vision is the rather crucial ability to see beyond current reality in such a way as to transform, in the present moment, into the future form. Of even greater significance, vision, more than any other factor, affects the choices the leader has to make. In fact, vision also dictates the way a leader spends her time. This is the reason why most great leaders often remind themselves that it hardly matters what they are doing if what they are doing is not what matters most.

Vision alone will not carry a leader very far. She must draw upon all the charisma and persuasive power she possesses to share her vision in order to raise and inspire her followers. This is the only way she can make impactful leadership a viable possibility. Effective communication skills are also fundamental to leadership success. Virtually every human interaction requires strong communication skills, and leaders with formidable communication skills usually enjoy better interpersonal relationships with their followers. Usually, quite convinced of the possibilities and potential contained in their vision, leaders refuse to back down or be discouraged by the challenges that are inevitably thrown on their path. Rather, they maintain a positive and unrelenting attitude as they seek to drive change with their capacity for converting obstacles into tools which they employ to work in their favor.

The quintessential leader combines an infectious charisma with sound character and excellent human relations, which all jointly invoke a sense of commitment, loyalty and respect from followers. Her high index of integrity breeds a mutual trust with the led, and this in turn increases effectiveness, as her followers begin to possess an individualistic ownership of her vision and are prepared to go the extra mile with her. This is the power of synergy at play. The word synergy comes from the Greek word *synergia* which means working together.

In essence, therefore, synergy is the interaction of two or more agents or forces so that their combined effect is greater than the sum of their individual effects. It has also been said that the power of synergy is exponential as it doesn't work through addition but rather through multiplication. In the context of effective leadership, since a cohesive group is more than the sum of its parts, synergy is the ability of a group to outperform even its best individual member. That is one of the most enduring mysteries of iconic leadership.

Yet, great leaders are humble enough to admit errors when they occur, to responsibly consider the views of their followers, and to share their success and the legacy with them. The leader humbly refuses to take all the glory for her accomplishments and insists on giving everyone the grace and opportunity to share not only in the story behind the glory but also the glory after the story. A great deal of humility is required for cultivating healthy interpersonal relationships. In fact, one of the greatest causes of leadership failure is a lack of humility. A true leader brings genuine insight and understanding to interpersonal relationships. Human interrelationship is generally regarded as being very complex, yet it is really quite simple, and the reason most people do not appreciate others is principally due to a lack of humility.

As an overview, genuine leadership will have to involve four attributes that have been and will remain virtually timeless. These are the ability to adapt, the ability to engage others in the shared meaning of an enduring vision, the ability to speak with an authentic voice, and the existence of a positive purpose. What this tells us is that, while people will generally have their own notions of the characteristics that have marked leaders throughout human history, most would agree that leadership skills must be honed to meet the specific challenges of the environments in which they have to operate.

There are certain core competencies that one must possess to lead effectively in today's world. These are communication skills, the ability to raise and inspire another generation of leaders, creativity and innovation, a passionate drive for results, thorough knowledge of the operating environment, being a role model for noble values, a strong ethical disposition, and the ability to build and foster mutually beneficial human relations.

Yet, we must also note that the stereotypical view of a leader is the hero-leader, one who portrays a larger than life image. This view tends to place the unnecessary burden of striving to meet unrealistic expectations on leaders. The rule of thumb is to understand that there is no one "correct" leadership style. Leadership, at the most fundamental level, is much better defined as a process in which a person fits in with the job that needs to be done, influences the right people at the right time to do that job, and gets the job done right, and in the right manner.

Conclusively, upon reflecting on the lives of the great female leaders featured in this book, one is reminded that the true measure of a successful leader's impact is not in the number of awards or accolades she receives but by the number of lives she ends up changing for the better by her unstinting dedication to a noble cause. Invariably, such selfless dedication results from certain experiences that have shaped a leader's perspective on what real impact is, and what it is not.

It is this totally refined perspective that equips a leader to discover her true legacy and her lasting place in history. As it is with creating any type of change, the true leader must first become a repository of that change, for it is from that fountain of change that she can liberally offer the best she has to offer her own followers.

A Summary of the Concept of Leadership

1. Everyone is capable of being a leader.

2. To be a leader, you merely have to be the best version of who you already are. That also means awakening yourself to your own highest potential.

3. Leadership is a process.

4. Leadership involves influence.

5. Leadership is not isolated to individual considerations. It involves the sharing of common goals for the greater good.

6. A leader needs followers.

7. Iconic leadership incorporates an ability to motivate others, an enduring vision, the combination of honesty and integrity, a certain decisiveness and the ability to effectively manage crisis situations.

8. Vision is the fundamental emotive force that drives everything else in a leader's life.

9. A great leader is humble enough to insist on giving everyone the grace and opportunity to share not only in the story behind the glory but also the glory after the story.

10. Genuine leadership involves the ability to adapt, the ability to engage others in the shared meaning of an enduring vision, the ability to speak with an authentic voice, and the existence of a positive purpose.

11. A leader's skills must be honed to meet the specific challenges of the environment in which she operates.

12. While recognition and appreciation are both inescapable and totally expected along the path of extraordinary leadership, the true measure of a successful leader's impact is not in the number of awards or accolades received but by the number of lives she ends up changing for the better.

CHAPTER 2

THE QUALITIES OF A LEADER

"If your actions create a legacy that inspires others to dream more, learn more, do more and become more, then you are an excellent leader."

DOLLY PARTON

The first chapter of this book, in attempting to proffer a working definition for "leadership," has delved, to some degree, into the qualities of a good leader. Yet, the subject itself is deemed of sufficient importance to warrant an entire chapter devoted to it, and in such a manner that those qualities stand out in bold relief for the benefit of committed students of leadership.

Good leadership is undoubtedly the fuel that enables society to progress along all known fronts of human development. The myth that "leaders are born" is not necessarily true, and leadership can be learned by anyone who aspires to make a significant mark in life. Indeed, irrespective of qualification and educational merit, anyone can become a leader of note. Certainly, the great women leaders featured in this book come from disparate social, economic and educational backgrounds.

Robin S. Sharma, a leadership speaker and author of the best-selling novel *The Monk Who Sold His Ferrari* wrote: *"Leadership is not about a title or a designation. It's about impact, influence, and inspiration. Impact involves getting results, influence is about spreading the passion you have for your work, and you have to inspire teammates and customers."* That statement is as authentic as one will ever get on the essence of leadership. A real leader is one who not only inspires others but also understands each member of her team, sometimes to the finest point of detail.

While communication, attitude and commitment to get the work done are the essential ingredients of a good leader, other traits and characteristics that enable real leadership in a person are creativity, empathy, ethical conduct, the ability to take responsibility and the ability to challenge failure.

A positive mental attitude is one of the most significant characteristics that define leadership. A positive attitude is the essential driving energy that a leader must have. In fact, it is a positive attitude that shapes a leader, since being not absolutely necessary that each member of a leader's team has the same drive for achievement, imbibing the leader's positive attitude can be life transforming for her followers. A positive attitude is a philosophy in itself, and it is to have an optimistic disposition in every situation. It tends to attract positive change and increases achievement on all conceivable fronts. It continues to seek, find and execute ways to find a desirable outcome, regardless of the circumstances. It opposes negativity, defeatism and hopelessness. A positive mental attitude is also the belief that one can increase achievement through optimistic thought processes. Essentially, it is a process of choosing positive emotions, and its objective is to create an outlook that translates into a new or a better chosen reality.

For most people, to "pass the buck" on to others in adverse situations is the easy and convenient thing to do. However, taking the responsibility and being accountable for all one's actions and inactions is what separates a real leader from the motley crowd. Accountability and transparency go hand in hand. The story is famously told of an American hedge fund manager who once wrote an apology letter to his investors explaining his failure to turn their funds into profit. Then he started another hedge fund company without charging any brokerage fee to his beloved investors. His noble action is accountability defined.

Accountability is answerability, blameworthiness, liability, and the expectation of account giving. In leadership, accountability is the acknowledgment and assumption of responsibility for actions, decisions and policies. This is a hallmark of outstanding leadership. Indeed, a good leader is never afraid or reluctant to take responsibility. This value in a leader not only shows that she is accountable and transparent but also inspires others to take responsibility for their own actions and inactions. In today's world, political leaders, in particular, ought to consider themselves as laboring under an obligation to offer nothing but good governance to the people of their country.

A leader is a compassionate being. A leader is an emotionally intelligent individual. Quite explicably, compassion and emotional intelligence would appear to be two wheels of a cart, as they both demand that a leader relate with others from within the heart. Most people might view the usage of the heart perspective as being unnecessarily sentimental in a book that seriously discusses leadership. In the circumstances, there are two reasons why that should not unduly bother one. The first reason is that if the word heart was not that significant in discussions about human predilection to compassion and kindness, the word heartless would not have assumed prominence in describing one who is unfeeling, unkind and unsympathetic. The second reason is that this is a book about women, and women do operate from the heart.

Most great women leaders are also immensely emotionally intelligent. Emotional intelligence is the ability to be able to monitor one's own and other people's emotions, to discriminate between different emotions and label them appropriately, and to use emotional information to guide one's thinking and behavior. Inherent in this definition of emotional intelligence are four components or abilities that are distinct, yet related. These are the ability to perceive, the ability to apply a skill, the ability to comprehend and the ability to appropriately manage emotions. Emotional intelligence also reflects a leader's ability to join intelligence, empathy and emotions to enhance thought and understanding of interpersonal dynamics.

Communication, as the definition goes, is the process of disseminating information from one party to another. A leader must possess the ability to communicate her vision to her followers in a definite and precise manner. Even the minutest gap in communication can lead to chaos in leadership and governance. That is why the commonest denominator that threads throughout this book among the women leaders featured is the ability to communicate effectively. The ability to engage in clear and coherent thought and speech, and the ability to communicate concepts in a clear and crisp manner so that the entire team shares the same vision and goals, are both indispensable tools in the arsenal of the effective leader.

Failure is an inevitability on the leadership journey, and any leader who would lay claim to one victory after the other, without some dose of defeat along the way, is not being altogether sincere. The ability to manage failure effectively is an indispensable skill for the aspiring leader. In fact, a leader must learn how to fail successfully. A good leader relates with failure not as an adversary but as a friend. She sees failure merely as a temporary obstacle on her way to attaining her goals. Her failures actually bring her closer to her goal since they will teach her valuable lessons on planning, strategy and methodology. Viewed from this perspective, failures are actually an authentic source of power for eventual accomplishment.

The more a leader is focused, the better the outcome of her engagement with her followers. Even in a cabinet meeting, government ministers will typically follow the point of discussion set forth by the president. If the head of state is diffuse in her discussion and approach to governance, the rest of the government will be diffuse in the execution of policy. Focus is a leadership trait that defines the pace of productivity and the commitment of a leader's team toward her objectives. Therefore, it is imperative for the leader to ensure that her focus is crystal clear and that priorities are clearly spelt out. Distraction from focus will only eventually lead to ineffectuality in the accomplishment of set goals.

Innovation is the life and blood of leadership. In fact, the only aspect of leadership that can rather quickly decide the fate of an individual in a position of influence is the ability to innovate new thinking and fresh concepts. Innovation drives on the vehicle of unique ideas. What good is an idea if it remains an idea? A leader must conduct experiments with potentially viable concepts and ideas. A leader must iterate, fail and then try again. That is the only way to change the world. A leader brings in a host of innovative ideas that will inspire her subordinates, as well as ideate on such an original scale as to remain well ahead of her competition. Innovation as a strategy is always on top of a leader's agenda. Creativity and innovation are two sides of the same coin, as they simply cannot be separated from one another.

Finally, the point must be stressed that the age-old and universal myth that leaders are born and not made is no more accurate, given the examples of the several great leaders that we have in today's world. There is no denying the fact that just about anyone can become a leader, although it also remains quite true that not every leader can be an extraordinarily outstanding one. However, the traits described in this chapter must be instinctual in anyone who wishes to lead and be followed. On the one hand, a mere boss is one who shifts all her responsibilities on to a leader. On the other hand, a leader is one who takes up all those responsibilities and discharges them to the best of her ability. That is why authentic success and real leadership are totally synonymous.

A Summary of the Qualities of a Leader

1. A leader inspires.

2. A leader is creative.

3. A leader has empathy.

4. A leader has ethics.

5. A leader has a positive mental attitude.

6. A leader takes responsibility.

7. A leader is accountable.

8. A leader is compassionate.

9. A leader is emotionally intelligent.

10. A leader is an effective communicator.

11. A leader is a good manager of failure.

12. A leader is focused.

13. A leader is innovative.

CHAPTER 3

THE POWER OF VISION

"A bird doesn't sing because it has an answer,
it sings because it has a song."

MAYA ANGELOU

It all starts with a vision. This book seeks to explore any and all conceivable platforms on which the female leaders of this generation and past generations can be properly assessed within the context of what constitutes effective leadership. By whatever parameters we elect to define effective leadership, and by whatever empirical standard we choose to set a benchmark for what constitutes a lofty example of leadership, and indeed no matter how impressive the performance of a leader might be, the starting point of authentic leadership will always be a vision. That is why the first of the Power Secrets is visionary leadership.

Vision is necessarily the vehicle on which the entire leadership engine runs. A leader in this century, or in past centuries for that matter, must possess a clear and crisp picture of an ambitious goal, and a good cause. That means she can lucidly envision what the desired end will look like. This vision is indelibly etched on the screen of her imagination, very much like how a consummate artist renders an enduring image on the canvas on her easel. It is this visionary imagination, this visionary work of art, that provides her with the driving impetus to drive her team effectively, to not only align with her goals but to also emotionally commit to their attainment.

Vision is born of creative imagination. If anything can be ultimately demonstrated to be the fundamental emotive force that drives everything else in a leader's life, it will have to be vision. That cannot be otherwise, because without an iota of doubt, the most potent motive for a leader's actions is vision. Vision is the vital ability to see beyond the current reality. Eventually, vision becomes a leader's compelling propensity to create. Put differently, vision is the leader's innovative competence to invent that which is not yet in existence. Stretched further, vision is the acumen to transform, in the present moment, into the future form. That is why it is vision that allows leaders to live out of their imagination rather than out of their memories. It also allows them not only to exist in the present moment but to also go beyond their present reality.

Vision, more than any other factor, invariably affects the choices a leader makes. Naturally, that is why vision also dictates, to a significant degree, how a leader deploys her time and energy. That is why the average visionary leader, more often than not, might constantly remind herself that it hardly matters what she is doing if what she is doing is not what matters most. It is also the reason why, at any point in time, such a leader would always pause to ask herself what the most valuable use of her time is at that instant. The visionary leader must draw upon all the charisma and persuasive power at her disposal to share her vision in order to raise and inspire her team. This is the only way she can possibly empower herself with the resources and tools she needs to even remotely make impactful leadership a viable possibility. That is why, for truly effective leadership, effective and persuasive communication must share a groove with vision. In other words, effective communication skills are fundamental to the success of the leader.

Every human interaction is powered by communication. Effective communication is a key interpersonal skill, and by learning how we can improve our communication we reap inestimable benefits. Since communication is a two-way process, improving communication involves both how we send and receive messages. A visionary is, for all practical purposes, a dreamer. Convinced of the possibilities and potential of their dreams, visionary leaders refuse to back down from, or be discouraged by, the challenges that are inevitably thrown on their path. Instead of throwing in the towel, they find a way to sustain the positive and unrelenting attitude that allows them to continue to drive change. That is why visionary leaders have a legendary capacity for converting obstacles into the tools that end up working in their favor.

The significant advances that will be made in the foreseeable future in the area of gender equality, and by extension the future leadership prospects of the world's women, will necessarily ride on the vehicle of visionary leadership by women themselves. This was the stark reality that stared me fully in the face as I was exposed to certain disconcerting revelations on the continued marginalization of women about five years ago. It was not long after this that I felt myself sufficiently challenged to embark on my own leadership initiatives in the direction of empowering women and young girls.

The story started when I took the baton from Mrs Cherie Blair, wife of former British Prime Minister Tony Blair, to launch the 2014 edition of the *"Because I am a Girl"* report, which takes an incisive and critical look at the state of girls in the world. Mrs Blair had launched the 2013 report. The theme of the report I launched was *"Pathways to Power: Creating Sustainable Change for Adolescent Girls."* I was appalled by that report's statistics on the state of girls. I was dumbfounded to discover that in the 21st century only 25 out of 500 FTSE companies are led by women. Worse, girls were still way behind boys in exposure to educational facilities, and when I added this to the unacceptably high number of girls that were given out in marriage before the age of 18, the number of girls enduring gender-based violence and other negative human development and economic indicators, I could only throw up my arms in agonizing despair.

My sensibilities would be further traumatized in March 2015 when I attended the 59th United Nations Commission on the Status of Women (CSW) which undertook a 20-Year Review of the Beijing Declaration and Platform for Action. Sadly, CSW59 revealed a sustained deficit in women's wealth and a glaring lack of effective women's representation and contributions at high levels of the decision-making process in practically all walks of life, including business, politics, society, environment, academia, science and technology. I was shocked to the point where I found myself marching in what was once again called a "Historical March for Gender Equality."

I recall that my mind was in near-violent turmoil. I wondered in utter despair how long women were going to keep marching in the quest for gender equality. I wondered what it would take for women and girls to achieve this gender equality that had eluded them for centuries. I am mother to a millennium baby. My daughter was born in the year 2000, the beginning of the century. She was born at the inception of the United Nations' very ambitious Millennium Development Goals. This millennium baby has now emerged out of her teen years. In fact, by the time the Sustainable Development Goals replaced the Millennium Development Goals in 2016, the young lady was already 16 years old.

What is, however, even more instructive is that this millennium baby and all other children born at the beginning of the millennium will be fully grown adults at the conclusion of the Sustainable Development Goals in 2030. These millennium babies will be 30 years old by the year 2030. As adults, they will be the decision makers, policy makers, business leaders and political leaders of that era.

That was when I arrived at my own momentous point of commitment to visionary leadership. I decided that, as a mother, I would simply not wish to see my millennium baby and her peers marching for gender equality in the year 2030 and beyond. However, should they find it necessary to march at all, I would prefer them not to march with their feet but to march with their mind; a mind fully equipped with the necessary skills, knowledge and information to compete on an equal footing with their male counterparts. As a consequence of this resolution, I came back from CSW59 to launch the Justina Mutale Foundation.

The Foundation has program areas focused on achieving gender equality and the empowerment of women and girls. The program areas are Political Participation, Education, and Economic Empowerment as well as Leadership and Entrepreneurship Training and Mentorship. To win the gender battle, our millennium girls will need to be truly equipped on a functionally intellectual level, and that is why the Justina Mutale Foundation is so critically focused on education. In the firm belief that the provision of quality education is non-negotiable for the eradication of poverty and its feminization, the Foundation offers overseas scholarships for the tertiary education of disadvantaged young women and girls from Africa. Unreservedly believing that every girl is blessed with tremendous potential, it remains my unwavering hope and prayer that someday in this age, every girl will have access to the quality education that will enable her to reach that potential.

As long as women can escape the shackles of poverty and live fulfilling lives, they can contribute and participate meaningfully and positively in an ever changing global economy. The world is currently experiencing an exciting moment in time, at the center of which is an ever changing global economy in which women are truly ready to make a remarkable difference. We are on the verge of the fourth industrial revolution, and it has been estimated that by 2030 there will be over 1.5 billion new jobs requiring new skills. Therefore, the girl-child needs to be fully equipped with the necessary tools and skills she will need for employment and participation in such a vibrant economy of the future.

It remains my firm belief that the 21st century is a time to awaken the feminine spirit. The 21st century woman, therefore, needs to unlearn the traditions and cultures that have held women back over the centuries. The next generation of women need to learn to lead without seeking permission. They need to be adequately empowered, and to have the unshakeable self-belief that will allow them to break down those barriers that have inhibited feminine initiative, potential and leadership from as far back in time as we can recall.

My own vision, therefore, is to leave a legacy that will prepare our young women and girls to withstand the uncertainty and challenges of an ever changing social, economic and political global landscape. To do this, I believe we need to equip our women and girls with the essential political, social and economic empowerment skills, tools, knowledge and global power networks to enable them to participate successfully in the economy, politics and society of the future.

We need to inspire our women and girls to be more innovative, and to build those resilient mindsets that will equip them with the capacity to identify and create career opportunities for themselves, because the age of the token woman is over. We do not want women to just make up the numbers. We want a generation of women who can muster the courage, character, skills and confidence to command respect and authority. We therefore need to nurture women who can have real power and real authority to make and influence real decisions in the boardroom, in parliament, in the home and in all areas of the global agenda and their own lives.

Many visionary women leaders have, through their exemplary lives, laid a solid foundation for the sustained emancipation of women on all conceivable fronts. One of such women possessed one of the greatest feminine minds in the world's contemporary history. She was a woman who envisioned a more equitable place for women in the world by using her formidable literary gifts to chart a vision for a humanitarian cause for mankind as a whole. Her name was Maya Angelou.

Maya Angelou was an acclaimed author, poet, dancer, actress, singer, producer and activist. Indeed, her life totally celebrated the vision that a woman can fit into as many shoes as she chooses in her lifetime. She was so exceptionally visionary even in her own life that she consistently and futuristically said yes to life. She discovered who she was, and taught the same philosophy to women all over the world, by saying yes to all opportunities. To quote her, *"If I'm asked, 'Can you do this?' I think, if I don't do it, it'll be ten years before another Black woman is asked to do it. And I say, 'Yes, yes, when do you want me to do it?'"*

Born Marguerite Annie Johnson on April 4, 1928, in St. Louis, Missouri, United States of America, this great American visionary leader died on May 28, 2014. In what must qualify as one of the most inspiring lives ever lived by a woman in the contemporary history of mankind, Maya Angelou published seven autobiographies, three books of essays, several books of poetry, and is credited with a list of plays, movies and television shows spanning over 50 years. She received a multiplicity of awards and more than 30 honorary degrees.

Her series of seven autobiographies are focused on her childhood and early adult experiences. The first, *I Know Why The Caged Bird Sings*, tells of her life up to the age of 17 years and brought her instant international recognition and acclaim. She recited her poem *On The Pulse of Morning* at President Bill Clinton's inauguration on January 20, 1993, making her the first poet to make an inaugural recitation since Robert Frost's rendition at the 1961 inauguration of President John F. Kennedy.

She became a poet and writer after a series of occupations as a young adult. These occupations included fry cook, nightclub dancer and performer, cast member of an opera, coordinator for the Southern Christian Leadership Conference, and journalistic stints in Egypt and Ghana during the eventful period of Africa's decolonization. She was also an actress, writer, director, and the producer of plays, movies and public television programs.

In 1982, she was named the first Reynolds Professor of American Studies at Wake Forest University in Winston-Salem, North Carolina. As one of the great visionaries who spearheaded the social emancipation of Black people in segregationist America, she was active in the Civil Rights Movement, working alongside Martin Luther King Jr. and Malcom X. By the time she was in her octogenarian years, she was making in excess of 80 appearances a year on the lecture circuit.

Angelou was said to possess a clear gaze when she looked at others, almost proclaiming her extraordinary power of visionary influence at the same instant. She also spoke with a rich and cultured voice that seemed to lay her life bare for others to draw inspiration from. She possessed an unapologetic honesty that resonated with those, especially women, who had been silenced in their own pain, helping to give much needed life to their voice. Even in old age, Angelou's physique and erect carriage was a dignified expression of survival that others could aim to achieve.

Angelou was a Renaissance woman because, through the multiple roles she played, she lived a life of rebirth. Childhood sexual abuse, poverty and teenage motherhood did not limit her possibilities in life. In fact, she seemed to have made her life an entire vision of awe-inspiring transformation that she shared with the audience that read her poems and books, listened to her lectures, and witnessed her performances on the theater stage. By the time she died, she had accumulated a formidable catalogue of works.

In her lifetime, she received a Tony Award nomination, won three Grammy Awards for spoken work production, and was presented with the 2011 Presidential Medal of Freedom. Angelou, who never attended a university, was an educator who once told Oprah Winfrey, *"When you learn, teach, when you get, give."*

Angelou was both a visionary and a humanitarian, a dual trait that was evident in her determination to learn the languages of the different places she visited across the globe. In the 1960s she performed and raised funds for civil rights organizations, and became the Northern Coordinator for the Southern Christian Leadership Conference. For a time, she lived and worked in Cairo, Egypt and Accra, Ghana, as a theatrical performer, freelance journalist and university administrator. Back in the United States in the mid to late 1960s, Angelou worked alongside Malcolm X to create the Organization of Afro-American Unity shortly before his assassination in 1965, and she was just getting ready to help organize a march for Martin Luther King when he was assassinated in 1968.

International acclaim for her literary works began shortly after this painful period, with the publishing of *I Know Why The Caged Bird Sings* in 1969. She would devote the succeeding years writing additional memoirs and poetry that all directly spoke to the human experience, with more than passing reference to the Black woman's experience. She then proceeded to act in movies, including Alex Haley's *Roots* in 1977, while her poetry was featured, along with her own appearances, in John Singleton's *Poetic Justice* of 1993 and Tyler Perry's *Madea's Family Reunion* of 2006. Angelou also directed *Down in the Delta* in 1998.

Angelou was one of the greatest apostles of human dignity in her generation, and she wove that thread into all her performances and literary works. To date, she remains one of the greatest sources of quotable quotes in the world. Her repository of quotes was as vast as it was phenomenal and includes famous ones like: *"There is no greater agony than bearing an untold story inside you." "When someone shows you who they are, believe them the first time." "A bird doesn't sing because it has an answer, it sings because it has a song."* In fact, so revered were her inspirational words that they were developed into a Hallmark greeting card collection in the early 2000s. Also, so soul-inspiring were her poems that young women all across America recited them in talent shows, beauty pageants and poetry renditions.

Only a visionary and a humanitarian of the highest caliber could have earned the sort of publicly televised funeral with which Angelou was memorialized at her death. Oprah Winfrey, who saw Maya Angelou as a mentor, once said, *"Maya Angelou is not what she has done or written or spoken, it's how she did it all. She moved through the world with unshakeable calm, confidence, and a fiery, fierce grace and abounding love."*

Angelou was truly a visionary, and her first book, *I Know Why the Caged Bird Sings*, is eloquent testimony to this fact because the book has found particular relevance in the current national conversation about sexual abuse in the United States. Long before the #MeToo and #TimesUp movements brought sexual assault into national focus, Angelou had written in that 1969 book about her own experience with sexual trauma, and how her mother's boyfriend raped her when she was just a child. He was convicted and imprisoned.

She had other visionary firsts to her illustrious name. She was one of the first African-American female members in the Directors Guild of America, which she joined in 1975, shortly after writing the 1972 movie *Georgia, Georgia,* and made her official debut as movie director at the age of 70 with *Down in the Delta*, a 1998 movie about a mother who sent her children away from Chicago to live with family in rural Mississippi so that they could learn about their roots.

As Bill Clinton himself would nostalgically relate, Maya Angelou grew up in Stamps, Arkansas, a mere 30 minutes south of Clinton's own birthplace in Hope, Arkansas, and her work reminded him of the grocery store that his grandfather managed in a predominantly African-American neighborhood. The former President said, *"When I read 'I Know Why the Caged Bird Sings' I knew exactly who she was talking about and what she was talking about in that book."*

Angelou was also a prolific award winner. She won three Grammy Awards and five nominations for best spoken word albums: in 1993, 1995 and 2002, for *On The Pulse Of Morning, Phenomenal Woman* and *A Song Flung Up To Heaven* respectively. She was also nominated for a 1973 Tony Award for Best Supporting or Featured Actress for her role in Jerome Kilty's 1972 play *Look Away.*

Given the extraordinarily active life that she lived, it's perhaps not surprising that she wrote a total of seven autobiographies, the last one being released just a year before her death. One is hard put to name any other person, living or dead, who accomplished this uncommon feat. To the best of one's informed knowledge, most people write an average of just one autobiography. As Angelou told *TIME* magazine, *"I'll probably be writing when the Lord says 'Maya, Maya Angelou, it's time.'"* Indeed, she wrote until the very end of one of the most remarkable lifetimes recorded in the modern history of womanhood.

The only befitting eulogy with which one could satisfactorily end this treatise on Maya Angelou is a reproduction of one of her greatest poems, *Still I Rise*, which was first published in her similarly titled 1978 book of poetry *And Still I Rise*.

You may write me down in history

With your bitter, twisted lies,

You may trod me in the very dirt

But still, like dust, I'll rise.

Does my sassiness upset you?

Why are you beset with gloom?

'Cause I walk like I've got oil wells

Pumping in my living room.

Just like moons and like suns,

With the certainty of tides,

Just like hopes springing high,

Still I'll rise.

Did you want to see me broken?

Bowed head and lowered eyes?

Shoulders falling down like teardrops,

Weakened by my soulful cries?

Does my haughtiness offend you?

Don't you take it awful hard

'Cause I laugh like I've got gold mines

Diggin' in my own backyard.

You may shoot me with your words,

You may cut me with your eyes,

You may kill me with your hatefulness,

But still, like air, I'll rise.

Does my sexiness upset you?

Does it come as a surprise

That I dance like I've got diamonds

At the meeting of my thighs?

Out of the huts of history's shame

I rise

Up from a past that's rooted in pain

I rise

I'm a black ocean, leaping and wide,

Welling and swelling I bear in the tide.

Leaving behind nights of terror and fear

I rise

Into a daybreak that's wondrously clear

I rise

Bringing the gifts that my ancestors gave,

I am the dream and the hope of the slave.

I rise

I rise

I rise.

On a conclusive note, it is pertinent to stress that the world will continue to need those leaders who are capable of not only creating a compelling vision but also communicating that vision to others, and engaging them around it. The world will continue to need great visionary leaders who are able to communicate what lies beyond the horizon and inspire confidence in those in their generation, and in generations yet unborn. In real terms, the potential for the sustained greatness of our planet will continue to ride on the vehicle of the extraordinary vision of such leaders.

How to Gain Access to Your Power of Vision

1. In your thinking, live fully in the present moment but also attempt to go beyond your present reality to the possibilities of the future.

2. Fully engage your faculty of creative imagination as often as you can, resolving firmly to build an empire in your mind, fully aware that the only way to build an empire in your mind is to dream big dreams. Be a creative daydreamer of big dreams.

3. Constantly remind yourself that it hardly matters what you are doing if what you are doing is not what matters most. Always pause to ask yourself what the most valuable use of your time is at that instant.

4. Effective and persuasive communication are key interpersonal skills you must cultivate to be able to share your vision with others, and to convince them to subscribe to it.

5. Commit to converting lemon into lemonade, which means converting obstacles into the tools that you will use to succeed.

6. Respond to opportunities with enthusiasm and agreeability because, more often than not, you never really know you can do it until you try to do it.

7. Insist on living a life of unapologetic intellectual honesty with which you consistently speak the truth to yourself and to others.

8. Teach others what you are taught, and give others what you get.

9. Identify those natural gifts and inclinations that bring out a sense of purpose in you, and deploy them for the benefit of others.

10. Become the light that glows so brightly that others easily navigate their way through life.

CHAPTER 4

THE POWER OF CREATIVITY

"Power without a nation's confidence is nothing."

CATHERINE THE GREAT

Creativity, in many respects, totally defines itself. This is because, boiled down to its composites, it easily translates to "the activity of creating something." It is the creation of an idea, product or concept that is fundamentally novel and original, and is at the same time meaningful or useful. Not unnaturally, when we view creativity in this light we are excluding ideas and concepts that are poached from others, second-hand or copied. However, no matter how original a concept is, if it has no utilitarian value, it is essentially meaningless and ultimately lacks creative merit.

One quickly reminds oneself that a leader is basically someone who leads or commands an organization or a country. Yet, a leader is also someone who holds a dominant or superior position within a circle of influence, and is able to exercise a high degree of control or influence over others within this circle. Therefore, we can safely say that a creative leader is someone who leads in such a way as to create extraordinarily novel, original and meaningful ideas for the betterment of her people.

Creative leaders tend to think and act differently. They are courageous and curious. They are confident and positive. They are inspiring and passionate. They are open-minded and flexible. They are focused and balanced. Very significantly, they live in the present moment, refusing to revel in past glory or fret about a future that is still ahead. What is more, because they are generally always creatively preoccupied, they consistently come up with breakthrough ideas to create extraordinary results that have a positive impact on the lives of their people. Leadership is and was never an easy task. That is why few people rise up to bear its flag. Yet, leaders are still ordinary people who decide at one point or another to rise up to do extraordinary things.

Anyone who would be outstandingly creative as a leader must be prepared to rattle a few cages. The only thing about life that is constant is change. In politics and in governance, and in any other thing for that matter, the only thing that remains the same is the fact that nothing remains the same. While most people wait until they are propelled into leadership roles by the forces around them, creative leaders are more inclined to provoke themselves into action. Because they are constantly imagining new possibilities and fresh horizons, they proactively instigate change that they envision even when others do not. Yet, the only major difference between such leaders and the average person is that they are willing to take massive action rather than allow circumstances dictate action for them. That is what is meant by rattling cages. It means shaking up long-standing beliefs and institutions, and the fact that this is never an easy, nor is it a well-received, initiative is what makes such leaders great.

Creative leaders are very intuitive people. As humans, there are things we *know* to be true and things we *feel* to be true. Due to our education, most of us lean on our acquired knowledge to solve problems and make decisions. But the greatest leaders are those who realize that the things they sense, those possibilities that seem to lie just beyond the realm of what they know, are of inestimable value too, and that listening to them is how creative ideas occur to them.

We mostly have problems balancing logic with intuition, yet the truth is that those faculties are neither mutually exclusive nor are they in opposition to each other. Most truly creative leaders seem to perfect the art of blending logic with intuition to obtain phenomenal results. In truth, intellect without intuition results in a smart person without much impact, while intuition without intellect results merely in a spontaneous person who may be lacking in direction.

Creative leaders know that perfection, both in themselves and in their results, is quite impossible, and that the pursuit of perfection often stands in the way of progress. Leadership requires making consistent strides, no matter how small, and the quicker the stride, the greater the progress. Therefore, not only do they act swiftly but they also act with conviction. But conviction is rare. That is why creative leaders are also not very common. Creative leaders are decisive in their conviction. They are also able to step out of the common view and imagine new possibilities that set the course for others to follow. Creative leaders are usually willing to go beyond what is required of them to do things that are truly inspiring, both to them and others. Ultimately, the vital difference between creative leaders and those they lead is action.

Sometime in the 18th century, an Empress of Russia rose to unprecedented prominence to become the long-awaited social and political reformer who would infuse an uncommonly large dose of originality and creativity into the art of governance. Born Sophie of Anhalt-Zerbst in Poland in 1729, Catherine II was a German princess who later became Empress of Russia, ruling from 1762 to 1796, a period in which she would become the most powerful female figure in the world of her time. Totally incapable of conducting barely passable conversation in the Russian language, and with not even the remotest hereditary linkage to the throne when she moved to Russia at the age of 14, Catherine II was determined to integrate herself into Russian society and to learn Russian so that she could communicate and interact with the people.

She came to power in the aftermath of a coup she executed to overthrow her husband, Peter III. Catherine II, Russia's longest ruling female ruler, and one of the most influential rulers the country had ever had, revitalized a nation that easily became so large and strong as to be recognized as one of the great powers of Europe and Asia. Under her rule, the Russian Empire was extended south and west to include Crimea, Belarus and Lithuania.

In a nutshell, her creativity was such that she ended up wielding formidable influence to totally modernize Russia. In an administrative initiative that lacked precedence, she organized and convened a legislative commission for the sole purpose of modifying the laws of the country. Her reign was so significantly progressive that it was eulogized as the "Golden Era of the Russian Empire." During her reign, she foresaw and approved the issue of the Freedom Manifesto of the Nobility, a statute that exempted Russian nobles from military service.

Catherine II believed in and advocated for education and culture, and because she loved to read, she sustained excellent relations with some of Russia's great thinkers of her time, and erudite French scholars like Voltaire and Diderot. Her advocacy for the empowerment of women and girls found a vehicle of promotion in her love for art, and in aligning with the idea of the Enlightenment, she gave full support for the establishment of the Smolny Institute, Russia's first-ever state-financed higher education institution for women.

The capacity of Catherine II for innovation and creativity knew no bounds. She was credited for showing more originality than any other previous ruler of Russia, and in any other part of Europe for that matter. Her creative originality was in patent display in the way she radically transformed the nature and structure of the central government of Russia to alter, in a manner that might have previously been considered inconceivable, the relationship between the central power and the corporate forces in Russian society.

She was also innovative enough to take inspiration from the laws of England, personally drafting changes to the constitutional structure of Russia, which she then proposed and introduced. She passionately believed in her reforms, and while she still managed to identify with many great administrators who aligned with her innovations, most of the officials she could rely on did not quite live up to her high expectations. Yet, in wielding such absolute authority, the people of Russia were left with no choice than to accept the legitimacy of Catherine II's rule, regardless of their disagreement with most of her policies.

The creativity in her model of governance was fascinating. Her government was operated as a partnership between the crown, the nobility and the townspeople. She was the first ruler of Russia to ever conceive of drawing up legislation to set out the corporate rights of the nobles and the townspeople, as well as the civil rights of the free populations of her country. She gave the nobility, the townspeople and the peasants a legal framework within which their rights could be accessed. Catherine II was also the first ruler to establish courts of law to which peasants had access to sue merchants and nobles. Moreover, during her reign, the individual, other than the serf or the soldier, was allowed more dignity, more security, more responsibility and more space, thereby allowing the people to escape from the overwhelming pressure of the militarization that had been imposed by Peter I, and later restored by Paul I.

The final verdict on Catherine II will have to be that she was an inspirational leader who overcame both language barrier and religious skepticism to become one of the greatest rulers in Russia's history. An efficient and effective leader, she introduced social and economic reforms that made Russia wealthier. Through grants to farmers and landowners she introduced the application of modern scientific methods and new machinery to the agriculture industry in Russia.

Another brilliant innovation of Catherine II was in how she boosted Russia's population. At the start of her reign, Russia was grossly underpopulated. As soon as she consolidated herself on the throne, she embarked on a program in which she used foreign newspapers to encourage immigration to her country. She offered enticing initiatives to people from different parts of Europe to settle in Russia to help increase the population. As an intellectual, she founded the first-ever school of mines in St. Petersburg and the Smolny Institute for women's education, inspiring people not only to move to Russia but to also expand their educational and economic opportunities as they settled in Russia.

Catherine II has been hailed as a woman who had an optimistic and cheerful temperament. She used her skills to build magnificent alliances that ingratiated her with the Russian people. Throughout her life, despite her exalted status of nobility, she exhibited great communication and interpersonal skills that allowed her to bond on unusual levels of friendship with people from all walks of life. For instance, apart from paying close attention to public opinion on her various travels around Russia where she was always well received by the common people, it is also believed that her servants adored her and remained loyal to her for many years.

A couple of centuries later, the world was presented with uncommonly creative leadership again, this time on the Asian continent. Park Geun-hye is the first-ever female President of South Korea, and she served from 2013 to 2017. She is also the first-ever woman to be elected a head of state in East Asia. She was listed by *Forbes* in its World's 100 Most Powerful Women in 2013 and 2014 consecutively, and the most powerful woman in East Asia. Park did not necessarily come into the spotlight because of her ascension to office as President. She had already been in public focus and consciousness as the daughter of the late Park Chung-hee, the President of South Korea who was assassinated in 1979.

Born in 1952 in Samdeok-dong of Jung District Daegu in South Korea, she received a Bachelor's degree in Engineering from Sogang University. She also studied at Joseph Fourier in France but had to terminate her studies to return to South Korea when her mother was killed. Later she would be conferred with honorary doctorate degrees from the Chinese Culture University in Taiwan, Pukyong National University and KAIST, Sogang University and TU Dresden University.

She was compelled to take on the role of hostess as a replacement for her mother who was First Lady and was killed in a failed assassination attempt on her father. After her father's death, she remained active in public life and served as Chair of the Educational and Cultural Foundations of South Korea.

Park was sworn in as the 18th President of South Korea in February 2013, at a time when the country was facing external security threats. This specter of external aggression, accompanied by internal constraints associated with reorganization of the government, led to a rather slow start to her administration. Changes in the National Assembly that were intended to promote bipartisanship ended in an administrative gridlock. There were other challenges, including high national household debt figures and tensions with North Korea, China and Japan.

Park actually rode on the vehicle of the stereotyping of women as problem-solvers to open the doors for her own entry into the political arena. She was adept at stressing her positive feminine traits to overcome the perceived weaknesses of female politicians. In addition, she exploited her long political credentials and strengths in diplomacy, and in national security issues, and this presentation of herself as an embodiment of both experience and change struck a favorable note with the public.

She ran for election and won a seat in the National Assembly to represent Talssong (Dalesong) District in 1998 under the conservative Grand National Party. She was re-elected for a further four terms from 1998 to 2012. She also served as Chair of her party between 2004 and 2006. Under her leadership, the party achieved unprecedented electoral gains against very difficult odds. In fact, she was credited for her party's victory in all of the 40 re-elections and by-elections held between 2004 and 2006.

Park's enduring political legacy will have to be the remarkable creativity she deployed to buoying up the dwindling fortunes of her party at a very critical period in its history. In what will have to pass for one of the most remarkable, if not totally deft, maneuvers in partisan politics, when her party, the Grand National Party, was experiencing dwindling approval ratings, the party under her leadership formed an emergency committee and renamed the party Saenuri Party, which means "new frontier," and Park emerged as Chair and de facto Leader of the party.

The renamed party, now invigorated by a new identity and a renewed sense of political purpose, went ahead to achieve a series of surprising victories against the opposing Democratic United Party in the 2012 general elections, winning 152 seats and retaining its majority position. During the campaign period, Park had traveled extensively throughout South Korea, visiting more than 100 constituencies. She became a leading candidate in every national poll in South Korea with her approval ratings rising to the highest possible level.

Quite apart from the refreshing flavor of originality that she brought into politics, Park reaped immense benefits from building a good, if not absolutely admirable, public image that made her stand far aloof and above the fray of the politics of the day. Maintaining an unusually high index of integrity, she was renowned for her strict adherence to keeping political promises. Upon assuming office, she emphasized the right of the people to pursue happiness, a democratic economy and customized welfare services for the people of South Korea. With a focus on conservative, market-oriented policies, she set out to cut taxes, reduce regulation, and establish strong law and order mechanisms.

Park's vision of her new government was focused on a rather creative slogan, *"A new era of hope and happiness,"* that incorporated five cardinal administrative goals, including a job-centered creative economy, tailored employment and welfare, creativity-oriented education and cultural enrichment, a safe and united society, and strong security measures for sustainable peace on the Korean Peninsula. Her government planned to create a trustworthy, clean and capable administration through carrying out these goals along with related strategies and relevant tasks.

In her inauguration speech, she expressed her hope that North Korea would give up its nuclear arms to walk on the path of peace and mutual development. She declared that a foundation for a happy era of unification would be built through the Korean Peninsula Trust-building Process, and in which all Korean people would be able to enjoy prosperity and freedom for the realization of their dreams. In furtherance of this objective, she articulated four guiding principles for her administration to be able to realize her vision. These were economic prosperity, people's happiness, cultural enrichment and the establishment of the foundation for peaceful unification.

She also vowed that South Korea would break away from the developmental model it had long pursued, which centered around the nation, and would instead shift the focus to the individual citizenry. She hoped that through this process the structure of co-prosperity would be established in which citizens would become happy and unimpeded national development would occur as a result.

During her visit to Harvard University in Cambridge, Massachusetts in the United States, she vowed to a packed audience to save South Korea and advocated for stronger relationships between South Korea and the United States. The United States and South Korea later adopted a joint declaration for the American-South Korean Alliance at a summit held at the White House, at which ways were discussed to further develop bilateral relations in a future-forward manner. Ways to promote cooperation in peace building in the north-east Asian regions, and to strengthen the partnerships between Seoul and Washington were also discussed.

In addition, South Korea and the United States agreed to adopt a joint statement on comprehensive energy cooperation that would build a foundation for a future growth engine, while they established a policy cooperation committee on information and communication technologies. Park seized the opportunity to urge the United States to expand the annual

American visa quota for South Korean professionals so as to promote the co-development of both economies.

As President, Park promised to restore a high level of economic growth to her country. She publicly apologized to those who had suffered under her father's regime and regretted the treatment of activists. She also vowed to unite the country and address stark income disparities. What was most commendable about Park's creative leadership was that her vision and basic principles for governing South Korea were firmly outlined in her policy plans for the economy, society, welfare, diplomacy and unification. She also consistently deployed the usage of key words and phrases to succinctly encapsulate her policy directions. For instance, her administration's key words for managing the affairs of the state were people, happiness, trust, co-prosperity and principles.

Creativity will always remain important, and the creative leader will always remain in premium demand. In fact, some would argue that creativity is the single most important leadership skill in a world that is more volatile, more uncertain and more complex than at any time before. The one thing that is clear is that the challenge is to embrace the innovator within. Leaders will continually need to embrace originality, and to focus on quality in everything they do. There is always room for improvement. There is always a better way, if we are willing to seek it. Creativity is coming up with ideas, while innovation is bringing those ideas to life. Anything less than a constant flow of life-changing ideas won't be sufficient in a world in constant flux.

Our world is more overwhelming than ever before. The future is more unpredictable than ever, and global resources seem to be getting scarcer. The world will continue to need those who express a certain willingness to be creative change-makers. To come up with ideas and bring them to life is one of the greatest challenges of the contemporary woman leader.

How to Access Your Power of Creativity

1. To be a creative leader you have to be prepared to lead in such a way as to create novel, original and meaningful ideas.

2. Remain alive in the present moment, for it is only in the present moment that action has any real meaning.

3. Free up your mind from negativity so that your mind can become like a garden whose soil is free from the weeds that can prevent the germination of creative seeds.

4. Always have it at the back of your mind that the past is history, the future a mystery, and this moment is a gift. That is why this moment is also called the present. Maximize your power of creativity by living in the present.

5. Be prepared to rattle a few cages, which means shaking up long-standing beliefs and institutions to come up with fresh perspectives.

6. Learn to cultivate, and to place trust in your intuitive abilities.

7. Avoid the pursuit of perfection, for you will never attain it. Instead, take that stride, no matter how small, with a decisive sense of conviction.

8. Be prepared to innovate new ideas while being open to adapt the concepts of others to create yours.

CHAPTER 5

THE POWER OF COMPETENCE

"The best man for the job is a woman."

MARGARET THATCHER

No matter how universally impressive a leader's skill set may be, she will need to be a fundamentally competent individual for her impact as a deployer of human, material and intellectual resources to be felt to any significant degree. Competence is that set of recognizable and demonstrable skills and characteristics that both enable and improve the efficiency and performance of a task.

Some thinkers see competence as a combination of practical and theoretical knowledge, behavior and cognitive skills, and values that are vital to the improvement of performance. Yet, on the everyday practical level, it is unarguably the state or quality of being adequately or well-qualified for a job. It also connotes possessing the ability to perform a specific role. An example of this is seen in management competence, which might incorporate skills like strategic thinking, emotional intelligence, influence and negotiation.

At best, competence, especially in the realm of political leadership, presents a very complicated and broad concept, and that is why it can end up meaning different things to different people. For some people, competence can include knowledge, motivation, social characteristics and roles. For others, it may connote the skills of one particular person in accordance with the demands of their office. Yet, for others, competence can mean a combination of two parameters: personal competence and merit. That is still not the end of the story of competence. Some will define it as that holistic group of knowledge, personal attitudes, skills and related experiences which are needed for a leader's success.

Whichever way we choose to view it, as long as a leader is able to carry out set tasks at an expected, or better still, exceptional level of proficiency, she can safely be considered a competent leader. On a broader level of consideration, however, competence, as an ability, demonstrates itself in different manners in different situations. Also, in emergencies, competent people tend to respond based on their own behaviors that they have found to be effective in the past. That also suggests that to be competent, a leader must be able to interpret a situation in accurate context, and to have options of possible actions to take, and be essentially formally or self-trained in those possible actions. Overall, competence tends to grow through both experience and the inclination of a leader toward learning and adaption.

As mankind has evolved over the centuries, so has the need for competent leadership gained increasing prominence, if only because of the critical need to provide effective guidance and direction to people with whom they do not necessarily come into direct contact. A competent leader displays the capability to dynamically sense and respond to changes in the governance environment, and responds with actions that are focused, fast and decisive.

A competent leader has the knowledge, skills and motivation to be productive and to produce results. Such a leader is necessarily rewarded with the maximization of her influence, genuine progress toward her highest potential, and the firm and unquestioned establishment of her own authority. Ultimately, she reaps the rewards of her efforts as her constituents uphold her tenure of leadership by casting a solid vote of confidence in her ability to lead, which in the context of contemporary democracy translates to re-election to office.

Competent leaders never settle for good or average results, whether it is in the effort of their team or themselves. They are purpose driven to invest the effort that will produce great results. This mindset strives for decisions and work of such superior quality that they may seem to be arrested by a compulsive desire for perfectionism. Even if that were true, however, it still does not mean that the slightest tendency toward perfectionism prevents them from delivering results. They never settle for the average when they can deliver greatness. That is why such leaders not only pay scrupulous attention to detail but also consistently display nothing short of peak performance through every season of leadership, whether they are the good, the bad or the ugly times of leading.

Toward the close of the last century, perhaps no other leader in the contemporary history of governance in Western civilization exemplified the classic traits of competent leadership better than Margaret Hilda Thatcher, later to become Her Ladyship Baroness Thatcher, Britain's first female Prime Minister. Rapidly rising from a place of relative obscurity as a junior minister, she confounded pundits to break the glass ceiling by becoming Leader of the Conservative Party in 1975 in a country and political party strongly dominated by men, and later rocked the British political establishment to be elected Britain's first female Prime Minister in 1979.

Thatcher demonstrated uncommon competence in leadership that was characterized by a ruthless decisiveness never before seen in a usually staid British establishment that prided itself on its loyalty to cherished values of delicacy and diplomacy. She was also a strong believer in individual choice and personal responsibility. Margaret Thatcher holds the record of the longest-serving Prime Minister of the United Kingdom. She also has the distinction of being the country's first-ever woman to serve as Prime Minister and Leader of the Conservative Party.

Born in 1925, just a year before her sovereign Queen Elizabeth II was born, Thatcher had an early upbringing in Lincolnshire in England. She studied Chemistry at Oxford University and briefly worked as a research chemist. She later proceeded to read Law and qualified as a barrister. Thatcher was appointed a junior minister for pensions in 1961, after her election to a seat in the House of Commons in 1959. Following a remarkable political career she was elected UK Prime Minister in 1979.

Thatcher's rise to political prominence is all the more remarkable because in a country whose political leadership had always been dominated by men, she broke through the ranks of what had hitherto been a gender-specific privilege to overcome male chauvinism. She would serve a total of just over 11 years to attain the distinction of the longest-serving Prime Minister of the United Kingdom in the last 100 years. Perhaps of even greater significance, her long political career was characterized by an indisputable competence that was defined by a combination of ruthless decisiveness, a strong belief in individual choice and personal responsibility, and an unwavering commitment to free markets and small government.

Although Thatcher's leadership was characterized as being altogether autocratic, and polarized public opinion in such a pervasive manner as to leave Britain literally gasping at her audacity, it was that leadership style that gave her the ability to take decisions firmly, swiftly and efficiently. This extraordinary degree of competence rendered her uncommonly effective in those high-pressure situations in which procrastination or hesitation might have proved damaging, if not outright dangerous, and Britain was always the better off for it.

The world's greatest examples of exemplary feats in governance prove conclusively that this leadership style is what has always enabled powerful and confident leaders to take firm charge of crisis situations to extract stability out of volatility. Thatcher utilized these qualities to tremendous advantage in the key moments of her tenure as Prime Minister. Her unparalleled courage, which will earn her the privilege of further mention in another section of this book, would be demonstrated in her unwavering resolve during her government's disputes with the trade unions in the 1980s, unequivocally sealing her reputation as a determined and fearless leader.

As it happened, by the time she assumed office as Prime Minister, public services in the United Kingdom had all but ground to an ignominious halt due to recurring trade union disputes and strikes over remunerations. In what is, to this day, considered one of the most decisive actions taken to curtail the pervasive influence of unions, Thatcher took unprecedentedly uncompromising charge and introduced legislation that severely whittled down the power of the unions, totally refusing to accede with accustomed ease to their demands. The miners' strike of 1984 to 1985 provides a perfect example of Thatcher's decisive competence. Stockpiling on coal in massive amounts prior to what might have turned out a breaking point for her government during the dispute, she simply refused to give in to their demands and finally succeeded in breaking up their prolonged strike.

Her determination turned the United Kingdom from a three-day working week due to electricity shortages in the country to an AAA-rated financial powerhouse. Also, her leadership saw to the transformation and revitalization of foreign investments in the United Kingdom, enhancing the fortunes of the private sector and providing an opportunity for less affluent citizens to buy their own houses.

Thatcher's leadership was the word competence defined. It probably fueled her ability to set goals and see them through to a logical conclusion. What principally characterized her tenure was her confidence in her ideals, because of which she was able to govern based on a rare sort of conviction politics that was largely driven by her own values. It was this totally individualistic political philosophy that would later earn her system of governance the brand name of "Thatcherism," a unique admixture of policies that encompassed, among others, privatization, tax cuts, home ownership and free market economics.

Because of her leadership style and conviction, she was able to build the strong relationships and forge strong political alliances which ensured that the United Kingdom continued to remain a force to be reckoned with in foreign and global affairs. For instance, riding on the vehicle of her strong ideological affinity with then President Ronald Reagan of the United States, she was able to rekindle Britain's unique and special relationship with America. Indeed, it was as an ally of the United States that Thatcher was able to win widespread support for her decisive role in the Falklands War of 1982, a defining moment in her political career and which led to her being re-elected to office in 1983.

Thatcher's uncompromising politics and leadership style was considered quite revolutionary for her time, possibly because of her unswerving and clear moral suasion. Certainly, she was hailed for exhibiting personality traits that included self-confidence, pragmatism, ambition, aggressiveness and a strong moral belief in her own peculiar manner of discharging duties and obligations. She left no one in doubt as to her single-minded quest for the combined power and authority that unequivocally allowed her to take unchallenged charge of control over decision making in her government. She always seemed to have a crystal clear direction of where she planned to take the country and how to get there. When unemployment rates plummeted during her early years in office, she realized rather quickly that so-called tested policies were stifling the British economy and that there was a need for a radical departure from the past. She persevered and successfully revived the British economy through her conviction and actions.

Thatcher had very little patience for group discussions, consensus seeking and a protracted decision-making process. Not unnaturally, this inclination prevented her from entertaining what she saw as unnecessary and long-winded expressions of opinion, because of which she was able to pare down inefficiency to its barest minimum. Consequently, as a confident leader and sole decision maker, she could authoritatively lay down her priorities and policies and fully expected people to align themselves to them. Expressed differently, she ensured that her goals were achieved within the full ambit of her own control and direction.

While her determination helped her to stand up to tyranny, it was her self-confidence that gave her the enormous respect she commanded at her every turn, and it was the resolute tone in her voice that gave her the ability to stand up and be listened to. As a woman leading a group of men, she earned a respect and an influence that was not only local but which also had a global reach. These days, many are quick to admit that without the firm conviction in her belief in her own abilities, Thatcher would not have been as successful as she was in bringing about the long-lasting positive change that she so efficiently and effectively bequeathed to the United Kingdom as a lasting legacy.

Thatcher was resolute in her beliefs. It was this resoluteness, added to a deep personal conviction, that served to restore the entrepreneurial spirit of the people of the United Kingdom. She deregulated the London Stock Exchange in 1986 and spring-boarded the City of London to the forefront of global finance. Ultimately, Thatcher, "The Iron Lady of Great Britain," fully recognized that, as a leader, the responsibility for all her decisions lay with her, and her alone. Thatcher's legacy lives on.

Another "Iron Lady of Competence" ruled Russia a clear two centuries before Thatcher appeared on Britain's firmament. In the chapter preceding this one, that great Empress of Russia was credited with the power of uncommon creative leadership. Only a few of the women leaders presented in this book have the rare privilege of appearing in two chapters. Catherine the Great is one of those women leaders.

Catherine the Great was born Sophie of Anhalt-Zerbst in Poland in 1729. Also known as Catherine II, she was a German princess who later became Empress of Russia, and was widely acknowledged as the most powerful woman in the world in her time. Possessing not even rudimentary knowledge of the Russian language, and absolutely no hereditary claim to the throne by the time she arrived in Russia at the relatively tender age of 14, Catherine II cultivated a surprisingly juvenile determination to learn the Russian language so that she could communicate and interact with the people of Russia.

Much later, she ascended to monarchical power in a palace coup that she executed against her husband, and to date remains one of the very few female rulers of her time who reigned for such a long period in Russia. She was also one of the most influential rulers of Russia, achieving the unprecedented feat of expansion of Russia's borders. During her reign the Russian Empire was extended south and west to include Crimea, Belarus and Lithuania.

Catherine II managed to elevate the twin leadership styles of unbridled autocracy and raw competence to an unprecedented level. Indeed, she was an autocratic leader who wielded her power with a very competent and a very authoritarian approach to leadership. She insisted on retaining absolute control over the country, with every decision regarding Russia being approved or initiated by herself. She reinforced her authority through absolute power and rigid discipline, and she remained consistent in this leadership style throughout her reign.

The manner of her rise to power in a foreign country was conclusive demonstration of her personal qualities of unequalled ambition, confidence, courage, intelligence and logic. She staged a coup against her husband, Peter III, at a time when he had started losing popularity and making enemies within the church and the military. She had initially intended to take over the throne on behalf of her young son and relinquish the throne as soon as her son had attained majority. However, she later opted instead to hold on to power and ended up ruling Russia for over 34 years, earning herself the title "Catherine the Great."

It is no exaggeration to say that she earned the title Catherine the Great. Catherine II was both a social and a political reformer who exerted her tremendous influence to radically modernize Russia. It is also true that she was immensely creative. She organized a legislative commission to modify the laws of the country. It is little wonder that her reign is largely perceived as the Golden Era of the Russian Empire. It was also the golden era of Russian nobility, as during her reign she foresaw the compelling need for, and approved the policy of, the Freedom Manifesto of the Nobility, an aristocratic-centered privilege that exempted Russian nobles from military service.

Catherine II believed in and advocated for education and culture. She loved to read and maintained good relations with some of Russia's great thinkers of the day, as well as erudite French scholars like Voltaire and Diderot. She also advocated for the empowerment of women and girls. In fact, falling back on her abiding love for art, she lent her support to the idea of the Enlightenment, during which time the Smolny Institute, the first state-financed higher education institution for women, was established in Russia.

An intelligent woman who demonstrated that competent leadership rides on the vehicle of courage, Catherine II employed logic to seize opportunities for the benefit of her people. Certainly, nothing could have seemed more logical than her introduction of inoculation against smallpox to Russia. When she learned that there was a new inoculation treatment for smallpox in England, she paid the pioneer of the inoculations to come to Russia to inoculate herself, her son and grandson.

What she did qualified itself as an enormous risk, as the experiment might have resulted in her death and that of her offspring. Risking her dynasty in this manner drew world attention to Catherine II, and it inspired millions of Russians and other Europeans to get vaccinated against smallpox. That public act of courage on her part saved millions of people who would have otherwise died or been badly scarred by the disease. It is little wonder that the people of Russia loved Catherine II so much, and she became known as the most benevolent ruler Russia had ever known.

Catherine II was a reformer. She introduced extensive social and economic reforms to make Russia a wealthier country. Through grants to farmers and landowners, she introduced the application of modern scientific methods and new machinery to the agriculture industry in Russia. At the start of her reign, Russia was grossly underpopulated. Engaging in a very original approach to the problem, Catherine II embarked on a program in which she involved foreign newspapers, using them to invite and offer enticing initiatives to people from different parts of Europe to settle in Russia, all in a refreshingly creative bid to help increase the country's population.

No less formidable was her competence in the area of intellectual empowerment. She founded the first-ever school of mines in St. Petersburg and the Smolny Institute that catered to the education of women. Clearly, she was an enlightened leader who strove on any conceivable front to change her country for the better, as was evident in her efforts to inspire people to move to Russia, and her expansion of educational frontiers for her people through the establishment of institutions, and the promotion and sponsorship of various art and cultural projects for the enlightenment of the people.

The world is now in a better position to properly analyze Catherine II's exceptional competence and leadership acumen in applying decision-making processes. As an autocratic Empress, Catherine II displayed a very authoritarian style of leadership in which she took care to retain total control over all of Russia. She reinforced her immense power through three strategies. Firstly, she ensured that every decision taken with regard to governance was either proposed or approved by her. Secondly, she stamped her authority on the polity through a combined power and discipline that remained consistent and unwavering. Thirdly, she earned the devoted loyalty and affection of her subjects because she made their needs her primary concern and dedicated her life pursuing those needs on their behalf.

Catherine II developed new laws for Russia, and strictly adhered to them. Yet, in one truly significant respect, her autocratic style was a marked departure from the norm of accustomed autocratic leadership. She not only embraced new ideas and theories but also welcomed freedom of speech, as long as that freedom did not go too far out of line to brazenly criticize the effectiveness of her rule and her reforms. Her leadership style may have been effective at that time because Russia was largely a disunited population of citizens who were dismally limited in their capabilities, and Catherine II herself possessed the incomparable vision, creativity and intellect that placed her on a pedestal that earned her unquestioned respect.

Catherine II's rise to power was carefully contrived, orchestrated and calculated. Right from the outset, her marriage had merely been one of political expediency. Her patience paid off in the long run when the then Empress of Russia, Elizabeth, died in 1762. Catherine II's husband, Peter, made a clean successful claim to the throne and succeeded Elizabeth to become the new emperor of Russia, a development that pleased Catherine II since it meant she was only one heartbeat away from becoming the sole ruler of Russia.

As it turned out, Peter III was a weak ruler whose political views alienated and frustrated Russia's nobles. His wife's friends and allies were beginning to grow weary of Peter, and this was just the opportunity she needed to seize power. She contrived a plan to stage a coup and force Peter to abdicate the throne, handing power over to herself. Clearly, she had put up long enough with the political weaknesses that precipitated her husband's destruction. After rallying up sufficient support for her aspiration, she kicked Peter off the throne by assembling a military force that arrested him and pressed him into signing control over to her. Catherine II had finally achieved her dream of becoming Empress of Russia.

Catherine II was an exceptionally competent ruler. She had spent her whole life preparing for her rule and she was determined not to trivialize the opportunity like her husband did. There had been some political pressure to install her seven-year-old son, Paul, as emperor. She fiercely resisted that move, knowing only too well that a child could easily be manipulated, and she was not going to let her reign be threatened by another coup. So, she focused on building her power base as quickly as practicable, a feat she was able to accomplish by increasing her strength among her allies, reducing the influence of her enemies and ensuring that she had the unalloyed loyalty of the military. Yet, ambitious as she was, she harbored the least desire to be a petty or cruel dictator.

An avid reader and enthusiastic learner, she had somehow arrived at the understanding that there was tremendous value in the concept of the Enlightenment, a political philosophy that, at that time, embraced knowledge and reason about superstition and faith. Russia, at this point in its history, was not particularly celebrated for a cultured, sophisticated or even educated citizenry. Indeed, in that era, most of Russia was composed of peasantry who were little more than subsistence farmers. Catherine II was determined to change the world's perception of Russia, and to embark on a process that would inexorably take Russia to its own place of pride and influence on the world stage.

She worked hard to expand Russian territory through a series of military campaigns that would eventually lead to the annexation of Crimea. Her initial intention had been to empower and increase the level of freedom of the serfs and ordinary people of Russia, but unfortunately those ideals had to be quickly discarded as they would have resulted in significant political upheaval among the nobility at the time. She had hoped that someday she would be able to empower her people such that all men would be equal, but it soon became obvious that such aspirations were simply too advanced for the prevailing culture.

She focused more on enlightenment, and she was adored by those in the Enlightenment era, for she had spent a great deal of time learning how to be cultured. She read broadly and voraciously, acquired a vast collection of works of art, as well as wrote plays, stories and musical pieces herself. She worked hard to cultivate the image of a sophisticated woman of taste and refinement, while simultaneously building up a formidable military machine which she used to expand Russia's influence. For instance, she gained control over Poland and placed her own lover in control of the Polish throne. Soon, she gained more territory from Poland, apart from gaining a level of political control over the country as well.

Her role in the expansion and legitimacy of Russia on the global turf can never be understated. Although Russia was not a particular favorite of the international community, other nations were compelled to develop a grudging respect for Russia as an emerging power. As she strove to increase the size and strength of the country, she also decided to empower the aristocracy, increase the size of government and simultaneously decrease the power of the Orthodox Church, being someone who was not particularly religious.

The decision to empower the nobility and ruling class even further was inspired by the chaos of the French Revolution, a development that convinced Catherine II that there was a great deal to be feared in the common man. For a time, she had subscribed to the ideals of equality, but a fear of loss of control had led her to change her mind, and for this reason she would ultimately not go down in history as a woman who cared greatly for the common people, despite the nobility of her intentions at the beginning of her reign.

Catherine II reigned for 38 years in what history adjudges an exceptionally successful career. She increased the size of Russia significantly, increased the power of the country's military, and gave the Russian state unprecedented legitimacy on the global stage. She lived an extraordinary life and died a relatively quiet death for a role that often ended in bloody coups and terrible rebellions. Of all the rulers of Russia she was considered to be one of the greatest, for she brought in a powerful military, increased the efficiency of the state and created the concept of an artistic and enlightened Russia.

Never in the checkered history of mankind has there been a greater need for competent and strong leadership on all fronts. It is competence that will determine whether followers will respect and follow a leader or not. Indeed, it is ultimately followers that decide whether a leader is great or not. Leaders have to cultivate a composite of decisiveness, hope, inspiration and trust for their followers to consider them capable, competent and strong. Every leader's followers must have the hope that their leader knows both the problems and the opportunities that abound in the society, and can explain both, and then offer effective strategies to solve and leverage both.

Also, followers must be sufficiently inspired to subscribe to their leader's vision and narrative as to how they, together, will confront and solve problems to turn them into opportunities. Furthermore, followers must place nothing less than implicit trust in their leader. Finally, followers must be in a state of assurance that their leader will act decisively any time decisive action is called for. Therein lies the overall challenge for a world in dire need of stronger and more competent leaders. Happily, the women leaders are stepping up to the plate.

How to Gain Access to Your Power of Competence

1. You must be able to dynamically sense and then respond with focused, fast and decisive action to changes in your circle of influence.

2. You will need to acquire the knowledge, skills and motivation to produce results.

3. You cannot afford to settle for average when you can deliver greatness.

4. Consistently remain a strong believer in individual choice and personal responsibility.

5. Take your decisions firmly, swiftly and efficiently, especially in high-pressure situations.

6. Cultivate courage. Courage is not the absence of fear. Courage is the mastery of fear.

7. Insist on setting clear and precise goals, and seeing them through to a logical conclusion.

8. Cultivate confidence in your ideals, and remain consistently driven by your values.

9. Insist on forging those strong alliances that can enhance your leadership efforts and win you support.

10. Have a crystal-clear direction of where you plan to take your followers and how to get there.

11. Assume full responsibility for all your decisions, actions and inactions.

12. Refuse to engage in pettiness, cruelty or insensitivity.

The Power of Emotional Intelligence

"I declare before you all that my whole life,
whether it be long or short, shall be devoted to
your service and the service of our great imperial
family, to which we all belong."

QUEEN ELIZABETH II

A good leader must lead from and with the heart. That is the source of the enduring beauty of feminine leadership. No known form of human leadership seeks expression through the power of emotional intelligence more than strong feminine influence. Emotional intelligence, being the ability to identify and manage one's own emotions, as well as the emotions of others, expresses itself through a combination of empathy, compassion, understanding, accommodation and appreciation.

Daniel Goleman is an American psychologist who helped to popularize the concept of emotional intelligence. He describes emotional intelligence as possessing the five key elements of *self-awareness, self-regulation, motivation, empathy and social skills.* Of the social skills, the most vital is appreciation. The greatest gift a leader can give her followers is that of genuine appreciation. Yet, for most people, conducting interpersonal human relationships with appreciation can be like trying to navigate uncharted waters. Therefore, like any good sailor, we need a North Star in our task of empathic and emotional navigation. The Golden Rule can be our North Star in this quest.

In its simplest and most lucid expression, the Golden Rule states: *"Do unto others as you would have others do unto you."* The Golden Rule cuts across cultural settings and religious boundaries to be embraced by people from every part of the world, and anyone who wishes to employ appreciative conduct in relating with others can easily find sufficient motivation in the Golden Rule.

This confidence in the universal applicability of the Golden Rule is predicated on certain bases. First, it will be quite difficult to find anyone saying, *"Please treat me worse than I treat you!"* On the contrary, everyone wants to be treated fairly and decently. It is merely a rational expectation to desire fair and decent treatment from others. Secondly, application of the Golden Rule is of such simplicity that one needs not be a philosopher to practice it. All one needs to do is imagine oneself in the place of another person. The third basis for its genuine utility is that it is a win-win philosophy. With the Golden Rule, everybody wins. If I treat you as well as I desire to be treated, you win; and if you treat me as well as you desire to be treated, I win.

We are all the same with respect to how we wish to be treated. We all want to be valued and appreciated. Most people who voluntarily leave their jobs do so because they feel undervalued and underappreciated. Encouragement is as vital to the human psyche as oxygen is to the soul. You can no more withhold encouragement from those you lead than you can prevent oxygen from entering their lungs. The two are near perfect corollaries. To value others, not even necessarily for performance, but simply because they are, first and foremost, human beings, is the hallmark of the Golden Rule.

People want to be genuinely appreciated for the skill and effort they deploy to their tasks. That what they do truly matters to others, and adds value to them is both a confidence booster and self-esteem elevator. We should always help people increase their self-esteem. A good leader must possess the skill of making other people feel important. There is no higher compliment one can pay another than helping her to be useful and to find satisfaction in that usefulness.

Also, people want to be trusted. Trust is the foundation of any worthwhile relationship. All profitable interactions, including friendship, business and marriage, require trust. In the absence of a foundation of trust in an organization, people cannot openly communicate their vision and values. Certainly, the led cannot be respected, and there can only be a focus on personal agenda rather than on shared goals. People can be made trustworthy only by trusting them.

People want to be respected. It is only when you truly appreciate someone that you can treat them with respect. Respect dignifies people. When leaders freely accord respect, it creates a totally positive working environment, and the more people are respected, the more and better they will perform.

The average person wants to be understood. Communication challenges are most often precipitated by a lack of understanding. People are too hasty in finding fault with others who do not conform to expected standards. Yet, with some effort at better understanding, we often discover that their way is not necessarily the wrong way, and that it is merely a different way. Others may perform differently because they haven't had the advantages we have had. On the other hand, they may be reacting to conditions that are totally beyond their control. As soon as we surmount these interpersonal constraints, we can achieve an emotional connectedness with others, and this is the meaning of genuine understanding.

When dealing with others, we must always seek to first understand and then to be understood. This is the fifth habit in the highly acclaimed book by Stephen Covey, *The Seven Habits of Highly Effective People*. The ability to seek first to understand others before being understood demands a dual attitude of emotional flexibility and humility. To properly understand another person will involve learning from that person. Also, to understand another person you must meet the person on their own level, and place the entire burden of establishing a human connection entirely on yourself and not on the other person. In fact, this is the real basis for the skilled practice of empathic communication.

Ultimately, we all need to be constantly reminded of the need to treat others as we would like to be treated. When we have an accurate notion of how we want to be treated, which naturally is with trust, respect, dignity and understanding, we can easily articulate how we should treat others.

As a young and impressionable girl, my pre-eminent ambition was to be a Catholic nun. My juvenile mind had registered quite early the notion that being a nun, and serving God to the exclusion of all distraction, was the greatest possible service one could render humanity. I sincerely desired to serve God. I also wanted to serve and save humanity. I wanted to feed the hungry, comfort the poor and save sinners from *"burning in hell."* As I grew older, however, I came into the gradual realization that there were various other ways in which one could serve God and humanity, and that one did not necessarily need to be a nun to serve. Today, I describe myself as a humanitarian. I work in the NGO sector, trying my best to save humanity from *"hell on Earth"*, as it were, in the 21st century.

That I asserted myself quite early in life hardly came as a surprise. As I have already mentioned in the preface to this book, because I came from a strong background of powerful and assertive women who had defied the prevailing gender dynamics for centuries, I was a lucky exception to the universal rule of negative cultural and social conditioning as a woman. My mother was descended from the Namwanga-speaking people of Zambia, where a woman rules the kingdom. Quite understandably, I grew up with the belief that I would one day become Queen and rule over the land and its men. Even in my father's Bemba-speaking tribe of Zambia, where a man rules the kingdom, a strong woman named Alice Mulenga Lenshina still rose to start a powerful movement through which she gained a massive following that shook the political foundations of Zambia.

These early experiences and exposure to strong feminine influence shaped my belief that women, being the backbone of society and the world's most potent force, have the power to lead the world and mold it for better outcomes in the evolution of mankind. Women are such natural-born leaders because of a strong sense of community which they cultivate by engaging at a very emotional level with their community in all they are able to do within the narrow corridors of opportunity that are available to them in a male-dominated society. To put it succinctly, women possess an intrinsic generosity of spirit, and an innate high index of emotional intelligence that makes them sensitive to the needs of others. Because of this early influence, I was also to learn quickly how to utilize emotional intelligence, self-awareness and social awareness skills in my relationships with other people.

My early years were spent in a Catholic co-educational school. I also joined the Brownies, the Girl Guides, and the Cadets. As part of my finishing school curriculum at the age of 17, I underwent military training. A Catholic education meant a more than passing emphasis on empathy and selflessness. It also emphasized the Golden Rule of *"doing unto others what you would want them to do unto you"* by going beyond self-actualization and personal gratification to be of benefit to others.

My co-educational background, my military training and the strong women around me were all responsible for indoctrinating the belief in me that I am equal in all respects to the other gender. The military is an institution that does not accord respect based on gender. Gender being of no consequence whatsoever, one earns respect only through hard work, valor, focus, leadership and authority. To be effective in the military, one requires a high index of emotional intelligence.

In those early years, I learned to aim for and shoot at the bull's-eye of a target. I also learned how to lead a platoon into battle with the sole aim of winning the battle. I learned the importance of preparedness, precision, discipline, initiative, focus, diligence, tact, perseverance, endurance and resilience. I would, in later years, realize that although these are the traits and qualities that are required for effective leadership, a leader will not get very far without possessing emotional intelligence.

Growing up in Zambia, I witnessed first-hand the devastation that the HIV/AIDS pandemic wrought on families, communities and the entire country. At its peak, the HIV/AIDS pandemic pruned down the professional and intellectual resource base of Zambia and the rest of the African continent in an unprecedented level of devastation. In claiming the lives of Africa's top managers, decision makers and policy makers, it not only impacted negatively on continental development but also created a humongous population of orphans and street urchins.

Although the world had made tremendous technological and medical advancement in the quest to see people live comfortably with HIV, it was baffling to me that in 2011, after more than 30 years, the world continued to experience new HIV/AIDS infections, especially in the young generation under the age of 30. Ironically, this is the generation that had never known a time without effective HIV/AIDS therapy. New infections might indicate that not enough effort had been deployed to halting the spread of HIV/AIDS, or perhaps that the message had somehow gotten lost and was not getting across to these young people.

That was how it occurred to me that new and innovative ideas were needed to contribute to the fight against the spread of HIV/AIDS so as to secure an AIDS-free world and an AIDS-free generation. Also believing in the age-old adage *"Prevention is better than cure"* I founded POSITIVE RUNWAY: Global Catwalk to Stop the Spread. This is a worldwide HIV/AIDS response campaign that aims to contribute to the global effort to stop the spread of HIV/AIDS by speaking the same language as the younger generation, and by utilizing the select media, including fashion and celebrity allure, that can arrest and hold their attention long enough for the message to be delivered effectively.

Ours is now a borderless world where both emerging markets and the developed world are creating multiple opportunities for greater global impact. With infinite ease of travel and communication now at our disposal, it is easy to seize these opportunities, cross borders and position one's brand for global visibility. That is why my organization currently boasts of a global presence spanning six continents. Yet, to adequately access the opportunities presented by globalization, one needs certain attributes, and high emotional intelligence is one of them. Emotional intelligence, more than any other, is responsible for creating sustainable human and business relationships. Closely allied to this are the attributes of humility, tact, self-affirmation, faith, diligence, self-awareness and social awareness.

Through the Global Catwalk, my organization aims to deliver the HIV/ AIDS message in dialogue that is comprehensible to the 21st century young generation. In working with a diverse global community of young people, we have to deal with varying cultures, behaviors, attitudes, traditions and beliefs, and this poses many challenges. Therefore, in leading POSITIVE RUNWAY, I focus on some key attributes of inspirational leadership, some of which cut across my early years of training, by utilizing emotional intelligence and relating positively to others.

Also, through being aware of and understanding how others feel, I have strived to go beyond mere self-actualization and personal development to be of genuine benefit to others, in the process working hard to leave a credible legacy that would have enhanced people's lives and made a sustainable difference that adds real value to their existence. I have also come to realize that one of the world's greatest setbacks is the erroneous belief that we are different and separate from each other. This mindset is the precursor to all human suffering, global hunger, poverty, conflict and socio-economic and gender inequalities.

In the course of my life and career, I have not found it such a daunting challenge to consistently subscribe to emotional intelligence, perhaps because of its similarities to the spirit of Ubuntu. I am, after all, an African, and Ubuntu is a traditional African philosophy that offers an understanding of ourselves solely in relation to the rest of the world.

According to the Ubuntu philosophy, *"a person is a person through other persons."* The philosophy proclaims the existence of a common bond between us all. It also teaches us wholeness and compassion, providing the assurance that since we belong to a greater whole, the suffering of others is not only our own suffering but ours is also theirs.

Norman Schwarzkopf, the American General who commanded Operation Desert Storm, once said, *"Leadership is a potent combination of strategy and character. But if you must be without one, be without strategy."* To many people, this statement might sound ill-placed, considering that we now live in a world where all too often leadership is focused solely on strategy, expediency and pragmatism. As I was to discover, however, the challenge for leaders in the NGO sector such as myself is not only to ensure effective delivery of daily tasks to a high standard of completion but to also win the commitment of our teams. This is because many of the talented and dedicated staff and volunteers who work with us do so for the noble cause of improving other people's lives rather than merely working to earn a paycheck.

Our roles in civil society organizations demand that we strive to make a difference in a way that governments and profit-oriented businesses cannot. NGOs have an ethos that places social and environmental considerations far above political or economic ones, since they are committed to reaching out to marginalized or excluded communities to provide innovative solutions to their problems. It is for this singular reason that NGOs, as the primary voices of social, economic and environmental justice, and the deliverers of innovative services to vulnerable people, must carry out their work armed with emotional intelligence and the spirit of Ubuntu.

My experience in steering the affairs of an organization with charitable objectives is that to lead effectively I need to inspire and engage others to give of their very best. This is not always an easy feat to achieve in a world filled with complex business and geopolitical challenges. That is where formidable emotional intelligence comes in. I have found it the most invaluable tool for inspiring people to go the extra mile, and to take work performance far beyond what was initially deemed humanly impossible.

Leadership expert Tim Irwin states in his book *Impact: Great Leadership Changes Everything* that the ability to inspire others to give themselves unreservedly to the mission is not a management technique but a leadership one. He further explains that management is positional, while leadership is personal. Equally, emotional intelligence is widely recognized as the driving force behind the majority of leadership skills, including time management and decision making. This, according to Bradberry and Jean Greaves, authors of *Emotional Intelligence 2.0,* makes emotional intelligence the single biggest predicator of performance at the workplace.

According to expert Daniel Goleman, emotional intelligence is *"the new science of human relationships,"* because its self-awareness and social awareness skills give leaders the ability to recognize emotions in themselves and in others. This understanding has given me the tremendous ability to manage behavior and relationships in the course of my work with a diverse global community. It has also helped me evolve a clear understanding of what I do at a superlative level, what motivates and satisfies me, and which people and situations propel me to peak performance.

In turn, this has enabled my team at POSITIVE RUNWAY and myself to pursue the right opportunities, and to put our strengths to work to achieve our highest potential by working as a high-performing team with a clear and compelling direction and an engaging and productive culture that allows us to respond effectively to threats and opportunities. Although POSITIVE RUNWAY started as an HIV/AIDS response campaign, the organization has now evolved into an international social development organization that operates in perfect alignment with demands from the various campaigns that seem to believe in our innovative approaches and methods of getting messages across to the 21st century young generation.

Emotional intelligence taps into that aspect of the human psyche that is distinct from the intellect and instead focuses on having a strong heart as well as a strong mind. It is also the ability to perceive, control and evaluate emotions. It is the seat of one's character, conscience, thoughts, feelings, attitudes, desires, considerations and volition. Various studies have demonstrated that healthy self-examination is a common denominator among leaders who forge great legacies. As such, accurate self-awareness has been an essential element of my leadership journey and personal effectiveness.

The possession of a high index of emotional intelligence has given me the ability to understand my strengths and vulnerabilities, equipping me with the capability to deploy my strengths toward challenges in my leadership role. In utilizing the self-awareness and social awareness skills of emotional intelligence, I have come to learn that people are generally more inclined to follow leaders who demonstrate a high degree of commitment and who pursue a clear and compelling purpose. Consequently, I recognize that to lead my organization effectively I have to inspire and engage others to give their highest and best effort to the cause at hand, and this requires a unique combination of authenticity, humility, self-discipline, courage and all the other attributes incident to a conviction of purpose.

No contemporary leader in the recorded history of mankind epitomizes the power of emotional intelligence in leadership as much as a remarkable woman who is also the longest-serving female head of state in world history, and the world's oldest living monarch, longest-reigning monarch and oldest and longest-serving current head of state. Born Elizabeth Alexandra Mary in Mayfair, London on April 21, 1926, Her Royal Majesty Queen Elizabeth II is officially and formally known as Queen Elizabeth II, by the Grace of God, Queen and Sovereign of the United Kingdom of Great Britain and Northern Ireland, and of Her other Realms and Territories, and Supreme Governor of The Church of England, Head of the Commonwealth, Defender of the Faith.

The Princess Elizabeth, as she was known before ascending the throne, was the elder daughter of King George VI. At her birth in 1926, she was clearly not in the direct line of ascendancy to the throne of Britain. As it happened, it was an unusual set of domestic circumstances that would usher in what is arguably the most epochal era of sovereign rule in the modern history of Great Britain.

Elizabeth's uncle, King Edward VIII, had willingly abdicated the throne to pursue his desire to marry American divorcee, Mrs Wallis Simpson, in defiance to the contrary opinion of parliament. Elizabeth's father, the Duke of York, was the King's younger brother and next in line to the throne. He was crowned King George VI. His daughter, Princess Elizabeth, was instantly thrown on to the global spotlight. At the death of her father in 1952, she was crowned Queen of England at the tender age of 25. In a reign that totally defines the phenomenon of royal epoch, Queen Elizabeth II has reigned for more than six decades, making her the world's oldest monarch and longest-serving sovereign.

Queen Elizabeth II is the delight of many an editor across the globe. That cannot be otherwise, for she has witnessed the tenure in power of 14 British prime ministers, 14 American presidents, seven popes and nine United Nations secretaries-general. If Queen Elizabeth II does not exemplify the servant-leadership ethos that is considered the hallmark of emotional intelligence in a leader, then no one does. A monarch who has always considered her work a service to humanity, her unshakeable commitment to duty appears to drive a proactivity that keeps her intensely busy, even as she lends her patronage to more than 600 charities, public service organizations and military associations.

At the ascension of Queen Elizabeth II to the throne, the United Kingdom was still reeling from the traumatic throes of World War II, during which she had served in the Auxiliary Territorial Service, having trained alongside other women to become an expert mechanic and driver. Although she ascended to the throne at a very young age, Elizabeth II has exhibited maturity, character, determination and commitment of the highest order in her role as Queen.

She found herself ruler of an empire that extended to all corners of the globe, and even in this modern age that empire has transformed into a Commonwealth of Nations that includes 54 member states that are nearly all former territories of the British Empire, spread across the different regions of the world, with different traditions, cultures, religions and beliefs, yet sharing the common language of English. Queen Elizabeth II is the Head of that Commonwealth. Over the decades, she has led and inspired Commonwealth member countries to work together with shared goals, values and principles, in a bid to promote prosperity, democracy and peace in a world in constant flux.

Queen Elizabeth II has demonstrated emotional intelligence at its most formidable. As a leader, she manages to display a sense of profound respect in her relationship with others. Her inquisitive and curious mind inclines her to always ask questions when she meets members of the public, and she not only attentively listens to the answers but also shows a keen interest in understanding those answers. Her legendary communication and interpersonal skills have stood her in good stead in her comfortable interactions with other world leaders. Over the years, successive prime ministers of Britain have given glowing testimonies that in formal briefings at the palace Queen Elizabeth II has consistently remained a great source of wisdom and reassurance.

As a modern-day leader, Queen Elizabeth II has exhibited a remarkable ability to embrace change and adapt herself to the changing times. When she ascended to the throne in 1953, she opted to have her Coronation at Westminster Abbey televised rather than broadcast on radio, overruling Prime Minister Winston Churchill's advice to conform to the convention of a radio broadcast. She chose to televise her Coronation as she was keen to make use of new media to modernize the monarchy, and to connect with people at a more personal level. Her decision was to actually prove wildly popular and was welcomed by a public that was given the hitherto rare opportunity to view one of the world's most historic moments of the day on television.

Queen Elizabeth II has since kept abreast with all aspects of the changing face of information technology. It is on record that when email was introduced she was the first head of state to send out an email, and today the monarch utilizes social media to connect with people and engagements.

Queen Elizabeth II's leadership style is a classic study in stoicism, and the enduring testimony to an unyielding spirit filled with courage and diligence. Following the terrorist bombings of the London public transport system on July 7, 2005, she addressed the country and called on the British people to stand together in the face of adversity. If in her Coronation speech she had clearly set out her vision with a great sense of duty, stating a total commitment to devoting her life to serve her people, the latter day calls for her to abdicate the throne in favor of her son have only strengthened her firm resolve to keep faith to her promise and commitment to her oath to spend her entire lifetime in the service of the people. Queen Elizabeth II continues this steadfast leadership with a great focus on national identity, unity and pride. It is not a matter for debate that the leadership of Queen Elizabeth II has been a source of stability and continuity for the British people and the people of the Commonwealth of Nations.

The high index of emotional intelligence of Queen Elizabeth II has found definition on both the microscopic and macroscopic levels. As the world's longest reigning monarch, she has enjoyed an incomparably positive public image in the United Kingdom, around the Commonwealth and across the globe. Her greatness as a leader lies in her ability to create a delicate balance between a healthy respect for the different traditions, cultures and customs of the different parts of the world with the need for the monarchy to embrace modern life and social change in such a way as to sustain the relevance of the same monarchy.

As monarch of Great Britain and Head of the Commonwealth, Queen Elizabeth II is one of the most traveled monarchs in history, having visited over 116 countries in the world. She has sponsored hundreds of charities and still attends numerous engagements every year. Queen Elizabeth II has many firsts to her name. She is the first-ever reigning British sovereign to have visited Saudi Arabia, China and Moscow's Red Square in 1979, 1986 and 1994 respectively. She is also the first British monarch to set foot inside a mosque, a Hindu temple and the Vatican.

In addition, Queen Elizabeth II was the first British monarch to open the Canadian Parliament, televise a Christmas address and fly in a helicopter. Furthermore, Queen Elizabeth II was the first British monarch to visit the Republic of Ireland since that country's struggle for independence started during the reign of her grandfather, King George V. Within the domestic affairs of the monarchy, she approved changes to the laws of succession, compelled the royal family to start paying income tax and opened up Buckingham Palace to public tours.

Queen Elizabeth II's leadership style has been characterized as measured and deliberate, and while it is arguable that she may not have anticipated being on the throne as long as she has been, she is still serving with dedication, commitment and diligence, even as she remains popular with the British people, the Commonwealth and the rest of the world.

In demonstrating a keen sense of awareness of her place in history as the current custodian of a long line of British sovereigns, her long-term bent of thinking and her formidable leadership style have helped her survive the ups and downs that come with her position, including the post-World War II depression, family upheavals in the Royal House of Windsor, a devastating fire at Windsor Castle, the anti-monarchy calls of the 1980s and 1990s that led to the royal family paying taxes, the death of Diana, Princess of Wales, and recently, the separation of her grandson, Prince Harry, from the rest of the royal family. Through all of these, Queen Elizabeth II has not only survived and thrived but has also remained steadfast and unscathed in her leadership.

In conclusion, one can only surmise that emotional intelligence is a very potent tool in effective leadership. It gives one the ability to understand the feelings of others at a very profound level, and thereby relate with them on an uncommonly positive pedestal. The world will increasingly thirst for emotionally intelligent leaders. This is because to fully exploit those empowering opportunities that globalization presents, leaders will need certain attributes, and high emotional intelligence is most definitely and definitively one of them.

Emotional intelligence, more than any other, will be responsible for creating those sustainable human and business relationships that will be instrumental to the economic integrity of our planet. Thankfully, more and more female leaders, quite in keeping with the natural feminine instinct for empathy, are rising up to fill the vacuum.

How to Gain Access to Your Power of Emotional Intelligence

1. You will need to cultivate the ability to identify and manage your own emotions as well as the emotions of others.

2. The traits of empathy, compassion, understanding, accommodation and appreciation are indispensable to the aspiring emotionally intelligent leader.

3. You will need to develop the core components of self-awareness, self-regulation, motivation, empathy and social skills.

4. You must be an appreciative leader. The greatest gift a leader can give her followers is that of genuine appreciation.

5. You must subscribe to the Golden Rule, which unequivocally states: *"Do unto others as you would have others do unto you."*

6. You must commit to valuing and encouraging others, not necessarily for performance but simply because they are, first and foremost, human beings. That, in fact, is the hallmark of the Golden Rule.

7. Cultivate the skill of making other people feel important. There is no higher compliment you can pay another person than helping her to be useful and to find satisfaction in that usefulness.

8. Learn to trust others. People, very much like you, want to be trusted. Trust is the foundation of any worthwhile relationship.

9. When dealing with others, you must always seek to first understand and then to be understood.

10. Commit to leaving a credible legacy that would have enhanced people's lives and made a sustainable difference that adds real value to their existence.

CHAPTER 7

THE POWER OF VERSATILITY

"I hope fathers and mothers of little girls will look at them and say, 'Yes, women can!'"

DILMA ROUSEFF

Versatility is the ability to adapt to many different functions, possibly in the course of a very eventful leadership career. In this particularly unique phase of mankind's evolution, a leader has a distinct advantage if she has versatility. Versatile leaders are not only able to manage several functions but they also demonstrate an ability to do so with admirable balance. It is becoming clearer that most people stepping into a leadership role need to understand the importance of versatility. This is because a leader may be asked to wear different hats during her tenure in a particular office, or she may have to display diverse competencies while traversing many diverse offices along the course of a rewarding and ambitious political career.

While it is true that leaders cannot be everywhere at the same time, their vision, goals and objectives should, quite frankly, be able to speak for them on different platforms. The most remarkable feature of the versatile leader is that she is able to deploy her leadership effortlessly to fit the people and situations she wants to influence. This is because she is more than likely to possess a range of approaches which she can adapt as required, rather than attempting to employ just a single rigid way of leading others, or interacting with them. The world has so much benefited from versatile female leaders that they are often branded the best leaders. Yet, such women themselves have also benefited in such tremendous ways that have rendered them even better leaders.

Firstly, a versatile leader acquires more and more knowledge in the course of her career. Having, in all probability, handled so many different leadership roles in the past, she is able to oversee multiple projects from start to finish. While one is not by any means suggesting that the versatile leader possesses knowledge of everything or is even remotely able to master everything, it does mean she has to be educated in areas where she was once uninformed. Once the versatile leader is enlightened with new knowledge, she never stops learning in those areas.

Secondly, the versatile leader increases her value in the realm of politics and governance. Although a versatile leader may be specialized in one or two areas of leadership strength, she also, along the line, discovers ways of improving her areas of weakness such that she decreases her degree of vulnerability within the sphere of governance. After months, years, and sometimes decades, such a leader invariably becomes an expert in her areas of strength and weaknesses because of hard work and an impeccable work ethic. That is why the versatile leader is ultimately sought after by governments and organizations, paid better, and more importantly, given even more and greater opportunities to become more versatile.

Thirdly, and more significantly, the versatile leader manages to stand out beyond her own immediate sphere of influence. That is why, no matter what environment a leader finds herself in, she should forever remain an avid learner and someone who uncompromisingly subscribes to an exceptional work ethic. There is no doubt that the world will forever remain in admiration of the leadership trait of versatility.

Patricia Janet Scotland, Baroness Scotland of Asthal, is one such versatile leader. Simply and incontrovertibly a feminine source of pride to the United Kingdom, Baroness Scotland made history when she was elected the first-ever female Secretary-General of the Commonwealth of Nations at the 2015 Commonwealth Heads of Government Meeting, in the process becoming the sixth Secretary-General of the Commonwealth of Nations as she took office in April 2016. Prior to that, Baroness Scotland had chalked up quite a few firsts and many accomplishments to her name. She had held the office of Attorney General for England and Wales, becoming the first woman to hold that office since its inception in 1315.

Born in Dominica and of dual British and Dominican nationality, she obtained a Bachelor of Laws from the University of London and was called to the Bar at the Middle Temple in 1977 to specialize in family law. She was also called to the Dominican Bar in 1978. In 1991, Baroness Scotland became the first Black woman to be appointed a Queen's Counsel. She established the Gray's Inn Square Barristers Chambers in London. She was later elected a Bencher of the Middle Temple and was named a millennium commissioner in 1994. She received a life peerage to become a member of the House of Lords with her creation as Baroness Scotland of Asthal in the county of Oxfordshire in 1997.

Baroness Scotland served as Parliamentary Under-Secretary of State at the Foreign and Commonwealth Office from 1999 to 2001. Among her duties in this role, she was responsible for the United Kingdom's diplomatic relations with North America, the Caribbean Islands, Overseas Territories, Consular Division, the British Council administration and all parliamentary business in the House of Lords. In that capacity, she successfully introduced the International Criminal Court Bill to ratify the jurisdiction of the International Criminal Court into UK law. She also created an overseas Territory Council for the Caribbean Islands, and reformed and restructured the Consular Division of the Foreign and Commonwealth Office to allow the office to respond more effectively to emergencies and disasters from abroad, such as the 9/11 attacks of 2001.

As a qualified lawyer, Baroness Scotland established the Pro Bono Lawyers Panel, comprising British-based lawyers who could provide legal advice on a pro bono basis to UK citizens who might find themselves imprisoned in foreign countries.

In 2001, Baroness Scotland was appointed Parliamentary Secretary in the Lord Chancellor's Department and became a member of the Privy Council of the United Kingdom. As a minister, she had the responsibility for civil justice and the reform of civil law, which included reforms to the Land Registrations Act 2002. In addition, she was responsible for international affairs at the Lord Chancellor's Department.

Baroness Scotland was later appointed the United Kingdom's alternate representative to the European Convention, with the primary task of heading negotiations in relation to the Charter of the Rights, which concluded in 2003. Employing her astute leadership skills, she used the period to consolidate on the strong relations forged with all applicant countries through the FAHR program and member states. She was subsequently awarded the Polish Medal for her contribution to the reform and the development of law in Poland.

Baroness Scotland went on to become Minister of State for the Criminal Justice System and Law Reform at the Home Office, and acted as Deputy to the Home Secretary from 2003 to 2007. At the Home Office, she was responsible for major reforms of the criminal justice system, and she established the Office of Criminal Justice Reform, which supported the creation of the National Criminal Justice Board and the Local Criminal Justice Board. As acting chair, she created the Corporate, Civic and Faith-Based Alliance to reduce reoffending.

She also created the Corporate Alliance Against Domestic Violence and the advisory group on victims, as well as the Criminal Justice Centre, Victims and Witness Units. She established the Inside Justice Week and the Justice Award. She introduced the Crime and Victims Act, which drafted the new offense of familial homicide. She represented the United Kingdom in various international negotiations, including the Extradition Treaty with the United States of America, which was signed in March 2003. In this regard, Baroness Scotland had the responsibility of promoting the necessary legislation in the House of Lords.

In 2007, Baroness Scotland was appointed Attorney General for England and Wales where she continued to promote pro bono work by lawyers, establishing an international Schools Pro Bono Committee, which was given the responsibility for coordinating pro bono work. She further created the Pro Bono Awards and Pro Bono Heroes, as well as the Attorney General's Youth Network.

Baroness Scotland was the last Attorney General for England and Wales, and also Attorney General for Northern Ireland before the devolution of justice powers to the Northern Ireland Assembly and the eventual appointment of a separate Attorney General for Northern Ireland. She subsequently became advocate general for Northern Ireland and the United Kingdom's chief government advisor on Northern Ireland law.

Baroness Scotland also served at local government level when she was elected the Alderman for the Ward of Bishopsgate in the City of London. In 2015, she was elected Secretary-General of the Commonwealth at the Commonwealth Heads of Government Meeting. As she took office in April 2016, she declared, *"As I take up the responsibilities entrusted to me by the Heads of Government, I want you to know that I am determined to put the Commonwealth back at center stage as we act collectively to uphold democracy, advance development and celebrate diversity."*

Baroness Scotland serves on several charities and organizations. She is patron of the Corporate Alliance Against Domestic Violence and the Chineke! Foundation. She is also the joint patron of Mission, the Catholic Church's charity organization for overseas missions, in addition to being patron of the Children's and Families Across Borders, a charity dedicated to reuniting children with families from whom they have been separated.

Her outstanding service, leadership skills and contribution to law reform in the United Kingdom and abroad have earned her numerous international awards, honors and accolades. She was awarded the Polish Medal for her contribution to the reform and development of law in Poland and was voted as Parliamentarian of the Year by the *Spectator* magazine and the Political Studies Association. She was also voted Peer of the Year by Channel 4's house magazine. In addition, an honorary doctorate degree was conferred on her by the University of East London in 2005.

Baroness Scotland has been ranked the most influential Black Briton in the annual Powerlist, having been ranked first in 2007, 2008 and 2010. Furthermore, she was decreed and invested as a Dame of Merit with the Star of Sacred Military Constantinian Order of Saint George by Prince Carlo, Duke of Castro in 2003. In 2014, Baroness Scotland was appointed to the Council of British and Irish Delegation of the Constantinian Order, and promoted to the rank of Dame Grand Cross of Merit. She serves as Chancellor of the University of Greenwich and is listed in the BBC 100 Women.

Latin America provides another example of a versatile leader. Dilma Vana Rouseff is the first-ever female President of Brazil. She was elected President twice - first as the 36th President of Brazil in 2011 and again in 2014. Rouseff started her political journey as a teenager when she was involved in the left wing opposition to the government of the day, and became associated with the National Liberation Command. She was a member of the student union that organized protests against military rule and which led to Brazil's coup d'état of 1964. In 1967, she joined the organization that demanded a constitutional assembly. She worked in the Rio Grande do Sul stage government for the Democratic Labor Party and helped with the presidential campaigns for the Revolucionária Marxista Política Operária, an extra-parliamentary opposition that was focused on bringing down military rule in Brazil.

An economist turned politician, Rousseff graduated with a Bachelor's Degree in Economics from the Universidade Federal do Rio Grande do Sul in Porto Alegre. She later earned a Ph.D. in Economics. She served in various government portfolios, including as Finance Secretary of Porto Alegre, Minister of Mines and Energy, and Chair of Petrobras, Brazil's state-run oil concern, and was tasked with the portfolio of Head of Growth Acceleration Program, before being appointed Chief of Staff in the Office of the President. While an expanding economy and shrinking poverty level boosted the then President's popularity, the constitution limited him to only two terms in office. Rouseff was then groomed to be the President's successor and was nominated as the presidential candidate in the ensuing presidential elections which she won. She was sworn into office in January 2011.

On taking office, Rouseff outlined a domestic agenda that focused on the maintenance of economic stability, political reform, tax reform, poverty eradication and job creation. On the foreign policy turf, she emphasized the observation of human rights, peace, multilateralism and non-intervention. She signed a landmark law that established a truth commission to investigate human rights abuses and the disappearances of people during military rule.

Rouseff launched a new industry policy titled "Larger Brazil" which was designed to make Brazil more self-reliant by encouraging Brazilian manufacturing industries through tax cuts, while also enticing Brazilian citizens to buy products made in Brazil. When the economy started to decline, the Brazilian central bank under Rouseff pursued an aggressive policy to reduce the interest rate for lending, and lowered the reserve requirement for Brazilian banks. This boosted Rouseff's popularity because it injected liquidity into the country's economy and helped to keep the unemployment rates low. When pressured by the industrial sector to reduce the cost of electricity, Rouseff's government came up with a provisional measure that created a mechanism to reduce energy prices by an average of 20%.

As Minister of Mines and Energy, she introduced the Luz Para Todos, or Lights for All program, to make electricity available to all citizens of Brazil, including those in the rural areas. In preparation for the 2014 FIFA World Cup and the 2016 Summer Olympics, Rouseff's government focused on giving the world the best possible sporting experience. Her government spent billions of dollars to upgrade government infrastructure and build new stadiums to host the two competitions. To mitigate the shortage of physicians in Brazil, Rouseff recruited doctors from Cuba and other foreign countries. At the Climate Change Summit in New York, Brazil refused to be a signatory to the anti-deforestation pledge, which had been drafted without Brazil's participation.

Despite the political, economic and social problems that appeared to beset her government, Rouseff won a second term as President in 2014. Rouseff would become the first female world leader to open a United Nations General Assembly debate. She has been hailed for her versatile leadership profile and strong management strategies. She is also one of those extraordinary women leaders who dared to bring gender equality and other political, economic and social issues affecting women to the forefront of international discourse. Most certainly, she overcame oppression, broke the rules, re-imagined her world and waged a rebellion to become the first-ever female President of Brazil.

Some women leaders have risen as far as the headship of continental regional bodies. One such woman is Nkosazana Clarice Dlamini-Zuma. She is the first-ever woman to head the African Union Commission. She is also the first-ever woman to present herself as a presidential candidate in South Africa. Prior to becoming Chair of the African Union Commission, Dlamini-Zuma had already cut her teeth as a seasoned administrator in an impressive career in which she held various high-level positions in the political party she belonged to, and in the alternating governments of South Africa. She was a member of parliament and a National Executive Committee member of her party.

She was also a member of the Gender Advisory Committee during the Convention for a Democratic South Africa and served as Minister of Health in the Nelson Mandela presidency. She then went on to serve as Minister of Foreign Affairs from 1999 to 2009. As Minister of Foreign Affairs, she engaged in a very effective shuttle diplomacy to end the civil war in the Democratic Republic of Congo. Subsequently, she served as Minister of Home Affairs from 2009 to 2012.

Born in 1949 and raised in Natal in South Africa, she holds medical degrees from four universities: the Universities of Zululand and Natal in South Africa, and the Universities of Bristol and Liverpool in the United Kingdom. Her political activism started when she was a student, becoming an active member of the African National Congress, and serving as youth chair, while also serving as Deputy President of the South African Students Organization. Dlamini-Zuma has held top cabinet posts under every democratic leader of modern South Africa. Her wealth of experience, having served in so many high-profile government positions, made Dlamini-Zuma the most experienced candidate during the presidential elections of 2019.

She deployed her medical knowledge and experience to great use as Minister of Health under Nelson Mandela. She also served for ten years as Minister of Foreign Affairs under Thabo Mbeki, before becoming Minister of Home Affairs under Jacob Zuma. As Home Affairs Minister, she was instrumental in turning around the embattled ministry, and bequeathing it with a clean audit for the first time in over 16 years of widely acknowledged gross mismanagement. Surrounding herself with very sound and skilled personnel, she successfully implemented effective internal protocols and measures in the finance and supply chain management.

Dlamini-Zuma is a great supporter of radical economic transformation to create further employment for Black people and women in South Africa. She lent tremendous support to the re-appropriation of land to Black people from White settlers, and advocated for universal and affordable internet access for everyone in the country. She believes in quality education and has been calling for more universities and increased funding for tertiary education. Furthermore, she advocates strongly for public-private sector partnerships, and greater engagements for the creation of working partnerships between the private sector and the public.

She left government to serve as chair of the African Union Commission in 2012. At her epochal election as the first female African Union Commission Chair, she was hailed as a pan-Africanist hero. That was hardly surprising. She came from a solid background of pan-African continental diplomacy, having served as Thabo Mbeki's Foreign Minister from 1999 to 2009, at a time when Mbeki himself was actively pursuing his African Renaissance vision, and worked hard to establish peace in the Democratic Republic of Congo.

As Chair of the African Union between 2012 and 2017, she was widely credited with changing the operational environment of the African Union Headquarters in Addis Ababa for the better. She took a radically different approach than that taken by her male counterparts regarding African peace and security issues. She brought a gendered and holistic developmental approach to the problems faced by the African continent. She appointed the first Special Envoy on Women, Peace and Security, and spearheaded an international campaign against child marriage in Africa.

At the completion of her tenure as Chair of the African Union Commission, she made history once again as the first-ever woman to stand as a presidential candidate in South Africa. Her beliefs are underpinned by a Black consciousness and pan-Africanist philosophy. As a member of the South African Students Organization, she and her fellow activists endured intense police harassment for their political beliefs. In fact, she had to flee South Africa to go into exile in the United Kingdom in 1976.

Not one to shy away from a justified fight for the common good, Dlamini-Zuma, as a practicing medical doctor, fought big pharmaceuticals over the prices of medicines. She also pushed through laws to confine public smoking to only certain places. While in exile in the United Kingdom, Swaziland and other countries, she continued to work as a member of the African National Congress, even while studying and practicing medicine.

Unlike her political opponents who built their campaigns around the ubiquitous fight against corruption, she focused her campaign on skills development and the radical transformation of the economy to make it a more equitable playing ground for everyone. With six contenders on the ballot, Dlamini-Zuma came second, missing the presidency by a narrow margin. In 2013, the South African government conferred on Dlamini-Zuma the Order of Luthuli Award in Gold for her contributions to the liberation struggle. She currently serves as Minister of Cooperative Governance and Traditional Affairs in Cyril Ramaphosa's government.

One vital lesson we can take away from the foregoing accounts of these versatile female leaders is that if all a leader has on offer is a one-dimensional methodology for tackling challenges, she will be abysmally lacking in the multifaceted tactics necessary to inspire the led in this era of rapid generational changes in the dynamics of governance. It is becoming increasingly important for leaders to truly develop versatility as a key component on their leadership journey. In fact, it is simply not an overstatement to say that versatility is the single most important component of leading effectively today, if only because versatile leaders have a more engaged followership and higher performing teams.

Because leaders now find themselves in a truly global community, it has become imperative for them to learn to interact effectively with people of diverse backgrounds, and this requires a more well-rounded approach to problems and solutions. Definitely, the best way to acquire this key skill is to traverse a genuinely versatile path on the leadership journey.

How to Gain Access to Your Power of Versatility

1. You must aim at being able to manage several functions simultaneously with a demonstrable sense of balance.

2. Your vision, goals and objectives should be able to speak for you on many different platforms.

3. You should be able to deploy your leadership effortlessly to fit the people and situations you want to influence.

4. You will need a wide range of approaches which you can adapt as required, rather than attempting to employ just a single rigid way of leading others, or interacting with them.

5. You should strive to acquire more and more knowledge in the course of your career.

6. You will need to increase your value continually in your sphere of influence, and become an expert in your areas of strength and weaknesses through hard work and an impeccable work ethic.

7. Aim to stand out beyond your own immediate sphere of influence by remaining an avid learner and someone who uncompromisingly subscribes to an exceptional work ethic.

8. Refuse to subscribe to a one-dimensional methodology for tackling challenges.

9. Commit to learning how to interact effectively with people of diverse backgrounds.

10. Adopt a well-rounded approach to problems and solutions.

CHAPTER 8

THE POWER OF RESILIENCE

"Our struggle was not a flash in the pan. I had kept it alive with every means at my disposal."

WINNIE MANDELA

Resilience. The sound of the word itself innocently belies the inherent strength it proclaims. Resilience is the capacity to recover quickly from difficulties. It is because it is the ability to recover from or adjust with some ease to misfortune or change that it is also considered a synonym of toughness. A resilient person has the capability to cope in the face of daunting challenges, setbacks, barriers or limited resources. That is perhaps why resilience is easily also a measure of just how much one desires something, and how much one is willing to sacrifice, through a combination of ability and willingness, to get that thing, or attain that goal.

Without doubt, resilience demands a certain degree of emotional strength. That cannot be otherwise since resilience also hints at some core inner strength. In conjuring up the image of a ball bouncing back to its thrower, it means to survive in the School of Hard Knocks. Indeed, if human existence can be likened to the University of Life, then the resilient leader is necessarily one of its first class or summa cum laude graduates, depending on which side of the Atlantic you're on. Definitely, it means to be the proverbial cat with nine lives.

The resilient leader knows that life is not all about her alone. Quite often, such a leader is aware, possibly at a subconscious level, that she has been brought into this turbulent world to be an instrument of massive transformation in the lives of others. This can be a powerful source of motivation for survival in such people. It tends to give them the psychological strength to cope with stress, hardship and other vicissitudes of life. It also serves as the mental reservoir of strength that such leaders are able to draw upon in times of adversity.

Resilient leaders tend to remain in acute awareness of critical situations and the behavior of those around them. It is this awareness that allows them to maintain firm and effective control of a situation, while innovating fresh perspectives to solve problems. It takes courage to traverse the vicissitudes of life. That is why courage is almost synonymous with resilience.

Resilience, liberally aided by uncommon courage, is the only word that adequately sums up the remarkable life of one of the strongest female leaders to rise up on the African continent. Winnie Madikizela-Mandela was a freedom fighter and a former First Lady of South Africa. Her Xhosa tribal name was Nomzamo which literally translates to "She who tries." Indeed, her entire life was to turn out a perfect study in trials. Famously referred to as the Mother of the Nation, it is an equally famous refrain that no other woman, in history or the future, will ever be able to stride colossally across the terrain of South African politics in quite the same manner with which Winnie Mandela did. Her iconic status transcended geographical boundaries, generations and genders.

Born in September 1936 in Bizana, an Eastern Cape village in South Africa, she rose to global acclaim as a freedom fighter who eventually became the First Lady of independent South Africa. Prior to her marriage to the globally celebrated Nelson Mandela, the father of apartheid-free South Africa and the first Black President of the liberated country, she was already a remarkable woman in her own right. Against the backdrop of apartheid and rigid restrictions in the education of Black people, Mandela still managed to earn a degree to become the first-ever qualified Black social worker in South Africa, and who later engaged in pioneer work in infant mortality research.

Her experiences with extreme poverty, and the discrimination that was an inherent part of the apartheid system, led to her political awakening. As a child, she had learned from her parents about the Xhosa wars against the colonizers and was determined to position herself as an inheritor of her ancestors' legacy of activism. Shortly after her marriage, she joined thousands of women who took to the streets of Johannesburg to protest the issuing of pass books to Black women, a protocol that served to enforce racial segregation and which allowed the government to track and control the movements of Black people in a bid to prevent them from entering White areas. Her political power would later stem from connecting with the everyday lives of Black people in a racist country. She effortlessly embraced her dual role of a mother and the wife of a political leader, effectively fashioning it into a platform of her own, and from which she courageously challenged the apartheid state.

She was barely six years into her marriage when her husband was sentenced to life imprisonment. Mandela found herself inextricably involved in the politics and turbulence of the liberation movement as a single parent. She joined the Federation of South African Women and the Women's League of the African National Congress (ANC) and participated in the various political campaigns. She served as Chair of the ANC Women's League and was a member of the provincial and national executive councils. In the 1970s, Winnie Mandela co-founded the Black Women's Federation. Although relatively short lived, the organization epitomized the sort and tone of township politics that was sweeping across the entire country at that time.

In the wake of the 1976 Soweto uprising, she built bridges between different political factions. She also brokered alliances between moderates and radicals in the ANC and its breakaways. She utilized gender politics, certainly by virtue of her status as an acknowledged mother of the nation, to unite warring factions and to hold together their political family to maintain peace. As an effective speaker, she had the natural gift for winning the hearts and minds of her audiences. Blessed with a high index of emotional intelligence, she was empathically attuned to the mood of the people, offering a form of intimate political leadership that allowed her to align herself with people in distress.

Mandela faced persecution to an unparalleled degree, but she remained fearless in the face of those attempts by the state to silence her. Right from the beginning of the 27 years that her husband would remain incarcerated in prison, she became the target of police harassment and brutality. Her children were expelled from school for no tangible reason, and she was forced to relinquish her job as a social worker. Her home became the focus of repeated invasions and unwarranted searches by the authorities. She was variously arrested, assaulted, imprisoned and placed in solitary confinement at different times.

Later, she was uprooted from her family and community in Soweto and sent into exile. While in exile, she established a sewing club, soup kitchen, gardening cooperative, mobile health unit, day care center and an organization for orphaned and juvenile delinquents. She also used her time in exile to come into a realization of the power that could be derived from directly associating atrocities committed against her with the policies of the state. As it turned out, her own political party was becoming increasingly intolerant of her radical voice and powerful leadership.

Additionally, she regularly stepped outside the agreed parameters of the official party line to assert her independence. Yet, this fierce independence was what allowed her to build alliances with new and emerging voices. Like many women in the movement, Mandela was marginalized from the decision-making power structures of the ANC and her personal life was constantly brought under the spotlight and subjected to rather harsh judgment.

At the end of apartheid, the release of her husband from prison, and the subsequent independence of South Africa, Winnie Mandela's role changed as her husband became a global focus of attention. She, however, continued to campaign for social issues affecting African women and girls. She was appointed ANC's Head of Social Welfare and she made significant contributions to the fight against HIV/AIDS in South Africa, adding her voice to those that were calling on the government to provide free anti-retroviral medicines for those infected with HIV. She continued to act as a voice for the weak and voiceless, and brought attention to the high number of women and girls in South Africa that were contracting HIV/AIDS due to cultural, social and economic inequalities.

Winnie Mandela's life was a contrasting mix of early glory and eventual dishonor, throughout all of which she remained an iconic figure in South Africa's politics. Despite a life that was stalked with tragedy and political drama, she was resilient enough to remain an enigmatic figure in South African society and in the country's history. She has inspired acclaim, both as a force of nature and as mother of the nation. In enduring the agonies of the apartheid era, she is seen as a guiding light for women and girls, and the vulnerable people of South Africa. She has been hailed as someone whose commitment to equity, justice, the vulnerable and the disadvantaged cannot be disputed.

Her courage and bravery as a woman made her an outstanding leader, even as she led with true dedication, holding the fort while her husband was away in prison for 27 years. Winnie Mandela has been duly credited with reshaping the narrative of what it meant to be a female activist in her time, and for paving the way for generations of women and girls who would come to walk the same path. She resolutely refused to live in the shadows of her famous husband, and created her own identity outside the confines of her marriage to become an icon in her own right. Winnie Mandela was a highly motivated leader who demonstrated an exceptional ability to stay the course with a tenacity that was as inexhaustible as her capacity to refuse to become demoralized.

Winnie Mandela was resilience personified. Years of constant police harassment, prison terms and intimidation did nothing to quash her revolutionary spirit, rather making her conviction even stronger and more enduring. Her fight was a fight for every woman and girl raised in apartheid South Africa. When society demanded that she play a subservient role, she refused to be a passive bystander who would be content to wait patiently for her husband's release from prison. Rather than fearfully slink into the shadows with the unobtrusiveness that the authorities and the party expected, she held the spotlight high and became a living and visible symbol of the struggle for equity and justice.

Her resilience in the face of brutality from a government that was meant to protect her rights as a civilian resonated with millions of South African women and girls, as well as the vulnerable. Fearless in the face of torture, imprisonment, banishment and betrayal, Winnie Mandela stood firm in her conviction that apartheid could be brought down. For the women and girls of South Africa she was the guiding light who taught them to be defiant, fearless, powerful and to embody strength, fortitude and conviction. It is indubitable that she earned her title of South Africa's Mother of the Nation, if only for the exceptional role she played in shaping the future of South Africa.

Across the Atlantic, in an entirely different socio-political culture, another strong feminine character-leader of authentic staying power rode on the heels, yet again, of a political leader spouse, to a position of self-contrived prominence in the affairs of her country of birth. Hillary Rodham Clinton would make history as the first-ever female presidential candidate in the 2016 presidential elections of the United States of America. She read law to become a successful attorney in both the private and public sectors.

As First Lady of the State of Arkansas, she worked hard to see her husband elected President of the United States. Having served eight years in the White House as First Lady, she went on to become Secretary of State from 2008 to 2016. Instead of resting on her past achievements, Clinton ventured into the murky waters of politics and gained the depth and breadth of knowledge required to govern the country. In fact, it is a testimony to the sheer political sagacity of his wife that when former President Bill Clinton was campaigning for the presidency some years ago, he told Americans that if they voted for him it would only be to their eternal credit, since they *"would have bought one and got one free!"*

What he meant was that his wife, Hillary, was as good a presidential material as he was, and if they voted for him they would have the benefit of two presidents working for the country. He was not only proved right but was uncannily prophetic in his assertion. Hillary Clinton went on to become, in quick succession, a Senator of the United States, a Secretary of State, and one of the most formidable presidential candidates in the recent history of the United States, just missing occupancy of the White House by the narrow margin of a loss at the electoral college.

As presidential candidate, she conducted a vigorous campaign that many easily remember as one of the most difficult and challenging in the history of the United States. Her extensive political network, combined with remarkable leadership skills, gave her campaign the required impetus to be a mission which was as much a mission to break the glass ceiling as it was one that threatened to upturn the status quo of male pre-eminence at the highest level of executive authority in the United States. Throughout what inevitably turned out to be one of the most exciting and breathtaking campaigns in American history, she deployed enormous courage, a deep conviction, unrivaled determination and remarkable leadership skills to her mission. She articulated a vision that was accepted by millions of Americans, and despite the numerous and seemingly insurmountable challenges that strewed her path, she demonstrated nothing short of strength, resilience and an indomitable spirit.

As President Barack Obama's Secretary of State, Clinton had to deal with enormous global problems. She faced each daunting situation head on, and with the resolution and toughness that confounded her most ardent critics. Never once did she deflect blame for her own perceived inadequacies, bravely admitting to and taking firm responsibilities for her errors. Her presidential campaign was what would decisively reveal the steel in her and her steadfastness as a consummate political player.

Demonstrating quite clearly that her tenures as a Senator and as Secretary of State counted for solid hands-on experience, she displayed an ability to communicate articulately in circumstances that demanded a constant love of learning and issue-based decision making based not on sentiments but on facts. Totally unafraid to change her course once she discovered that traditional thinking was taking her on the wrong trajectory, Clinton left no one in doubt that she was a consummate politician who perfectly understood the political process in Washington DC.

As a Senator, she displayed an admirable willingness and flexibility to work effectively with the opposition whenever necessary. In the face of vicious attacks during her presidential campaign, she demonstrated an uncanny ability to remain focused on the goal at hand, and on the key elements of her proposition to the people of the United States. She outlined an articulate blueprint for the future of the country, and would faithfully return to those fundamentals, even in the face of a relentless onslaught of criticisms and virulent attacks. Clinton's vision for the country was so clear and unambiguous that it also included how her presidency would differ from previous administrations in addressing the complexities and challenges that the United States and the rest of the world were facing.

Consistent with her leadership philosophy of inclusion and consensus building, prior to commencing her presidential campaign, Clinton addressed women in Silicon Valley, where she articulated what her presidency would look like. Rather than focusing on red and blue, the colors that are representative of America's political bipartisanship, she announced, in what instantly emerged as a brilliantly creative employment of the color metaphor, that she would "mix" both colors to create a nice warm purple space in which the United States could solve its problems as a united country. She expressed her willingness to build close relationships, and to work closely with the Republicans, her opponents, on real policy change for the betterment of the United States of America.

In what can only qualify as the survival of a cat with nine lives, she overcame near-unbelievable obstacles to become the frontrunner in that presidential race, including an FBI investigation into perceived misconduct during her term as Secretary of State, and spurious allegations against her family's non-profit foundation. Despite all these distractions, she maintained and sustained a focused and disciplined campaign strategy. Her political message was suitably crafted to appeal to the majority of the American people. She started out with a massive lead over her primary challengers, and despite the vicious attacks, she stayed focused on her positive platform, stoically biting her tongue to resist the urge to squander her lead by engaging in a mud-slinging contest.

Clinton refreshingly emerged a campaign veteran who demonstrated the ability to tweak even the smallest details to her own advantage. She appeared at campaign rallies looking resplendently presidential, and speaking effectively to her established platform, while strategically avoiding unplanned media questions. During that campaign, she absorbed attacks with clinical detachment, maximized every conceivable political opportunity, and formed powerful political coalitions as the opportunities to do so comfortably presented themselves.

Ultimately, as a courageous leader, she was prepared to stand faithfully for what she believed in, while confronting traditional ways of thinking, and rather than give in to fear, she took prudent risks that served to leverage her campaign on every exploitable front.

Clinton's unique leadership formula was the rare combination of a formidable intellect and an uncommon strength of character, and it helped her to gain meteoric rise as a politician of note. She has been hailed as an influential leader who systematically deployed that formula of success to devastating effect when she competed for the highest office in the United States. Her poise and composure reflected nothing short of total self-confidence and the capacity to assume the office of the President of the United States.

While navigating the swift and potentially overwhelming currents of personal pain and profound embarrassment, she remained focused and composed, and never gave up her self-respect and pride. Even at the end of a keenly fought race, she faced and accepted defeat with decency, dignity and compassion, expressing a sincere gratitude to all those who had believed in her leadership and message. She fought the good fight in an endeavor that was powerful, positive and personal.

Hillary Clinton gave a brilliant account of herself as a highly ambitious and competitive politician who was primarily concerned with getting things done to achieve desired results. She also valued continuous learning and was not afraid of making mid-course alterations in order to succeed in the face of circumstances that seemed insurmountable. Her words and actions definitely emanated from the place of a high index of resilience that allowed her to overcome and then thrive in adversity. Although she was a perfectionist who obsessed over every detail, taking preparation and organization to a rarely seen level of seriousness, she was still willing to listen and take advice from others. This much was evident in the way she worked and dealt with constituents, business leaders and heads of state to build consensus across multiple sectors.

Her enduring legacy will have to be a vision that rode on an unerring understanding of different constituencies to galvanize and unite the people that she would lead, while responding to their yearnings accordingly. In conclusion, Hillary Rodham Clinton remains one of the most formidable presidential candidates in the annals of American politics.

If Angela Dorothea Merkel (née Kasner), Germany's first-ever female Chancellor, is considered remotely qualified to wear the toga of a resilient leader, a statement that was once credited to her will suffice for that categorization. She once declared, *"I don't carry my early childhood trauma around with me."* She took office in 2005 and remains the longest serving Chancellor of the Federal Republic of Germany. *TIME* magazine named Merkel Person of the Year 2015, and in 2019 Harvard University conferred its honorary Doctor of Laws degree on her in advance of her keynote speech at the Ivy League institution's 368th commencement ceremony, with Harvard President Larry Bacow calling her one of the most *"influential statespeople of our time."*

Merkel has been leader of the ruling center-right Christian Democratic Union since the year 2000. Her political dominance of European politics has earned her the title of de-facto Leader of the European Union, and the most powerful woman in the world. She has also been hailed as the Leader of the Free World. She emerged one of the most admired and accomplished leaders in the history of both post-war and pre-war Germany, and in the history of the European continent.

Prior to becoming Chancellor, Merkel had served in various positions in the German government. *TIME* magazine, in naming her Person of the Year 2015, defined Merkel's life as a study in resilience. The magazine noted in a matter-of-fact manner that her political style was totally and clinically detached from the more common niceties and embellishments. The magazine's citation stated that Merkel brought no flair, no flourishes and no charisma to both politics and the art of governance, just the combination of a survivor's sharp sense of power and a scientist's devotion to data. The magazine was right. Merkel started off as a quantum chemist and was a foreigner in Western Germany who knew next to nothing about politics. Later finding herself in an all-masculine political party, she was left with no choice than to learn the political ropes rather quickly, and she kept on learning. Her most identifiable and effective traits were to be reasonable and to understand other people.

Merkel has been literally left gasping for breath in her meteoric rise to political prominence. As soon as she rose one step and began to get accustomed to her new role, the next level would be upon her. This occurred with such regularity that as soon as she had started to marginally grasp domestic politics as Minister of Women, she found herself moving up to become Minister of the Environment, a position that thrust her on to the global stage. Characteristically, she had barely settled into this role when she had to assume leadership of her party, and then soon became Chancellor of Germany.

Merkel is accustomed to minority platforms and has never been afraid of being a lone voice. A divorced Protestant who found herself in a Catholic political party, she came from East Germany to enter politics in the newly unified Germany of the 1990s at a time in which East Germans were still considered aliens. With a background in quantum chemistry, in which she had earned a doctorate degree, her educational background had nothing to do with politics or international relations.

A woman in a party full of men, Merkel has been hailed as a master at leading from behind, the ultimate form of purpose-based leadership which focuses on purpose and not the leader, power or authority, to create and animate a community of followers. Her values of humanity, generosity and tolerance have helped to reverse Germany's reputation of a toxically nationalist and militarist nation, and to rescue it from its genocidal past.

Merkel's tenure has liberated Germany, forcing the country to stop hiding in the shadows of its own power, a past situation in which the government downplayed the country's strength to avoid standing alone on the international stage. When the United States began to relinquish its role as military and moral leader of the West, and embarked on the withdrawal of American involvement from conflicts in Europe, Merkel's Germany took over as the giant in the center of Europe.

Merkel's personality and her political leadership have intersected and matched each other to an unerring point of perfection. Seriousness has been a defining characteristic of her chancellorship. She has been a serious leader who has led her country with authentic seriousness of purpose. Merkel has been hailed for her preternatural calm. No matter the situation or circumstances, her hand on the wheel of leadership has remained steady, and her presentation of self has been devoid of all theatrics. She has been leader of her party for over 20 years and German Chancellor for over 15 years, and her longevity as a leader is an accomplishment in itself, given the many challenges that liberal democracies face today.

There is no doubt that Germans place implicit trust and confidence in this remarkable woman, as no single source of Merkel's power, authority and influence stands out as much as the degree to which she consciously or unconsciously embodies the yearnings of the people of Germany, who have always clamored for a greater role in NATO and the European Union. Under her leadership, Germans have generally been happy to be blessed with a remarkably stable democracy, a thriving economy and a strong social fabric. The majority of the population have been her loyal followers, constituents and supporters, to the extent of voting her as Chancellor for no less than four terms of office.

A remarkable political leader, she never indulges in grandstanding and authoritarianism. She has always created space for a cooperative, reason-based and network-oriented style of leadership for Europe. There are two important and overarching accomplishments, among many, that Merkel will be credited for. Firstly, when she leaves office as Chancellor of Germany, she will be leaving a strong and liberal democracy. Secondly, she will be leaving the country with the proud German testimony of taking responsibility in a world where evading responsibility has become the norm.

Merkel has redefined the meaning of strength, as her strength has nothing to do with arrogance, pride, a misplaced sense of honor, visible dominance, boastfulness, public humiliation and intimidation. Merkel's place in history is already guaranteed by her leadership of Germany and Europe. History will recognize Merkel as someone who has done more to shape Germany than any other post-war leader, with the capacity to rise to the occasion even when she ordinarily ought to have been caught napping, and no traumatic event illustrates this better than her response to the coronavirus pandemic of 2020.

Merkel's scientific thinking, which is essentially her deliberate probing of every piece of information, and her cautious consultation with experts, has remained integral to her decision-making process. In all probability, her measured and modest handling of Germany's affairs is partially responsible for her enjoyment of 15 uninterrupted years of the support of a nation whose understandable historical reverence for the scientific achievement of great minds like Albert Einstein is legendary. At no time during her leadership has this reliance on science and evidence-based reasoning played a greater role than the coronavirus pandemic of 2020. Trusted by her people to navigate the outbreak's murky waters, Merkel has proved to be both commander-in-chief and scientist-in-chief. She deployed her characteristic rationality to guide Germany through what was adjudged a relatively successful battle against COVID-19.

Without doubt, the pandemic proved to be the crowning challenge for a politician whose leadership style has been consistently described as clinical, analytical, unemotional and cautious. Although her quest for socio-economic stability during the outbreak was aided by the advantage of a well-coordinated system of scientific and medical expertise all across Germany, the hard-earned trust of the German populace allowed Merkel's steady and sensible leadership to flourish. Coming from 30 years of experience in political leadership, and facing such an enormous challenge that demanded calm and reasoned thinking, Merkel was at peak performance in her modeling of the humble credibility of a brilliant scientist at work.

In conclusion, one can safely say that at no other time in the 5,000 years of recorded history of mankind has there been a greater need for strong leaders. More to the point, given the remarkable strides that have been made in the area of gender equality and empowerment, we now need upcoming women leaders to be uninhibitedly inspired by the resilience of women like Winnie Mandela, Hillary Clinton and Angela Merkel. This is because, as the future embodiments of authentic feminine strength, the hope for a solid consolidation of the gains of efforts to emancipate women from the shackles of male domination and marginalization rests squarely on their shoulders.

How to Gain Access to Your Power of Resilience

1. Develop the capacity and capability to recover rapidly from difficulties.

2. Come into the knowledge that resilience is synonymous with toughness. Therefore, resilience is also your capability to cope in the face of daunting challenges, setbacks, barriers or limited resources.

3. Be prepared to sacrifice time, effort and resources, because resilience is also a measure of just how much you desire your objective, and how much you are willing to sacrifice to achieve it.

4. Be prepared to deploy a combination of ability and willingness to achieve your goal.

5. Resilience will demand a great deal of emotional strength from you.

6. Be prepared to be an instrument of massive transformation in the lives of others.

7. Be prepared to remain in awareness of critical situations, and the behavior of those around you.

8. Develop courage, because courage, also, is almost synonymous with resilience.

CHAPTER 9

THE POWER OF COMPASSION

"It is not how much you do, but how much love you put into what you do that counts."

MOTHER TERESA, PATRON SAINT OF CALCUTTA

A very significant reason why women tend to execute their leadership roles in a manner that is a marked departure from male stereotyped models is that, fundamentally displaying genuine compassion in leadership, women possess both an uncommonly strong sense of community and the ability to selflessly deploy that connection to their community in whatever they do. Even the most unrepentant skeptic would find it difficult to controvert the widely held belief that, relative to men, women have an inbuilt generosity of spirit and the high degree of emotional intelligence that allows them to be acutely sensitive to the needs of others.

Another perfectly valid reason why women might have evolved into the more compassionate of the genders is that the self-serving considerations of winner-takes-all gratification, competition and an unbridled quest for profits at the expense of grave human and social consequences are traits that are largely absent from the feminine psyche. While men remain preoccupied with the need to continually demonstrate physical superiority through the incessant war-mongering that leads to endless human suffering, women, on the other hand, have through the ages demonstrated nothing short of a limitless strength that is founded on the values of compassion and humility that are born of genuine strength of character.

Expressed differently, women continue to use their inherent emotional strength and wisdom to display a strength that is more enduring and certainly more productive than the physical. This combined emotional strength and wisdom finds expression in compassion. It is this compassion that some great women have used to both assist others in traversing everyday challenges, and to continue with the human struggle where men's physical strength appears to have failed the world.

What motivates some leaders to become such big-hearted people is one of the mysteries of human predilection. While some leaders remain comfortably ensconced in their mansions, wallowing in all the obscene luxury that their means can afford, others are toiling hard to ease the pains of people in distress. The source of the motivation to give so selflessly of time and resources is compassion. There is little doubt that compassion is one of the purest forms of the expression of love for humanity. It would seem as if such great leaders feel left with little choice than to strive to be the very epitome of the practice of that very elevated form of love.

Often, people equate compassion with kindness, but the meaning and the scope of application transcends mere kindness. In fact, kindness is only an elemental component of compassion. The expression of compassion by anyone is a wholesome reflection of the potential bigness of the human heart. More often than not, this expression involves the willingness to do four things. The first is to place oneself in someone else's shoes, so to speak. The second is to take the focus off oneself and one's personal needs and desires. The third is to creatively and emotionally imagine what it might be like to be in someone else's predicament. The fourth is to feel love for that person.

There is no doubt that true compassion can only be found in those deep, subterranean depths of the human condition, and that is why its qualification in any individual is such a rarity. That cannot be otherwise. Compassion is profoundly silent. Compassion is indescribably tender. Compassion manifests itself as a constantly self-relinquishing and gentle demeanor. It is only compassion that truly elevates leaders above a self-centered existence. It allows leaders to finally reside in the hearts of others, and to think and feel what they feel.

A surgeon during the Second World War was celebrated for his total devotion to tending wounded soldiers at a military hospital. He was quoted to have said, *"I do not ask the wounded person how he feels, rather I become the wounded person."* He was right. Compassion feels the agony of others and is solely preoccupied with seeking to alleviate it. That is compassion at its most elevated level of practice. This was the type of compassion displayed throughout the remarkable life of one of the greatest female figures to have traversed the surface of this earth in the last century. She was famously known as Mother Teresa.

She was born Agnes Gonxha Bojaxhiu in Skopje, Macedonia, of Albanian extraction, in 1910. At the age of 12, she felt what she would later characterize as "the call of God." Realizing she had to be a missionary to be able to spread the love of Jesus Christ effectively, she left her family home in Skopje at the age of 18 to join the Sisters of Loreto, a Dublin-based Irish community of nuns founded in the 17th century, and which ran missions in India. Following a few months of training in Dublin, she was sent to India, where on May 24, 1931 she took her initial vows as a nun and was given the name of Teresa, in honor of Saint Thérèse of Lisieux.

From 1931 to 1948 she taught at St. Mary's High School in Calcutta, India. However, the sheer human suffering and poverty she witnessed outside the convent walls made such a deep impression on her that in 1948 she obtained permission from her superiors to leave the convent school to devote herself to working among the poorest of the poor in the slums of Calcutta. Although she had no funds, she depended solely on Divine Providence to sustain her rather arduous mission, which also involved running an open-air school for slum children. Her efforts did not go unnoticed or unappreciated, and she was soon joined by voluntary helpers, while financial support also started trickling in, making it possible for her to expand the scope of her work such that she could establish the Missionaries of Charity, a religious order of nuns based in Calcutta.

Through the Missionaries of Charity, Mother Teresa sacrificed even the most basic of life's necessities to live like the poor and the destitute. In a life that can only qualify as one of the most fascinating and highly revered in the 20th century, Mother Teresa dedicated all that life to serving the poor, the sick and the dying in India and other parts of the world. Through the years, her selfless work in helping the needy would earn her global acclaim and numerous honors, awards and accolades. The United Nations later adopted the anniversary of her death as the International Day of Charity.

Mother Teresa's greatest strength lay in her relentless commitment to stay focused on the core mission and vision of her organization, Missions of Charity. Her dedication to serving the least materially endowed of God's creations brought out the natural saint in Mother Teresa. She saw herself as nothing more than a servant of those she helped, an attitude that turned her into a total embodiment of servant-leadership. She paid ardent attention to what people had to say. She accepted others and totally empathized with them. Also possessing uncommon foresight and intuition, she was immensely socially aware and perceptive. Additionally, she possessed such powers of persuasion that she could communicate her thoughts and concepts to her target audience with effortless ease. Mother Teresa exercised very high levels of moral authority and was able to exert great healing influence on individuals and communities.

To many, Mother Teresa was an icon of love and care. She was also a great role model who exemplified transformational leadership for those who wished to pursue a career in helping others. In attaining very high levels of performance for herself and her organization, she motivated her followers to achieve the vision of her organization. She was able to influence them to transcend their personal interest for the sake of the greater good. She was also a charismatic leader who inspired people around the world to help the less privileged and those in need.

Through the sheer force of her faith and determination, Mother Teresa saved and changed countless lives around the world. A highly esteemed and confident leader who displayed extraordinary leadership qualities backed by a strong sense of purpose, she articulated goals and ideals which her followers subscribed to just by her sheer humility and her ability to inspire action in others using only simple words. Put differently, Mother Teresa exhibited an extraordinary form of moral suasion that influenced her followers to join her to deliver passionately on her mission.

Indeed, Mother Teresa was a passionate leader who spent over 50 years of her life working relentlessly to service the needs of the poor. Being sensitive to the needs and expectations of others were traits that strengthened her moral authority and inspired loyalty from both the people that she worked with and those that they, in turn, helped. She gave everything she had of herself to help the poor, in the process becoming a world changer and a history maker. At an early stage in her life, she had decided that the needs of the poor were more important than hers, and this mindset launched her into ministering to the poor, the sick and destitute.

Deploying one of the most profoundly moving and revolutionary interpretations of Christianity to her work, her vision and mission would change the face of faith in many profound ways, while her name would become synonymous with kindness, compassion and benevolence. In addition to the Nobel Peace Prize, which she received in 1979, Mother Teresa was also honored with the American Presidential Medal of Freedom in 1985, The Bharat Ratna Award, India's highest civilian award in 1980, and the Jawaharlal Nehru Award for International Understanding in 1972.

On deeper analysis, it is clear that Mother Teresa epitomized compassion as a composite of three innate qualities. These qualities are kindness, gentleness and insight. True kindness, the one that is seen in the great women leaders of compassion, is definitely not an ephemeral impulse but one of a quality that is enduring if only because it requires no external incentive to propel it into the good deed. Gentleness, on the other hand, the sort that Mother Teresa manifested to venerable degree, is one that confers a semblance of divinity on one, and speaks into one's tremendous self-discipline in the same instant. Finally, Mother Teresa's insight was indicative of a depth of understanding which allowed her rather than seeing only a man's clothes to see the man and not be concerned with his clothes. She was totally unprejudiced and free of bigotry in any guise whatsoever.

Like every leader of note, Mother Teresa was not lacking in critics. However, she carried on laying the foundations of her work, refusing to be deterred by pressure or criticism. Instead, she rose above it and succeeded in spite of the criticism. For over five decades, Mother Teresa devoted time and energy to establishing foundations all around the world, comprising orphanages, schools, hospices and care homes. By the time she won the Nobel Peace Prize in 1979, she already had 159 Missionaries of Charity foundations throughout the world.

Through the 1980s and 1990s she traveled around the world, bringing her work to those who were in desperate need of love and care. By 1997, she had well over 4,000 sisters in her order, and she had established 600 foundations in more than 100 countries across the globe. The sisters of her Missions of Charity also ran soup kitchens, dispensaries and mobile clinics. Theirs was a silent vow to give wholehearted and free service to the poorest of the poor on Earth. Their work was eloquent testimony to

Mother Teresa's influence in inspiring many people to push toward their unique greatness and to share their gifts with the world, in the process ensuring that her own powerful legacy would live on for generations.

When she died at the age of 87, Mother Teresa brought the world together in an unforgettable funeral that was attended by presidents, prime ministers, royalty, and hundreds of thousands of people from all walks of life and religious persuasions from all over the world. To cap her ecclesiastical glory, she would be canonized by the Catholic Church as Saint Teresa, the Patron Saint of Calcutta, on September 4, 2016.

Mother Teresa's leadership was a classic study in combined spiritual and secular statesmanship. Even as in her late 80s she continued to minister to the abject poor and downtrodden of the streets and ghettoes of Calcutta, a remarkable story was famously told about her.

As the story goes, Patricia, a Phoenix-based reporter, got ready for a scheduled radio interview with Mother Teresa. Shortly before the interview itself, Patricia asked, *"Mother Teresa, is there anything I can do to help with your cause? Can I help you to raise some money? Can I help you with some publicity?"*

"No, Pat," replied Mother Teresa. *"There is nothing you need do. My cause is not about publicity neither is it about money. Frankly, Pat, it is about something much higher."*

"Surely, there must be something I can do to help! I feel so helpless!" Patricia persisted.

After a momentary pause, Mother Teresa replied, *"Well, if you really want to help, Pat, get up tomorrow morning at 4am, and go out on the streets of Phoenix. Find someone who believes he is all alone in this world and convince him that he is not."*

Patricia was speechless, even as the compassionate nun continued speaking. *"Each waking moment of mine is occupied by encounters with Jesus Christ in all His distressing disguises. Pat, step out on to the streets of Phoenix for your own divine encounters. That is how you can help."*

In no other profession does compassion find such a powerful pedestal for expression than the nursing of the ill and infirm. While many of the great women in mankind's history have exhibited their remarkable leadership traits through civic governance and the humanitarian deed, one particular woman was to prove her own mettle through the compassionate care of the sick.

Florence Nightingale was a British social reformer and statistician. Born in 1820 in Florence, Italy, she received a good education, excelling in mathematics and learning to speak several languages. However, Nightingale is more renowned as the founder of modern nursing. She came to prominence when she was serving as manager and trainer of nurses during the Crimean War, where she helped organize care for wounded soldiers. In giving nursing the new image of a reputable profession that could be pursued for the good of humanity, she became an icon of Victorian culture. In 1860, to lay the foundation for professional nursing practice, she established the first secular nursing school in the world at St. Thomas's Hospital in London. The school is now part of King's College London, a prestigious university in the United Kingdom.

The Nightingale Pledge taken by nurses, and the Florence Nightingale Medal which until today remains the highest international distinction a nurse can possibly achieve, were both named in recognition of her pioneering work in nursing. The United Nations International Day of Nurses is celebrated on Nightingale's birthday. Yet, her social reforms transcended nursing to include improving healthcare for all sectors of British society. She also advocated for hunger relief in India and helped to abolish prostitution laws that were considered unduly harsh on women.

Widely remembered as the Lady with the Lamp, Nightingale was the first woman to be admitted as a Fellow of the Royal Statistical Society. She also redefined the role of the professional hospital administrator. With only the exception of today's high-tech medicine, almost all departments in today's hospitals can trace their roots back to innovations that were first introduced by Nightingale, who was also a scholar of religion. She remains history's first and most effective advocate for the healthcare rights of soldiers and veterans.

Not only was she an icon of nursing, but she also strongly advocated for the empowerment of women and girls by expanding acceptable norms of the day for female participation in the workforce. She was a versatile and prodigious writer, much of whose published work concerned the spread of medical knowledge. She was also a pioneer in data visualization with the use of infographics, using graphical presentations of statistical data. Much of her work was published posthumously, including extensive work on religion and mysticism. Her collection of letters is the largest in the British Library, surpassing even those of Sir Winston Churchill in magnitude.

As a leader of note, Florence Nightingale firmly established her role as the world's first professional hospital administrator in the midst of a healthcare crisis. During the Crimean War in 1854, Nightingale was called to duty in response to an outcry over the deplorable conditions under which British casualties received critical care.

She led a group of nurses to the Scutari Barrack Hospital in Turkey where they found thousands of sick and wounded British soldiers living in deplorable conditions, with some of them lying on blood-soaked straw mats along the facility's corridors, their clothes crawling with lice and vermin. Worse, drugs and medical consumables were unavailable, while adequate ventilation and fresh water were nonexistent luxuries.

Naturally, stale food and infections were the order of the day. The British soldiers had to endure amputations without anesthesia after most of them had succumbed to gangrene.

It was during this healthcare crisis that Nightingale established nursing as a respectable profession. She went on to develop modern nursing, pharmacy, laundry, sterilizing and nutrition services as the core components of a modern hospital as we know it today. She innovated meticulous record keeping to create today's medical and epidemiology records. Her efforts at charting infection and death rates among the soldiers at Scutari gave weight to her demand for the improvement of sanitary conditions in both military and civilian hospitals.

While Nightingale was a compassionate caregiver, she was at the same time a tough-minded manager. She had the intuitive understanding that emotions were contagious and would never tolerate gossip, complaining and other forms of toxic emotional negativity. She always insisted that people be treated with dignity. She never hesitated to point out that she had a mission and not a job. Therefore, she did not focus on pay and benefits before leading her team to Crimea, a place that would prove notorious for its intolerable working conditions.

Nightingale's legacy reminds the world that caring for the sick is more than just a job or a business. It can only qualify as a mission and a calling. She proved unstoppable and courageous in her work and did not allow opposition from the aristocracy or the antiquated views of imperious physicians and military leaders to detract her from carrying out set tasks with dedication and commitment. Through that calling, she changed the face of healthcare forever. She encouraged a recommitment to the profession and attracted idealistic young people into it. Whenever she ran into an obstacle, she would do everything to overcome that obstacle, sometimes appealing directly to the public for funding, and going to the Queen for political backing. Strongly believing that awareness and empathy were more paramount to quality healthcare, she calculated and reduced costs per patient per day.

Nightingale was an exceptional team builder who not only devoted rare compassion to the soldiers under her care but also cared passionately about the nurses who worked under her. While she was clearly a demanding leader, she exhibited an uncompromising commitment to the people that she led. She ensured that upon return from Scutari, every nurse who had worked with her was given employment by the British government. At her death, her coffin was escorted by octogenarian veterans of the Crimean War in honor of her legendary contribution to the healthcare and welfare of soldiers at the Crimean war front.

As a leader, Nightingale had a wonderful sense of humor with which she defused tense situations. She attributed her success to the proven fact that she never gave excuses not to do her work to the best of her ability, nor did she take excuses from others in the same regard. Refusing to rest on her laurels, she continually raised the bar of performance higher and higher. After ensuring that a more professional approach to nursing care would improve clinical outcomes, Nightingale helped to establish the first visiting nurses association, chartered the first modern school of professional nursing, and in her twilight years used her writing to help establish a professional standard for hospital management.

Famously known as the Lady with the Lamp because of many late-night nursing rounds in which the only source of illumination was the lamp she carried as she tended to wounded soldiers during the Crimean War, Nightingale has come to be judged by history as an influential leader who exhibited many admirable leadership traits. She had a clear vision and mission and selflessly provided care for others.

In the early 19th century, nursing was viewed merely as a lucrative domestic service that so-called and ill-trained nurses selected as a career path principally as a source of easy money. Nightingale, however, changed all that. She insisted that all nurses undergo formal training to develop both their knowledge and skills base. Of far greater significance, and posterity would seem to be in perfect accord with this, she possessed and pursued the conceptual vision that nursing was not just a service but a profession of indisputable utilitarian value to the wellbeing of mankind, and one to which she dedicated her entire life.

It is famously said that political leadership traditionally does not lend itself to the display of emotions of the soft kind, politicians being more inclined toward a generally brittle and stoic attitude in the rough and tumble world of power struggle. If one politician defied this norm, yet attained the heights of political leadership, it was Portia Lucretia Simpson-Miller, first female Prime Minister of the Caribbean island country of Jamaica.

Throughout her political career, Simpson-Miller would so decidedly earn herself the compassionate reputation of a voice for the poor and unemployed that she was dubbed the "Face of the Faceless." As an advocate for the poor, the dispossessed, the oppressed and all those who were voiceless and faceless, she was focused on the empowerment of the marginalized, including women and children, and the bringing together of all classes to tackle deep-rooted crime and economic underdevelopment. Her great passion for social justice was representative of the feminine compassion and empathy that she displayed throughout her career.

Born in the rural community of Wood Hall in St. Catherine in Jamaica, Portia Simpson-Miller is one of the most popular and most successful female politicians in Jamaica. She made history when she became the first female President of the People's National Party and was sworn in as Jamaica's first-ever female Prime Minister in 2006, a position in which she served twice, first from 2006 to 2007 and then from 2012-2016.

Simpson-Miller, who had once served as the country's Minister of Defense, holds a degree in public administration from the Union Institute of Miami, and which later conferred on her the honorary degree of Doctor of Humane Letters for her exemplary efforts at improving the quality of life of all Jamaican citizens, becoming the Institute's first recipient of an honorary doctorate. In addition, she completed the Leaders Development Executive Education Program at John F. Kennedy School of Government at Harvard University.

Simpson-Miller's political career started in 1974 when, on the platform of the People's National Party, she stood in the municipal elections representing the Trench Town area. Her success in that election led to her nomination as a candidate in the general elections in which she won a seat as member of parliament for South West St. Andrew. She later entered the cabinet as Minister of Labor, Welfare and Sports. Her empathy and compassion toward Jamaica's underserved and underprivileged was legendary.

A strong advocate for women and girls, she helped set up a network of childcare centers to encourage women to get into employment. Her administration abolished healthcare fees for children and pledged greater government support for first-time parents. As Minister of Labor, she took great interest in the working conditions of overseas farm workers. She reformed the program by working through the overseas recruitment center for farm workers to seek an improvement in the working conditions. She embarked on strategic investments of the insurance fund, which saw an increase in growth from $1.5m to $20m over a three-year period, an initiative that resulted in the significant growth in the national insurance fund, to the ultimate benefit of pensioners. Her agenda also included employment for the youth and women.

As former Minister of Labor, Welfare and Sports, and an avid supporter of Jamaican athletes, it was under her leadership that the country's indoor sports facilities were built and a sports development foundation established. She supported community and school sports programs and funded the building of stadiums and playing fields, and would often be seen dressed in national colors supporting sports events.

Simpson-Miller was also a great ambassador for Jamaica, as she represented the country on an international level as Director of the Commonwealth Local Government Reform, Vice-President of the Inter-American Network of Decentralization, Director of the Board of Trustees of the United Nations Center for Local Government and Chair of the Caribbean Local Government Ministers. She also served in several positions in the People's National Party, including being the party's Vice-President and head of the Women's Movement. She also served as spokesperson for women's affairs, pension, social security and consumer affairs. As Minister of Tourism, she worked hard to promote Jamaica in the wake of the September 11 terrorist attack to restore confidence in tourism by improving airport security.

Simpson-Miller's election as Prime Minister was hailed as a proud moment for the women of the region and the women of the world. She became Jamaica's seventh Prime Minister, its first-ever female Prime Minister and the third in the Anglophone Caribbean states, following in the footsteps of Eugenia Charles of Dominica and Janet Jagan of Guyana. Her election was largely seen as the beginning of a transformation for the Jamaican society and other Third World countries. During her tenure as Prime Minister, she was one of only seven women in the world out of 192 nation-states that were leaders of their nations.

At her inauguration, she emphasized her government's commitment to regional integration and cooperation, and later, with her proven leadership, management and progressive ideas, Simpson-Miller commanded the trust of Jamaicans. Quickly becoming a truly influential and courageous leader, she was honored with the Jamaican Order of the Nation. During her tenure in office, her administration began to reform Jamaica's drug laws and subsequently decriminalized the possession of marijuana in small amounts. As Prime Minister, she enabled the prosperity agenda for Jamaica, while a solid foundation was laid for the Jamaican economy to take off on a trajectory of sustainable growth. Simpson-Miller met the targets set by the cabinet and the International Monetary Fund, a feat that no other Jamaican Prime Minister had ever achieved.

A proud Jamaican, Simpson-Miller opened an inquiry into the proceedings surrounding Marcus Garvey's conviction, which had been largely viewed as being politically motivated at the time. When she spoke at Jamaica's 44th Independence Anniversary on a visit to New York, she invoked Garvey's memory and pledged that as Prime Minister she would work assiduously for a unified Jamaica. She regarded Garvey as a national hero, and his philosophy of self-reliance and pride for those descended from the victims of the Trans-Atlantic slave trade as part of Jamaica's proud heritage. In 2006, she opened the exhibition of Marcus Garvey at Liberty Hall in Kingston, Jamaica, as a fitting monument to the memory of the great national hero and his enduring vision for the advancement of the African Diaspora. Without doubt, Simpson-Miller's successful career as Prime Minister cast her in the mold of an authentic role model for women all over the world.

The Mother Teresas, Florence Nightingales and Portia Simpson-Millers of our world are a rare gift. They are a rare gift to the world because of the compassion that is an integral part of their nature yet happens to be the greatest force for good in the lives of many. As a necessary and core leadership trait, compassion itself teaches us that the simple things in life are quite often the most extraordinary. A spontaneous display of affection can bring the bloom back into someone's life. An unexpected gesture of kindness may yet turn out the soothing balm that a tortured and tormented person needs to continue to thrive in a harsh world.

Our women leaders remain an enduring hope for the rise of mankind from the ashes of mortal attrition and economic chaos because of that place of authentic love, compassion and empathy that they bring us to, and which will always and truly be the foundation for a better quality of life for the people of our planet.

How to Gain Access to Your Power of Compassion

1. You will need to develop a strong sense of community and the ability to deploy that connection to your community in whatever you do.

2. You will need to employ a generosity of spirit to be genuinely sensitive to the needs of others.

3. Avoid the winner-takes-all attitude, or the irrational competition that will render you insensitive to human suffering.

4. Develop the core values of humility and empathy that are indicative of enduring strength of character.

5. Continually tap into your inherent feminine emotional strength and wisdom to display a strength that is more enduring and certainly more productive than the physical.

6. Be prepared to assist others in traversing their own everyday challenges.

7. Recognize that compassion is one of the purest forms of the expression of love for humanity.

8. Remain aware of the critical difference between compassion and kindness, the latter being only an elemental component of compassion.

9. To be compassionate, you have to place yourself in someone else's shoes, so to speak.

10. To be compassionate, you have to take the focus off yourself and your own personal needs and desires.

11. To be compassionate, you have to creatively and emotionally imagine what it might be like to be in someone else's predicament.

12. To be compassionate, you have to feel genuine love for another person.

CHAPTER 10

THE POWER OF CHARISMA

"As First Lady, I have seen the very best of the American spirit. I've seen it in the incredible kindness and warmth of the people. I've seen it in teachers in a near-bankrupt school district who vowed to keep teaching without pay. I have seen it in people become heroes at a moment's notice, diving into harm's way to save others. I've seen it in our men and women in uniform and our proud military families. Every day, the people I meet inspire me. Every day they make me proud. Every day they remind me how blessed we are to live in the greatest nation on Earth."

MICHELLE OBAMA, FIRST LADY OF THE UNITED STATES
DEMOCRATIC NATIONAL CONVENTION, SEPTEMBER 4, 2012

The word charisma itself rolls off the tongue with a smoothness of ease that gives it an unmistakably attractive flavor. Charisma seeks its most authoritative definition from the Merriam-Webster dictionary, which states that *"it is a personal magic of leadership arousing special popular loyalty or enthusiasm for a public figure, especially a political leader."* Without doubt, it is the quality of being capable of attracting, charming and influencing those around one.

No one is so easy to identify as that person who is genuinely charismatic. If there are sometimes difficulties in saying exactly what skills or qualities charismatic people possess, it is often because there are different types of such people. Some may be more reticent, perhaps relying more on their personal charm than their words to influence others. Yet others are such passionate communicators that they tend to sweep others off their feet with their enthusiasm.

Ultimately, however, charismatic people find a common ground in the excellent communication and interpersonal skills that they possess. A highly developed charisma confers tremendous personal power on one. That is because, being more people-oriented and empathic than most, those who are charismatic on several different levels tend to bond more easily with people, allowing them to attract genuine goodwill in any situation in which they find themselves.

Charisma is also defined as a compelling attractiveness or charm that can inspire tremendous devotion in others. Expressed quite simply, charisma is that special quality that makes one a likable person. The classic picture of a charming person is not entirely alien to our experience. She is confident. She has incomparable poise. She is classy in that inconspicuous manner that still manages to transfix everyone around her. Her capacity to effortlessly entrance those in her orbit is comparable only to the way a magnet attracts steel to itself. She radiates a combined energy and confidence that genuinely draws the admiration of even the most reticent of individuals. Yet, as has been proven over and over again, she does not exude all that charm because of what she says or how she looks. The true essence of her charismatic energy is merely a function of someone who unwittingly and effortlessly inspires others, not only by her own ideas but by their own ideas, a remarkable feat that buds from her place of genuine empathy and infectious passion.

The charismatic leader tends to communicate with incomparable ease. She is socially adroit. She effortlessly projects an attractive and exciting image that others wish to cultivate. From whichever perspective we view it, charisma is simply the ability to exert a positive influence on others by bonding with them physically, emotionally and intellectually. It is charisma that compels others to like one. Charisma is what motivates people to enjoy being around a leader even when they have limited knowledge about her.

The charismatic leader carries herself with grace and confidence. She does not consider herself well-dressed unless she is also wearing a smile. Yet, she also readily paints her world with a smile at the slightest prompting. Being a compellingly persuasive person, she finds it infinitely easy to get people to align with her viewpoints. Apart from being a consummate communicator who is able to articulate her ideas properly for easy comprehension, she is also an excellent listener. In fact, she appears to possess the rare skill of listening her way into the hearts of other people.

Charismatic leaders are also peddlers of great ideas and lofty visions for their people. After all, no matter how persuasive a leader is, and no matter how skilled she is in connecting with others, if she has nothing of substance to say to her people, or no productive ventures she has to inspire them with, she will merely be an empty barrel.

If charisma is truly a magical trait that arouses unflinching devotion in people, then no political leader in ancient history exemplifies it more than one of the greatest and certainly one of the most beautiful female monarchs in the history of mankind.

Cleopatra VII Philopator was both a political ruler and a religious icon of ancient Egypt. Descendant of the founder of the Ptolemaic Kingdom of Egypt, Ptolemy I Soter, and a celebrated companion of Alexandra the Great, Cleopatra VII, who lived from 69BCE to 30BCE, was the last active and female pharaoh and ruler of that era, ending the Ptolemaic dynastic rule of nearly three centuries.

Cleopatra VII believed that broadmindedness was an absolute requirement for effective leadership. Revered for a beauty that was as arresting as it was stunning, she was also a highly intelligent and very ambitious person. It was her combination of ambition and fixity of purpose that would propel ancient Egypt into the rich, civilized and much more successful kingdom than it ever was, even if only in comparison with its status under previous Ptolemaic governments.

Fascinatingly, in the history of Egypt there were seven queens in the Ptolemaic dynasty, and they all bore the royal name of Cleopatra. Indeed, almost every pharaoh-queen of Egypt was named Cleopatra. However, Cleopatra VII, whose personality was essentially charisma at its finest point of definition, would elevate the place of the pharaoh-queen in history by establishing herself unequivocally as one of the most phenomenal women leaders in mankind's early history, in the process also declaring herself the quintessential symbol of female efficacy in leadership.

Cleopatra VII lived in an ancient, male-dominated world. Yet, she managed to distinguish herself by impacting on history, not only as a strong female leader but perhaps also as the most powerful female leader of her time, wielding unprecedented influence on the people of Egypt and the rest of the world.

Born of Macedonian Greek extraction in 69BCE, she had six brothers and grew up in Alexandria, the capital of Egypt. In the arts, Cleopatra VII has been more prominently depicted as a temptress and an adulteress who courted both Julius Caesar and Marc Antony, a notoriety that was responsible for many people being unaware that Cleopatra VII was actually a woman leader who demonstrated far greater leadership skills than many men of her time.

When she ascended to the throne at her father's death, she was only 18 years old, an age at which many were understandably skeptical of her leadership skills and her suitability to lead, with many considering her too young to be a sovereign queen. What many did not realize was that the young monarch was not only confident but also determined that with her beauty, charm and intelligence, she would make a great queen. To firmly establish herself as a unique monarch, she christened herself "The Sun-God's Daughter."

As queen, Cleopatra VII evolved a unique leadership style that lent itself to a remarkable case study in inspirational and inborn leadership. This point becomes all the more important when one realizes that Cleopatra VII reigned as Queen of Egypt in very turbulent times that included war, famine and the expansion of the Roman Empire. Although all these epochal events affected Cleopatra and her leadership in various ways, her leadership principles and core values were more largely influenced in very relevant context by the profound undercurrents of her own personal life.

Indeed, a very compelling tool that Cleopatra VII cultivated to a devastatingly effective level of utility was charisma. She believed that to be considered a worthy leader, she was under an uncompromising obligation to cultivate the impeccable appearance that is totally befitting of a leader. Cleopatra VII invested a great deal of time and effort in taking personal charisma to unprecedented levels. She asserted that a woman's appearance, especially that of the woman leader, was what fundamentally announced her as a leader. Furthermore, she insisted that it was an unimpeachably elegant appearance that confers such a leader with non-negotiable respectability before her own people, and before foreign royal leaders.

Cleopatra VII paid scrupulous attention to the most intricate detail of the clothes that she wore, and always ensured that she was the last word in elegance whenever and wherever she appeared for public and official royal duties. Additionally, her devotion, at least for the times, to an elaborate routine of personal hygiene was legendary. For an era in which body grooming was not in the least sophisticated, she bathed with soap and used perfumes and fragrances that were extracted from natural ingredients.

She was also very particular about her make-up, which remained always impeccable, indoors and outdoors, while her hair received the devoted attention of the greatest stylists of the day. To complement the beauty of her hair, she chose to wear a crown in the shape of a cobra, which also served as a protective symbol of sorts. Without doubt, her physical appearance made her a greatly admired figure, and must have contributed greatly to a leadership style that was widely celebrated as possessing immense charisma.

Cleopatra VII complemented her charismatic combination of beauty and intelligence with an uncommon dose of ambition. It is probably logical to assume that the principal trait to which a queen might wish to deploy compelling beauty and charm is ambition. The point can never be disputed that Cleopatra VII was consistent with her vision and mission to expand Egypt and make her rich. She was a passionate leader with great ambition who reclaimed the land in neighboring territories and ultimately succeeded in controlling Syria, Lebanon and a small part of Asia.

Broadmindedness and intelligence are components of leadership charisma. Cleopatra VII combined her beauty with broadmindedness and a scintillating intelligence. She understood right from the outset that intelligence would be an important factor for advancing the interests of the Egyptian empire. With that in mind, she used quality education to advance Egyptian civilization, founding a library in the royal capital of Alexandria which was to later become the world's largest library at that time. That was why the city of Alexandria was dubbed the "City of Learning." Cleopatra VII taught herself to speak Egyptian so that she could interact more effectively with the people of Egypt. Yet, she was famously known to be multilingual, with facility in three languages and the ability to speak several others with more than passing fluency. For this reason, several languages were spoken in Egypt during her reign.

Cleopatra VII was a fiercely independent ruler. She had total confidence that she could rule her kingdom without help from outside, making her one of the most admired rulers of her time. As a woman leader in a male-dominated world, Cleopatra VII was expected to be dependent on her male peers, such as Julius Caesar and Marc Antony who were both leaders of Rome. Instead of dependence, however, she complemented them. She forged military alliances with Marc Antony and they worked together at the Battle of Actium during the Octavian War.

Cleopatra VII took full military responsibility to consummately plan her battles. At the Battle of Actium for instance, Cleopatra realized that her forces and those of Marc Antony were about to lose long before Antony did. Cleopatra led her ships out of the battle and Antony followed with his fleet thereafter. She risked being killed several times during her reign, and she was only too aware that she could be poisoned at any time, since many people disagreed with her position on many issues. Nonetheless, she was always firm in her convictions and judged situations in accordance with those convictions.

Although both Caesar and Antony loved Cleopatra VII to the point of distraction, she managed to sustain her independence. She asked for help only when she absolutely needed it. Being only too aware of Egypt's shortcomings, she requested Julius Caesar's help at the crucial time when it became imminent to get her country out of the civil war that killed Ptolemy VIII. Cleopatra VII was never content with taking the back seat and allowing the men to take control.

In all, she left an enduring legacy as a great role model for other women leaders through her incomparable charismatic leadership skills. To this day, her leadership style is considered to have had one of the greatest impacts on the civilization of ancient Egypt.

More than 2,000 years later, Cleopatra's charismatic personality would be replicated, this time not in a political leader but the consort to one. Michelle LaVaughn Robinson Obama, First Lady of the United States and consort to the 44th President of the United States, made history when she became the first-ever African-American First Lady of the United States of America in 2008, when Americans voted in her husband as the first African-American President. From a one-bedroom apartment in the South Side of Chicago to the White House, a 132-room mansion at 1600 Pennsylvania Avenue in the nation's capital, she ended up becoming the standard bearer of totally refreshing charisma, unparalleled feminine dignity, classic elegance and casual chic for her generation. She would become the embodiment of every man and every woman in America, even as she strived to make the White House a totally accessible showcase of American diversity and down-to-earth living.

She orchestrated command performances at the White House, including, but not limited to, Earth Wind and Fire, Justin Beiber and Brad Paisley. The East Room played host to the finest strains of jazz and country music. She did push-ups on the Ellen Degeneres Show; jumped rope with Dr. Oz; wore J. Crew and Jimmy Choo; graced the covers of *Essence* and *Vanity Fair* magazines; and was listed as among Harvard's annual list of most influential alumni. Indeed, hers is the story of one of the most remarkable first ladies in America's contemporary history.

She was born Michelle LaVaughn Robinson on January 17, 1964. Although one would describe her as an American lawyer and writer, she earns more prominent recognition as a former First Lady of the United States, from 2009 to 2017. Her husband fondly calls her *"the girl from the South Side."* Michelle Obama was raised in the South Side of Chicago, Illinois. Although she was a First Lady, Obama became a charismatic and independent leader in her own right, away from the shadows of her husband.

Before becoming First Lady, she had already achieved her own outstanding accomplishments. She had graduated cum laude from Princeton University and went on to finish her law degree at Harvard. Upon leaving the White House, she completed her Ph.D. at Harvard. Prior to her arrival at the White House, Obama had been in various leadership roles. She was an Associate Dean of Student Services at the University of Chicago, a role that saw her introduce a community service program, and later Vice-President for Community and External Affairs of the University of Chicago Medical Center.

She married Barack Obama in 1992. Not unnaturally, she became a politician-by-marriage. She would vigorously campaign for her husband's presidential aspirations throughout 2007 and 2008, and even delivered a keynote address at the 2008 Democratic National Convention. She would repeat the same oratorical feat at the 2012 Democratic National Convention, and again at the 2016 Democratic National Convention in Philadelphia, at which she spoke glowingly in support of the Democratic presidential nominee and fellow First Lady, Hillary Clinton.

Michelle Obama left a remarkable legacy as a First Lady who succeeded in becoming a veritable role model for women, a strident voice in advocacy for poverty awareness, education, nutrition, healthy eating and physical activity for optimal wellness, and, in the process of all these, still managed to become a fashion icon of sorts. She tirelessly advocated for equal rights and championed education for girls, while pushing for healthy living and advocating for American families living in poverty. Her grace and grit earned her the title of "style icon" and she became a role model to millions of women and girls across the globe.

Obama stood out as one of the most accomplished and passionate first ladies in the history of the United States of America because of her charisma, compassion and powerful communication skills. She has been hailed as a risk-taker, who stepped outside traditional first lady stereotypes. By the time her husband's tenure as President of the United States was over in 2016, she had become more popular than her husband and she was even more loved and admired all over the world.

Prior to becoming First Lady, Obama was already an accomplished writer and community activist as a practicing lawyer who fought against injustice and addressed community social issues when she worked at Chicago City Hall. She had also established the Chicago Chapter of Public Allies, a national service network aimed at helping prepare young people for a career in the civil service. Her special combination of accomplishments and talents made Obama a role model to women and girls around the world.

Presented with the freedom to define her own roles as First Lady, she rose to the occasion by addressing the rights of women and girls, public health and racism. She became mom-in-chief, advocating for the education of children and the needs of military families and those living in poverty. Among numerous other initiatives, she launched the Let Girls Learn initiative to fund projects aimed at girls' education, tackling leadership skills and the alleviation of poverty. She also launched the Reach Higher initiative to inspire young people across the United States to put their education first, in addition to launching the Let's Move campaign against childhood obesity.

Obama achieved several other important milestones as First Lady, including passing a bipartisan School Lunches Program that provided free and reduced-price meals to children from low-income families. She urged young leaders to be the next generation's problem-solvers who should take up the responsibility of eradicating hunger, poverty, HIV/AIDS and other social ills. Behind the scenes, Obama was an insatiable supporter of her husband's presidency.

A powerful inspirational and motivational leader, Obama gave hope to people by relating with them at an uncommonly profound level. Her own story touched and resonated with many women and girls around the world, apart from empowering African-American women to knock down stereotypes that had held them back. As a great communicator and a powerful speaker, she publicly shared stories about her personal life, her first date with her husband and her hopes and aspirations for her daughters. Obama continuously rallied women across the United States to exercise their right to vote, and to strike a comfortable balance between motherhood, work and profession.

With a great sense of purpose, and by sustaining her faith in her convictions, Obama consistently stood up for what she believed in, and she lived by those values, regardless of opposition from various quarters. She gave powerful speeches on her experience as a Black woman competing in academia and did not shy away from calling out lewd behavior, including sexist remarks by politicians. She did all of these without ever losing her cool, as her voice continued to resonate with the hearts and minds of millions of people across the globe. As a strong leader, she always demonstrated the dual high level of self-respect and respect for other people as demonstrated by her use of words like integrity, dignity, decency and pride that she often employed in her speeches.

Obama's story demonstrates how a strong commitment to one's values can lead to desired change in the world. It is also remarkable that despite her multitude of engagements and accomplishments, she still made it a priority to manage her time in such a way as to focus on properly raising her two daughters. Arguably, Obama will be remembered as the most progressive

First Lady the United States has ever had. As a First Lady she was a star in her own right. She did not allow herself to be defined by her husband but rather by her own self. She was not merely seen but was engagingly heard to the point of breaking precedent.

With a personal story that was so inspirational that it made a great impact on millions of people around the world, she used her strong personality to motivate, inspire and call others to action, while her fearless character enabled her to fight relentlessly for social issues. She remained vocal and honest about the harsh realities that are faced by minority communities in America, regardless of how controversial those issues might be. In fact, so influential did she become that over the course of the Obama presidency, particularly during the second term, Michelle Obama was subject to speculation over whether she would run for the presidency herself, in similar fashion to her predecessor, Hillary Clinton.

Michelle Obama is so charismatic that, for all practical purposes, she can be described as an elegant intellectual. To draw on the title of the global hit song of the Commodores of the 70s, *Three Times A Lady*, Obama comfortably occupied three departments of ladyhood. In the eight glorious years of a remarkable phase in the history of the United States, she managed to deliver a command performance that was rich in all the trappings of a novel form of executive glamor.

In the first department, she held her audience spellbound with the very best that contemporary haute couture had on offer, in the process consistently assailing our vision with breathtaking creations in chic and elegant ensembles, appropriately matched by a regal carriage and a totally self-effacing manner.

In the second department, she completely disarmed America with a rare nobility of spirit, and an effortless easy disposition that demonstrated a compassionate consideration for others in making life infinitely easier for them, and totally respecting their sensibilities by displaying, at any conceivable opportunity, not only a flawless physical appearance but also a totally civil conduct.

In the last department, she totally demystified her lofty role of spouse to the Leader of the Free World by sustaining a simple and urbane dignity by consistently behaving in an enthralling manner that gloriously celebrated common sense and courtesy.

Charisma is very infectious. With her husband's rising profile as a politician of note, Michelle Obama gradually became a part of popular culture. In May 2006, *Essence* magazine listed her among 25 of the World's Most Inspiring Women. In July 2007, *Vanity Fair* listed her among 10 of the World's Best Dressed People. She was an honorary guest at Oprah Winfrey's Legends Ball as a "young 'un" paying tribute to the "Legends" who helped pave the way for African-American women. In July 2008, she made a repeat appearance on the *Vanity Fair* international best-dressed list. She also appeared on the 2008 *People* list of best-dressed women and was praised by the magazine for her "classic and confident" look.

At the time of her husband's election, some sources had already anticipated that as a high-profile African-American woman in a stable marriage, Michelle would turn out a positive role model who would influence the view the world has of African-Americans. They would be proved conclusively right on many fronts. Michelle's public support grew in her early months as First Lady, as she was increasingly accepted as a role model.

On her first trip abroad in April 2009, she toured a cancer ward with Sarah Brown, wife of British Prime Minister Gordon Brown. *Newsweek* would later describe her first trip abroad as an exhibition of her so-called "star power," while MSN described it as a display of sartorial elegance. Questions were raised by some in the American and British media regarding protocol when the Obamas met Queen Elizabeth II, and Michelle reciprocated a touch on her back by the Queen during a reception, purportedly against traditional royal etiquette. Palace sources, however, denied that any breach in etiquette had occurred.

Michelle Obama's sense of style has been variously compared to that of Jacqueline Kennedy, while her discipline, comportment and sense of decorum have been likened to that of Barbara Bush. Her style has been described as "fashion populist." In 2010, she wore many high-end clothes from more than 50 designers, and in the same year a study revealed that her patronage alone was worth an average of $14m to a design company. Michelle became a fashion trendsetter. In August 2011, she became the first woman ever to appear on the cover of *Better Homes and Gardens* magazine, and the first person in 48 years. During the 2013 Academy Awards, she became the first First Lady to announce the winner of an Oscar; Best Picture went to *Argo*.

Charisma can comfortably share a groove with wealth. If there was ever any contention about this fact, it has been conclusively laid to rest by an African-American woman who was born into poverty in rural Mississippi to a teenage single mother and later raised in inner-city Milwaukee. Today, dubbed the "Queen of All Media," Oprah Gail Winfrey rides the crest of fame and success as the world's No.1 television talk show host and the wealthiest self-made African-American woman in history. As an entertainment mogul, her famous shows have over the years attained global success and acclaim with millions of viewers from all corners of the world.

Oprah Winfrey serves as chair and chief executive officer of her own production company, Harpo Productions, and the Oprah Winfrey Network, an American television channel. She is also a renowned philanthropist, who is passionate about causes in education and the wellbeing of the African-American people. She graduated with a degree in communications from the Tennessee State University, where she had received a scholarship after winning a speech contest.

Her early work as a news anchor and talk show host led to the creation of the *Oprah Winfrey Show*, which would become a roaring success, attracting millions of viewers from all over the world. She went on to establish Harpo Productions and the *O Magazine*, accompanying it with a popular book club. She has also produced and acted in several Hollywood movies, at one point earning an Academy Award nomination for Best Supporting Actress. When her talk show closed in 2011, Oprah established the Oprah Winfrey Network (OWN) in partnership with the Discovery Network. Widely acknowledged as one of the most influential women of her generation, she was awarded the Presidential Medal of Freedom by the President of the United States in 2013.

If Oprah Winfrey is a transformational leader, she is an even greater charismatic one whose clear vision and mission has tremendously influenced others all over the world. What is perhaps most outstanding about Winfrey's circle of influence is the fact that it is not gender specific. She has positively influenced both men and women to the same significant degree. Her outstanding interpersonal and communication skills have enabled her to engage at a profound level with people from diverse backgrounds. Indeed, as an authentic communicator who operates on a firm platform of sound and enduring moral values, Winfrey's greatest legacy will remain an unerring ability to connect strongly with an audience. That she is always open to new ideas and experiences is evident in the many roles she has played in her life.

She is known to dissolve into tears during interviews on her shows, in emotive and unconscious response to the emotional stories of her guests, evoking a very human and humane side that connects with others. Known and addressed only by her first name by an adoring base of followers all over the world, Oprah has garnered numerous titles over the years. They include media proprietor, actress, producer, businesswoman and philanthropist, all of which come with the enormous responsibility that she appears to breeze through with effortless grace.

Not only is Oprah a woman of effortless and disarming charm, but she has also been hailed as one of the most powerful and influential women in the world, and who effects change in a positive way that inspires others to go the extra mile. She is the first woman in the United States to own her own television network, an initiative she has self-confidently employed to freely share her own stories of pain and joy, in the process changing millions of lives around the world.

Oprah's leadership style demonstrates a keen awareness of a vision that has enabled her to achieve her own big goals, while her listening skills and empathy have enabled her to inspire and motivate others. In many respects, Oprah has been fundamentally a relatable leader since many of her viewers find themselves, wittingly or unwittingly, relating to her personal stories of struggle with issues such as her weight gain and a childhood of poverty and pain. A deeply empathic and caring person, she fights for the common good and does not shy away from addressing injustice and humanitarian issues. She initiated the National Child Protection Act of 1991, and has transformed lives through remarkable education initiatives such as the Oprah Winfrey Leadership Academy for Girls, located in South Africa.

An enduring epitome of leadership by example, her focus has always been on being the best person that she can be, and it is based on this personal philosophy that she offers advice and suggestions to others in their times of need. Her quest to continue to improve herself, personally and professionally, remains a constant source of inspiration to people. To the millions of people who watch her shows, what comes through with incomparable ease is her energy, positivity, encouragement, outgoing personality, and an uncanny awareness and sensitivity to other people.

Oprah's most outstanding strength as a leader has been the creation of a vision for her own success, and her ability to communicate that vision to those around her. Resolute in the execution of that vision, she has also been brave enough to dream big enough to craft a focused brand for herself which she slowly grew by diversifying the distribution of that brand. While her underpinning was the television show, she diversified into movie production, subsidiary television shows, magazine publishing and a radio channel. She has also ventured into philanthropy through multiple charitable foundations.

Clearly, the personal values that Oprah has infused into each phase of her business are totally representative of the solid foundation of her success. She has deployed an intentional strategy that invests in top talent, seeks out smart teams, values customers and consistently nourishes all these relationships. Oprah has invested in loyal mentors, peers, employees and consumers to enable her outstanding success. Expressed differently, she has become the best by surrounding herself with the best. This cannot be otherwise since she has consistently insisted in hiring and supporting only talented people that she believes in, carefully selecting her top team to assure both competence and compatibility.

Oprah is a truly remarkable woman. To accomplish her humongous level of success has demanded insatiable drive, ambition and focus. Hailed as a leader worth emulating, Oprah has uniquely inspired her team and followers, and executed her vision, yet managed to maintain a mass appeal. Over a span of just three decades, Oprah has risen from the status of a young girl from rural Mississippi to a media mogul and tycoon, and most significantly, a world renowned brand. Despite an underprivileged background rooted in poverty and abuse, Oprah managed to establish a platform on which she built her talents to ultimately succeed beyond her own wildest expectations. She believed she could turn her dreams into reality, and she did. She had confidence in her own abilities, and she exploited that confidence to carve herself a place in posterity as a game changer.

Oprah's engaging charisma, interpersonal and communication skills, wisdom, courage and incomparable leadership skills have all combined to earn her numerous awards, honors, accolades and the respect of millions of people across the globe. In addition to the Presidential Medal of Freedom, the highest civil honor in the United States of America, *TIME* magazine named Oprah one of the most influential people on Earth for six consecutive years: 2004, 2005, 2006, 2007, 2008 and 2009.

Our world will continue to appreciate those women of power and influence who attractively embellish their leadership virtues with a certain compelling charm, if only to add some human esthetic polish to the often somewhat brittle sides of leadership, be it on the political terrain or even on the economic turf. Nothing quite beats the picture of an elegant, poised and totally graceful woman at the head of a boardroom table, or even striding purposefully down the hallowed corridors of an executive mansion. Therein lies the softer side of female leadership.

When all is said and done, we will have to accept that leadership excellence will increasingly be in premium demand, principally because the expectations of the led continue to rise to higher standards with every succeeding generation. All strata of political and business life are exacting skills that exceed mere competence to include charm, empathy and mutual human support. That is why charismatic leaders will always continue to stand out. Since they are empathic communicators who see things from the perspectives of others, they will also continue to seek the common ground in all their inter-human relationships, and for the ultimate good of mankind.

How to Gain Access to Your Power of Charisma

1. Develop the quality of being capable of attracting, charming and influencing those around you.

2. Your personal charm, more than your words, may be what makes you charismatic.

3. Your ability to communicate in a passionate manner may be what makes you irresistible to others.

4. To be charismatic, you must possess excellent communication and interpersonal skills.

5. Insist on being uncommonly people-oriented and empathic.

6. Explore ways by which you can bond easily with others, so as to attract genuine goodwill in any situation in which you find yourself.

7. Try to develop that compelling attractiveness or charm that can inspire tremendous devotion in others.

8. Develop the special quality of simply being a likable and agreeable person.

9. Remain confident, incomparably poised and classy in that inconspicuous manner that still manages to transfix everyone around you.

10. Harness that combined energy and confidence that genuinely draws the admiration of anyone who encounters you.

11. Come from your own place of genuine empathy and infectious passion to attempt to inspire others, not only by your own ideas but by their own ideas.

12. Attempt to effortlessly project that attractive and exciting image that others wish to cultivate.

13. Develop the ability to exert a positive influence on others by bonding with them physically, emotionally and intellectually.

14. Develop the ability to articulate your ideas properly for easy comprehension.

15. Develop the skill of keen and attentive listening.

16. Become a peddler of great ideas and lofty visions.

CHAPTER 11

THE POWER OF PURPOSE

"I knew what I wanted from an early age, and while I had no links into politics, I knew quite confidently that if you put your mind to wanting to do something, you will find the paths, meet the right people, and seek out the right opportunities."

SANDIP K. VERMA

The word "purpose" exists within two contextual meanings. The dictionary broadly defines it as the reason why something exists, an intended end, aim or goal, so to speak. It also has a connotation in which it is contextually defined in terms of one's life or activities. Accordingly, one might refer to one's actions as being carried out in a purposeful manner. In that context, purpose offers us a sense of direction, helping to guide our behavior and paths in alignment with our goals and objectives.

Purpose is the driving force behind a leader's actions. Outstanding leaders have a purpose that transcends the desire to merely gratify their own ego through the acquisition of fame and material gratification. Almost invariably, their purpose tends to appeal to the moral convictions of all who are stakeholders in their leadership journey, including both their followers and their peers. Naturally, it is a perfectly legitimate aspiration to seek both fame and fortune. Yet, the paradox of purpose lies in the rather pleasant coincidence that in aiming for something far more important than fame and fortune, such leaders actually come into both rewards with effortless ease, especially in the medium to long term.

There are possibly four moral pedestals on which strong leaders can most effectively drive purpose. The first platform is the *discovery* of a resolute path, in which they continually seek new and innovative paths to express their passion for impactful performance. The second platform is a passionate commitment to *excellence* in all they do. The third is genuine *altruism* in their motives for seeking political relevance, and through which they demonstrate genuine care for their constituents. The last platform is a form of *heroism* in which they truly and courageously lead at the front lines of political leadership. These four moral compasses help to produce leaders that truly stand the test of time, if only because they also tap into a general sense of what is noble, right and worthwhile.

Having a strong sense of purpose is vital to many aspects of leadership, including but not exclusive to an individual's overall morale, personal innovation and the cultivation of mutually beneficial relationships. Purpose, apart from providing focus and direction is also a source of inspiration for others. For instance, most purposeful leaders are able to galvanize others around a personal identity that is based on their purpose. More significantly, in aspiring to become leaders, such people are also able to identify the appropriate environments that seem to easily accommodate their purpose and bring out the best results from their potential as leaders. Purposeful leaders understand that in order for them to lead with purpose, and to achieve the results that are most important to them, they must get everyone else to live according to that purpose.

The one thing that purposeful leadership is not is a one-person show. It is a leadership parameter that ensures that a leader consistently lives in that purpose, and that she has made it unequivocally clear that she expects her primary constituents to hold her to it. In many respects, it is like entering into an article of faith, or covenant of credibility, with others. That is why leading with purpose takes a village. Leading with purpose is only for those who have the courage to make the difference they are committed to making by publicly announcing what their purpose is and working resolutely to achieve it.

In the epigraph to this chapter, an accomplished British politician tells us that she knew what she wanted from an early age, and even though she had absolutely no early links with politics, she remained secure in the confidence that she would eventually actualize her desire.

Sandip K. Verma leaves us in no doubt as to her early identification of her own purpose. Born Sandip K. Rana in Amritsar in Punjab, India, she moved to England with her parents as a child in 1960. Appointed to the British House of Lords as a Conservative life peer with the title Baroness Verma of Leicester in the County of Leicestershire in 2006, Verma is considered one of the United Kingdom's top female politicians, an influential business leader, a protector of women's rights, and a champion for the universal cause for diversity and inclusion.

A prominent voice in the fight that is tackling violence against women and girls, she serves as Chair of the UN Women's National Committee in the United Kingdom. She is also Chair of Domiciliary Care Services, and an independent, non-executive Director of the Renewable Energy Association. In addition, Baroness Verma is global Chair of the World

Wide Generations, and serves on the International Advisory Board of the Amity University International, and that of Sir John Cass Foundation. Coming from a successful career as a businesswoman, in the 1980s she had run a business in women's high-fashion wear with her husband. In 2000, she created Domiciliary Care Services, working with local authorities to support adults within the comfort of their homes.

Since becoming a member of the House of Lords, Baroness Verma has held various key ministerial appointments in the British government. She currently serves as chair of the Lords' European External Affairs Committee, and she is a member of the House of Lords European Union Select Committee.

Until the formation of the Conservative-Liberal Democrat coalition government following the May 2010 general election, Baroness Verma was an Opposition Whip and Conservative spokesperson in the House of Lords on Education and Skills, Health and Pensions. In 2010, she became a Government Whip and spokesperson for the Cabinet Office, International Development, and Equalities and Women's Issues. She has extensive experience in development and governance, and is a strong and committed advocate of diversity and inclusion. Baroness Verma has played an active and advisory role in policy formulation and development in the government of the United Kingdom.

In the four-year span of 2012 to 2016, Baroness Verma served as Minister for the Department of Energy and Climate Change, and later moved on to become Minister for International Development. Under her leadership, the Department of International Development saw a number of reform plans, in which she took a lifespan approach to policy development. She held vital consultations that led to the initiation and design of policy papers to tackle global violence against women and girls, with a focus on using men and boys as agents of change. As Minister of the Department for Energy and Climate Change, Baroness Verma introduced modernization plans and developed strong relationships with the unions, while also working on long-term business planning and budgeting.

In 2013, Baroness Verma created Powerful Women, an organization that works with various energy companies and associated businesses to address gender representation across the energy sector in middle and senior management roles. Under her leadership, Powerful Women developed a toolkit in partnership with Ernst and Young and the Energy Institute. She assisted in the launch of the Sellafield Women's Network and provided support in the setting up of the Women in Nuclear, United Kingdom Chapter.

Between 2015 and 2016, Baroness Verma served as Parliamentary Under-Secretary of State at the Department of International Development, having previously served as Parliamentary Under-Secretary of State at the Department of Climate Change. She was Opposition Whip from 2006 to 2010 and became Government Whip following the 2010 general elections.

Motivated by a strong ethos of hard work, Baroness Verma is a staunch protector of the rights of women and girls, with a focus on raising awareness and ending violence against women and girls. Her strong involvement in global activism for gender equality earned her the appointment as chair of UN Women, United Kingdom Chapter in 2018. She has received various honors, awards and accolades in recognition of her hard work in government, science, business and the feminist movement. She received the inaugural Women in Nuclear Award for her work in increasing the presence of women in senior roles in the nuclear sector. She was also honored with the Pravasi Bharat Samman Award by the President of India in 2011 for her role in building and strengthening business ties between India and the United Kingdom.

Baroness Verma holds honorary doctorate degrees from Wolverhampton University in the United Kingdom and Amity University of India. She was also conferred with an honorary fellowship by the Institute of Directors of India for her work in corporate social responsibility.

To become the first-ever female head of state on an entire continent is no mean feat. Yet, that is the kind of outcome that attends a career rich in purposeful leadership. Helen Sirleaf Johnson is Africa's first-ever female head of state. She was born in Monrovia, Liberia and was educated at the

College of West Africa and Harvard University. She was elected Liberia's President in 2005 and would serve 12 years in office. She was elected President at the critical period of Liberia's emergence from a devastating civil conflict, and symbolized the dawn of a new leadership era in the politics of the West African nation and that of the African continent as a whole.

Not unexpectedly, her ascendancy to the office of President in a patriarchal society came with enormous challenges in a war-ravaged country. Yet, even amidst those Herculean challenges, armed with a compelling vision to lift her country out of the debris of war, Johnson managed to stay focused and succeeded in restoring peace, and in advancing individual freedom across the country. Throughout her 12-year tenure in office she remained dedicated to bringing tremendous political, social and economic change to Liberia.

As a leader, Johnson inspired and motivated others with an uncompromising sense of purpose and direction. She was purpose-driven and exhibited loyalty to the people of Liberia. She encouraged tolerance across socio-cultural divides and valued the diversity of her people. Liberia had been buried in one of Africa's bloodiest civil wars for over a decade, and which claimed the lives of thousands of its citizens, while many others fled the country to refugee camps in neighboring countries. Johnson's transformational leadership style gave her the ability to reconcile a fractured society. A leader who sincerely valued freedom, and who sought to give a voice to the voiceless, she turned her vision into action in the way she governed the country, in the process revamping infrastructure that had been decimated by war.

Despite all the challenges that attended the leadership of a post-war country, Johnson combined integrity and an unflagging vigor for hard work with a fierce commitment to fiscal and economic discipline across her government and its ministries. Her vision came to life through the implementation of various strategic agenda for positive change directed at leading her country effectively. Running a war-torn country required diligence, loyalty, passion, vision and creativity, all of which Johnson demonstrated during her 12-year tenure as President. Johnson came to power not just at a time when Liberia was still nursing the wounds of civil war, but also at a period that witnessed rampant corruption, neglected infrastructure, a broken road network, collapsed health and education systems and massive unemployment.

The risk of the country relapsing into conflict stared President Johnson in the face, as scores of ex-combatants and unemployed youth roamed the streets aimlessly. However, driven by the desire to turn her vision into reality, she took specific and concrete actions to achieve her agenda for the country, and these included social, economic and political programs, with a focus on addressing vital issues such as creating jobs for the youth, who formed the majority of ex-combatants in the civil war, and providing free and compulsory education for all children in Liberia.

As a leader who valued freedom and free speech, Johnson provided a platform for media practitioners, civil society activists and the general public to engage in public debates on any given topical issues without fear of persecution from her government. She also vigorously campaigned for tolerance and respect for religious diversity, and advocated for a gender equality that insisted on genuine equity and equality at all levels of the society.

Johnson presented a compelling example of moral leadership. Prior to becoming President of Liberia, she was an activist even as a member of government. She served as junior minister in the Treasury Department. Her activism led to her imprisonment, and she later fled her country to the United States of America, where she worked at the United Nations and the World Bank before returning to Liberia.

Her legitimacy and authority were grounded in her knowledge of the treasury and finance. She also had great communication skills and believed in speaking truth to power. As President, she exhibited a rare moral leadership that earned her legitimacy. She also had a high index of emotional intelligence which gave her the ability to connect easily with international organizations, diplomats, plantation owners, union members and civilians. Johnson appointed women to high positions in her government, including the ministers of commerce, justice, finance and the national chief of police. She gracefully managed dissent and protests by disgruntled citizens, including retired soldiers, while building allies on the global turf.

A 2011 Nobel Peace Prize winner, Johnson has been globally hailed for the great leadership qualities that also won her many other honors, awards and accolades, including the Ibrahim Prize for Achievement in African Leadership. This is awarded to former African heads of state or government who have developed their countries, lifted their people out of poverty and paved the way for sustainable and equitable prosperity. The award also highlights exceptional role models for the continent and ensures that Africa continues to benefit from the experience and expertise of exceptional leaders when they leave national office, by enabling them to continue in other public roles on the continent.

In addition, Johnson has been awarded the Presidential Medal of Freedom, the highest civilian honor awarded by the President of the United States to recognize people who have made an especially meritorious contribution to the security or national interests of the United States, world peace, cultural or other significant public or private endeavors. She has also been awarded the Indira Gandhi Prize for Peace, Disarmament and Development, a prestigious award accorded to individuals or organizations in recognition of creative efforts toward promoting international peace, development and a new international economic order.

"The power of women in politics is a soft power." This profound yet subtly powerful statement was credited to the first-ever female President of Kosovo and the Balkan region, Atifete Jahjaga. She was elected Kosovo's President in April 2011. Born in Gjakova on April 20, 1975, Jahjaga was educated at the Law faculty of the University of Prishtina, from where she proceeded to do a postgraduate certificate program in Police Management and Criminal Law at the University of Leicester in the United Kingdom. She also undertook extensive professional training at the George C. Marshall European Center for Security Studies in Germany and the FBI National Academy in the United States of America, before earning a postgraduate certification in Crime Science at the University of Virginia.

After rising to the rank of Major General of the Kosovo Police Force, she assumed the presidency of the country at the age of 35, making history as the youngest woman to take up Kosovo's top leadership position, the first female Head of State in the modern Balkans, and the youngest female world leader to be elected to the highest office at the time. A member of the Council of Women World Leaders, which has active representation and participation of women in all walks of life, giving a strong voice to women's role in survival, professionalism and peace-building, Jahjaga is regularly invited to participate at global conferences that strengthen the role of women in society.

As Kosovo's first-ever consensual and non-partisan President in the history of the country, Jahjaga set out to depoliticize the Office of the President, which she opened up to all citizens and political parties. Her cabinet has been hailed as one of the world's best examples of transparency and accountability in government. During her tenure, the Office of the President was ranked as the most trusted institution by the citizens of Kosovo, because her cabinet advisers comprised non-partisan and experienced professionals.

Her focus was the healing of her country, fighting corruption, developing the economy, integrating a multi-ethnic post-war society and promoting alliances with Kosovo's neighboring Balkan states and the wider global community. On assuming office, she articulated her main goal of putting Kosovo on a safe path toward membership of the European Union and the United Nations.

Her government pursued reparations for war crimes perpetrated by Serbian militants against Kosovars, which included acts of ethnic cleansing and sexual violence. She led institutional efforts at rehabilitating and reintegrating survivors of sexual violence during conflict. Jahjaga focused on strengthening democratic institutions in Kosovo and securing greater international recognition for the country. She established the National Anti-Corruption Council in 2012 to coordinate the work and activities of the institutions and independent agencies to fight corruption.

She also advocated for the empowerment of women and girls throughout the Balkans. She advanced the role of women and girls by hosting the 2012 International Women's Summit. The summit presented a platform for the crossing of ethnic barriers and brought together women from the Balkan region, resulting in the creation of the Prima Principles, which affirmed the rights of women to political participation and representation, economic empowerment and access to security and justice, with calls to action to actualize these principles.

A year after taking office, Jahjaga requested parliament to review the Criminal Code by removing provisions pertaining to freedom of expression under the criminalization of defamation, and articles that compelled journalists to reveal their sources of information. She considered those measures to be a contradiction of freedom of expression, the constitution of the Republic of Kosovo and the European Convention on Human Rights. She also successfully coordinated and mobilized mechanisms of justice and central election commission to ensure democratic processes of fair, democratic and transparent electoral process.

When Kosovo was threatened with a constitutional deadlock that prevented formation of institutions and undermined the country's democratic processes, Jahjaga sought a solution to the political impasse and embarked on meetings with various political parties to find a formula for the establishment of a new parliament and formation of government in 2014. She played a key role in resolving the crisis to ensure democratic functioning institutions through transparent, credible and inclusive processes, while respecting the decisions of the constitutional court and legal procedures. As a determined leader, she sought broader consensus on the national agenda by establishing three National Councils to ensure inclusion of civil society, academia and the business community. When there was a wave of illegal migration of Kosovo citizens to Western Europe, Jahjaga visited the affected municipalities to address citizens' concerns.

During her tenure, Jahjaga sought to strengthen the democratic institutions of Kosovo. She led the Consultative Council for Communities, which made recommendations pertaining to the empowerment of communities in various fields, including education, economic development, employment, and social activities. Her leadership contributed to changing Kosovo's image abroad and promoting European and Euro-Atlantic agenda, reconciliation and tolerance, normalization of relations with neighboring countries, and starting foreign investment.

Jahjaga refined the role of the President in building the pluralistic and democratic life of Kosovo by continuously implementing the constitutional principles that form the basis for democracy. Through her participation in various international forums and numerous bilateral visits, she built new bridges of cooperation and gave Kosovo a voice on the international stage by sharing Kosovo's state-building experience and making her country a vital contributor to global debates. Her vision and moderate leadership in Kosovo and the Western Balkans earned Jahjaga unprecedented international support.

The final verdict on Atifete Jahjaga will incontestably have to be that she steered the affairs of Kosovo with single-minded purpose to leave the Balkan nation much better, in all spheres of activity, than she met it, and she achieved that singular purpose with unqualified success.

Creating purposeful leaders takes a village. That is because there must be an audience that will benefit from one's efforts at purposeful leadership. To attempt to lead with purpose forces leaders to take actions they are passionate about. It also connects them to the difference they wish to make, and the impact they wish to have. Becoming clear about one's leadership purpose requires immense courage. Yet, a leader becomes one through her unique strengths, passions and character. Ultimately, therefore, a true leader will have to unleash her purpose.

A purposeful leader attains her position of pre-eminence for the high intelligence and creativity that only she can bring. In this and future generations, purposeful leaders will be required to take risks and show the world what has never been done before. On a final note, such leaders will be required to prove conclusively that they were singled out for leadership to be their best, and to bring out the best in everyone around them.

How to Gain Access to Your Power of Purpose

1. You must transcend the desire to merely gratify your own ego through the acquisition of fame and material gratification.

2. The pleasant paradox is that in aiming for something far more important than fame and fortune, you will actually receive both rewards with effortless ease.

3. Make an attempt to appeal to the moral convictions of all who are stakeholders in your own leadership journey.

4. Aim to continually seek new and innovative paths to express your passion for impactful performance.

5. Passionately commit to excellence in all you do.

6. Ensure that your motives for seeking leadership relevance are pure and genuine, and that you demonstrate genuine care for your constituents.

7. Insist on truly and courageously leading at the front lines of leadership.

8. Accept with humility that purposeful leadership is not a one-person show, and that it is not just about you.

9. Consistently live in your purpose, and lead with it, while making it unequivocally clear that you expect your primary constituents to hold you to it.

10. Cultivate the courage to make the difference you are committed to making by publicly announcing what your purpose is and working resolutely toward achieving it.

CHAPTER 12

THE POWER OF FOCUS

"We have been waiting for 200 years.

Is that hurrying?"

GOLDA MEIR

There is tremendous power in focus. Leaders who have focus have an incredible ability to pick on an aspect of their work as a leader, dedicate a tremendous amount of energy to it, and then ensure that they drive it to completion. Focused leaders create. Focused leaders are committed to an authentic finish. Finally, they ensure that what they create is made available for the benefit of those who need it. A primary and unavoidable task of leadership is to direct the attention of those they lead. To do so, leaders must learn to focus their own attention. In its most fundamental definition, to be focused means to devote one's attention to one particular activity while filtering out distractions of any sort.

Experience and studies have shown that the world's most dedicated leaders first focus on themselves, ensuring that from an early stage in their career they earn the education and credentials, and cultivate the habits and traits they will need to lead and achieve set objectives in a focused manner. Next, they focus on others, identifying those areas in which they can contribute to make their lives better. Finally, they focus on the wider world, harnessing past experiences to exert even greater impact on the global turf.

This last tendency among focused leaders is easily evident in some outstanding leaders we will see in this chapter who started out as cabinet ministers, and then graduated to become heads of states of their countries, only to finally end up along the hallowed corridors of the United Nations as heads of some of the key functional organs of that pre-eminent global body. A platform from which they bring their years of leadership experience to bear on the lives of millions of people, within the ambit of a particular area of specialization, for example gender equality and women's rights.

From an intellectual angle, focusing on self-development first allows one to develop many essential leadership skills. Later, focusing constructively on others helps leaders to cultivate the primary elements of emotional intelligence. Finally, focusing on the wider world arena improves their ability to devise strategy, and to innovate and manage big organizations, as we discover in the case of national leaders who later find themselves at the helm of affairs at multinational organizations like key United Nations organs.

Directing attention toward where it needs to go is a primary task of leadership. The talent to achieve this lies in the ability to shift attention to the right place at the right time, and to sense prevailing trends, emerging realities, and wonderful opportunities.

A leader's field of attention, the particular issues and goals she focuses on, tends to guide the attention of those who follow her, whether or not the leader explicitly articulates it for them. Studies have unequivocally shown that people make their choices about what to focus on based on their perception of what matters most to their leaders. Therefore, a ripple effect is created which gives leaders added responsibility, meaning essentially that they are guiding not just their own attention but, to a large extent, that of the people they are leading. In the final analysis, when we say a leader has *focus*, we are referring to single-minded devotion to a cause that is for the ultimate benefit and the greater good of the led.

A female leader in the Middle East was to pursue a career in leadership that totally exemplified what it means to pursue a particular cause, with a total fixation of focused attention until its logical conclusion. Golda Meir was born Golda Mabovitch in 1898 in Kiev, Russia. She was elected Israel's fourth and first-ever female Prime Minister in 1969. She is also regarded as the founder of the Jewish State.

If it is true that each human being was created for a precise purpose, then Golda Meir must be a total personification of that fact. This is because the one singular cause to which her remarkable life was dedicated was the founding of a Jewish State, a geo-political place where the Jews could call a home, and a place where she believed Jews from all over the world could live free from anti-Semitism and persecution. She pursued this cause with a fixity of purpose that lends itself to a study in classic focus. Concurrently, she also strived to achieve peace in the Middle East.

Golda Meir worked diligently to inspire others to align with her cause, and would go to extra lengths to bring them to the table for the accomplishment of her dream. She clearly possessed those rare leadership traits of a hero who not only possessed the great personal influence with which she could unite her people toward a common cause, but also had the tremendous willpower to persevere through some of the toughest hurdles imaginable to be able to ultimately realize her dream. Deploying formidable leadership acumen, unwavering dedication and authentic inspiration, Meir managed to achieve the feat of uniting the entire nation toward a cause that were it not for her guidance and inspiration, many would have abandoned as a lost, if not a hopeless one.

In spite of odds and obstacles that might have overwhelmed a less resolute leader, and coupled with the various military assaults on Israel by neighboring Arab states, Meir refused to budge from her cause, and remained focused on her goal of establishing Israel as a legitimate nation, with its own sovereignty, security and the right to ward off threats of overt external aggression. In the build-up to the Yom Kippur War, military advisors and strategists were intent on a pre-emptive strike, but Meir made it clear that she would rather not be seen as the aggressor. Her principled stand would be vindicated when the Arab nations struck first. Meir won the support and sympathetic alliance of the United States, who subsequently assisted Israel with economic and military aid.

As Prime Minister, Meir was a strong unifying force for Israel. She was able to do this because she had great interpersonal skills that gave her an uncommon ability to influence influential people, and this helped to unify and strengthen the government of Israel. Perfectly content with remaining in a comfort zone as long as it served her purpose to do so, she fought for her beliefs and ideals by using her leadership skills to bring people together and to influence them. In demonstrating a firm leadership style that radiated faith and confidence, she consistently subordinated her own needs to those of the State of Israel, and expected no less a sacrifice from members of her cabinet. She also exhibited a combined kindness and courage that earned her the respect of the Israelis and that of the nationals of other countries around the world.

Meir was actually just an ordinary woman who rose to become an extraordinary leader. Born in Russia, she moved with her family to Wisconsin in the United States at the age of eight. When her parents balked at the notion of sending her to school, in obvious preference to marrying her off, she ran away to live with her sister in Denver, Colorado, where she went to school and eventually studied American history. At an older age, she returned to Milwaukee, Wisconsin, where she attended the Milwaukee Normal School for Teachers and became an active member of the Zionist Labor Movement in the Midwest. After her marriage, she moved to Tel Aviv, Israel, where she became secretary of the Women's Labor Council, and later became head of the Labor Federation's Political Department.

Meir was one of only two women to sign the Israeli Declaration of Independence. After Independence, she was appointed Israel's first ambassador to Moscow. Later, she became a member of the Israeli Parliament, and then went on to become Minister of Foreign Affairs and Israel's delegate to the United Nations. Ill health compelled Meir to retire from political office in 1968. However, her retirement would not last long, as fate would propel her to succeed Levi Eshkol in the office of Prime Minister, close on the heels of his death in 1969.

A very strong will had been evident in Meir right from the early age at which she had insisted on attending high school. Clearly, without that education she could not have become the first female Prime Minister of Israel, paving a path of political relevance for Israel's future women leaders. Meir's remarkable achievement as an influencer must be seen in the light of just how patently patriarchal Jewish society is. Having been a signatory to the Israeli Declaration for Independence, the first Israeli ambassador to Moscow, and having held countless political appointments in a cabinet dominated by men, Meir would later be given the tag "The Only Man in the Cabinet," as she had a greater presence and a stronger voice than most of her male counterparts in the cabinet.

Despite acknowledgement and praise for Meir for her ability to lead her people to a common goal while keeping the nation unified, Meir never became power hungry. For Meir, Israel always came first. Becoming one of the most prominent and one of the strongest leaders of her time, she led her country with uncompromising authority. A strong-willed and ambitious female politician, she fought for unrestricted Jewish immigration to Israel.

Without doubt, the core component of her conviction was the need to keep her nation together. She spent each single day of her four-year tenure as Prime Minister fighting for the recognition of Israel. As a politician and leader, her decisions were in correspondence with the needs of her people.

Although she was a firm leader, she was also flexible and open-minded whenever necessary. A combination of pragmatism and a rare form of intellectual honesty earned her unequalled respect from her peers. As a diplomat, she brilliantly strengthened Israel's ties with African countries during her tenure as Minister of Foreign Affairs. As Prime Minister, she secured military aid from the United States during the Yom Kippur War, signaling the start of a beneficial relationship that would establish Israel as a major nation of influence that would for years continue to dictate the direction of politics in the Middle East.

What is influence, if not the power to transform, motivate and inspire? Meir has been hailed as a transformational leader who sought to raise her followers to higher levels of motivation and inspiration. In that regard, her dedication to her country and her personal concern for her people were both legendary. Her place in history is unassailable. She was a charismatic leader who led Israel with total confidence at a time of heightened crisis. She has been described as exceptionally intelligent, capable, balanced and understanding. All that may well be true. What is of greater significance is that Meir was a formidable leader whose determination, resilience and perseverance were traits that aided her steady march toward the actualization of her vision for Israel.

Despite being under no illusion about living in a time of blatant gender inequality, Meir was not fixated on identifying with other women nor did she see herself publicly as a woman. However, despite this open indifference to feminism, she actually became an icon for American feminists, who now saw her as an emancipated and empowered woman. It is widely acknowledged that Meir's legacy and Israel's fate and future will forever be intertwined. It cannot be otherwise. Golda Meir will forever remain an integral part of Israel's political consciousness, emancipation and ultimate statehood.

Another woman leader of extraordinary focus was to make history when she was sworn into office as the first-ever female President of Taiwan in May 2016. Tsai Ing-wen, who was also chair of Taiwan's Democratic Progressive Party at the time she became President, was born in a coastal village in the south of Taiwan. She moved to the capital city, Taipei, at the age of 11. Her election to Taiwan's highest office was a landmark not only for Taiwanese politics but for the entire Asian region, as she did not have any political pedigree like most female political leaders in other Asian countries.

Tsai spent the first 30 years of her life in academic pursuit. She studied law, obtaining a Bachelor of Laws from the National Taiwan University, a Master of Laws from Cornell University in the United States, and a Ph.D. from the London School of Economics in the United Kingdom. She served in several roles in the government of Taiwan, including being a legal consultant and negotiator, national security advisor and vice premier. Because of her expertise and proficiency in the English language, she was called upon to become a legal consultant for Taiwan's entry negotiations into the World Trade Organization, and this launched her into a career in public life.

A former academic and Law professor, Tsai was appointed a policy advisor to the government, and rose to prominence when she was selected, along with other legal experts, to conduct research and come up with a two-state concept that validated the theory that Taiwan was not part of the People's Republic of China. She also briefly served as Vice-President of Taiwan.

A highly respected thinker and negotiator, with a reputation for aggression, Tsai is largely seen as someone who represents a sharp contrast to traditional politicians. She has won her people's hearts and minds with her intelligence, sincerity and tenacity of purpose. Tsai has always been steely in her belief that Taiwan's future should be determined by its own people and not as a province under China's jurisdiction. As Taiwan's national security adviser, Tsai helped draft the President's special state-to-state doctrine, defining relations between Beijing and Taipei. As Head of Mainland Affairs Council, she found a way to work with a hostile China, launching a landmark program that allows direct ferry transport and trade links between Taiwan's islands and mainland China. She later secured a permit for the first-ever chartered flights to commence between China and Taiwan.

Aware that the people of Taiwan were trading illegally with mainland China, she advised the government of Taiwan and its legislature to revise Taiwan's law governing the country's relations with China, so as to make it legal for Taiwanese businesses to invest in China. As a leader, Tsai has been praised for being practical and flexible with a focus on building consensus. She is not someone who would very easily take the initiative to go on stage. However, once she gets on the stage and sits at the table, she assumes a leadership role with infinite ease. She made it clear that Taiwan's democracy is dear to her heart when she agreed to take over the Democratic Progressive Party, believing that a strong opposition was necessary for democracy to thrive.

She has introduced unique initiatives such as the promotion of green energy, two days off the working week for all workers and the legalization of gay marriage. Taiwan has had the most progressive policies in Asia regarding LGBTQ rights and the legalization of same-sex marriage. Despite these landmark policy initiatives, Tsai's principal focus has been the protection and sustenance of Taiwan's sovereignty. Tsai has declared herself defender of Taiwan's sovereignty against a China that believes that someday Taiwan will be unified with mainland China. Her government has resolutely stood up to Beijing to keep Taiwan as an independent liberal democracy.

Her style of leadership has attracted young voters to her party. For instance, during her first term in office, she introduced a rise in the minimum wage and monthly salaries, with investments and stocks rising as well. Her government also provided a boost to social services like childcare, elderly care and public housing. She advanced the rights of women and supported the Gender Equality in Employment Act, a proposal that gave women a right to maternity leave, prohibited sex discrimination in employment, and strengthened anti-sexual harassment laws.

In the course of her presidency, Tsai has displayed attentiveness, tolerance, calm, flexibility and incomparable organizational skills to chart a course that stepped back from controversial economic policies. She has courageously and repeatedly rejected threats from mainland China. In fact, Tsai's government has been courageous enough to grant asylum to political refugees from Hong Kong, another territory that had a status similar to that of Taiwan.

In the final analysis, what has made Tsai such a powerful leader is that she is resolute in her fight for Taiwan's independence and its liberal democracy. She has succeeded in uniting an island that was often starkly divided by political allegiances. Despite her stand on Taiwan's sovereignty, she has sought reconciliation and cooperation with mainland China. She has always been a very patient leader, working steadily, practically and accurately to achieve her ideals. She insists that Taiwan must choose her own future and should stand with democracy and freedom.

She refused to acknowledge the 1992 consensus, a vaguely worded agreement stating that Taiwan is part of One China. Like most female political leaders, Tsai has been attacked from all sides for being too strong, or for not being strong enough, but she remained resolute in her vision. In all these, she has proved conclusively that she leads a government that is willing to listen to people, is more transparent and accountable, and certainly more capable of leading the country past its challenges.

Tsai won the 2020 re-election as President of Taiwan by a landslide, defeating the populist challenge of her pro-China opponent in a campaign dominated by how to handle growing pressure from Beijing. Her victory is significant for Taiwan, a self-governing island of 23 million people and the world's 21st biggest economy, with an influential technology hub. She is mistrusted by China's ruling Communist Party, which considers Taiwan a wayward province to be politically and economically reunited with mainland China, by force if necessary. Taiwan has governed itself since effectively splitting from the mainland in 1949, following China's civil war. Tsai's victory speech re-affirmed her consistent message of independence. *"Today I want to once again remind the Beijing authorities that peace, parity, democracy and dialogue are the keys to stability. I want the Beijing authorities to know that democratic Taiwan and our democratically elected government will never concede to threats."*

One of the most focused leaders of this generation was a woman who held quite a number of firsts in her Latin American country, in the process displaying a high degree of focus on public service that is rarely seen in political leaders. Veronica Michelle Bachelet Jeria made history when she was sworn in as the first-ever female President of the South American country of Chile in March 2006. She served a first term from 2006 to 2010, and returned to serve a second term from 2013 to 2018. Bachelet holds a number of firsts to her name. Prior to becoming the first female President of Chile, Bachelet served as the first female Minister of Health in 2000, and became the first female Minister of Defense in 2002. She was later appointed the first-ever Director of UN Women, the United Nations agency dedicated to fighting for the rights of women and girls around the world.

Born in Santiago, Chile, Bachelet grew up between Chile, Australia, the United States of America and Germany. She graduated with a medical degree in surgery from the University of Chile. She received a scholarship from the Chilean Association of Medicine to specialize in pediatrics and public health at the Roberto del Rio Hospital. Bachelet developed a rare drive for public service that later led her to become exceedingly focused on the desire to serve others and to help build her country. This focus on public service began when she became an active member of the Youth Socialist Group.

After a military coup d'état, Bachelet was held in detention centers with her mother and subsequently sent into exile in Australia and Germany, where she continued with her studies. Upon her return to Chile, she served in various social service positions and NGOs dedicated to providing professional help to children whose parents were detained and victimized by Chile's military regime.

When Chile returned to democracy, Bachelet worked in the country's health service, including the National AIDS Commission. She served as a consultant to the Pan-American Health Organization, and worked in the ministry of health, addressing issues related to improving primary healthcare and the management of healthcare services. In 2000, she was appointed Minister of Health. She laid the foundation for the overhauling of the healthcare system in the country and succeeded in reducing hospital waiting times for patients. She also presented and secured an agreement for the first legal proposal to reform healthcare workers' rights and responsibilities in a widespread and participatory process that included citizen forums, roundtable discussions, businesspeople, experts, academics, and health unions.

She studied military strategy at Chile's National Academy of Strategy and Policy and at the Inter-American Defense College in the United States, and was later appointed an advisor to the Ministry of Defense. For a woman who initially trained as a medical doctor and public health specialist to suddenly veer into defense and strategic studies must qualify as nothing short of a passionate desire to serve in as many capacities as the intellect will allow. Therein lies Bachelet's total commitment to, and focus on, public service.

Bachelet made history in Latin America when she became the first-ever female Minister of Defense in Chile and the entire South American region. While she was Defense Minister, she made significant changes and strengthened the role of the ministry and its staff, and the rights of women in the armed forces. She also made improvements to the country's police service and deployed more Chilean peacekeeping forces around the world. Her election as the first-ever female President of Chile marked the beginning of a period in which the Chilean government would focus on achieving greater gender equality and social inclusion in the country. Her presidency was marked with record citizen support and approval.

Upon leaving office, she established the Fundación Dialoga, through which she could continue to contribute to the betterment of Chile. The foundation served as a motivational forum for new leadership and the renewal of ideas. Bachelet also became the President of the Social Protection Floor Advisory Group, an initiative that worked in collaboration with the International Labor Organization and the World Health Organization for the promotion of social policies aimed at stimulating economic growth and social cohesion. Under her strategic leadership, the council published a report which served as a guide for the United Nations. It was titled *"Social Protection Floor for a Fair and Inclusive Globalization."*

When UN Women, the United Nations agency responsible for the global promotion of the rights of women and girls, was created in 2011, Bachelet was named the agency's first-ever Executive Director. She served in this position for two and half years, in which time she focused on working toward increasing women's political participation, women's economic empowerment and an end to violence against women. She left UN Women and returned to Chile in 2013 to reconfirm her dedication to public service, and announced her decision to stand for presidential elections once again. She won the election and was sworn in as President of Chile for a second time. During her second term, she created the Ministry of Women and Gender Equality. Her government also passed a new electoral law that required that at least 40% of candidates for elected office must be women.

Although she had to contend with a sexist and male-dominated culture that was characteristic of all Latin American countries, Bachelet's leadership still managed to leave an indelible mark, with women gaining unprecedented clout in unions and student movements. Bachelet unapologetically fashioned a leadership style that was inclined toward a feminist agenda and which promoted the greater inclusion and participation of women in Chilean democracy. She countered her opponents' attacks on her style of leadership by asserting that their attacks were a mere revelation of the continuing resistance to women's leadership and inclusion in decision-making positions and political leadership. She boldly drew on a gendered definition of political leadership and presented herself as the best qualified person to lead Chile, and one who possessed the necessary leadership credentials and skills that the country needed at the time.

A staunch advocate for the rights of women and girls, Bachelet will be remembered as the President who steered Chile toward becoming a more democratic country in many different ways. Her government adopted the quota system in an effort to increase the representation of women in government, and she pioneered the global push for a more equitable footing for women in politics and getting women elected to lead in influential democracies. Although Bachelet is not the first female head of state in Latin America, she is widely regarded as the first woman to be elected on her own merit, thereby establishing herself as a credible source of inspiration for women across South America and other parts of the world.

On September 1, 2018, Michelle Bachelet assumed office as the United Nations High Commissioner for Human Rights. The Office of the High Commissioner for Human Rights was established in 1993 and Bachelet will be its seventh and current High Commissioner.

To summarize what can only qualify as an uncommonly brilliant public service career, during her presidential tenures Bachelet promoted the rights of all, but particularly those of the most vulnerable in her country. Among her many achievements, education and tax reforms, as well as the creation of the National Institute for Human Rights and the Museum of Memory and Human Rights stand out, as do the establishment of the Ministry of Women and Gender Equality, the adoption of quotas to increase women's political participation, and the approval of Civil Union Act legislation, granting rights to same sex couples and thus advancing LGBT rights.

Economic empowerment and ending violence against women were also her priorities during her tenure. She has recently pledged to be a Gender Champion, committing to advance gender equality in OHCHR and in international forums. After finishing her second term as President in March 2018, she was named Chair of the Partnership for Maternal, Newborn and Child Health, an alliance of more than 1,000 organizations in 192 countries from the sexual, reproductive, maternal, newborn, child and adolescent health communities. As co-Chair of the High-Level Steering Group For Every Woman Every Child, Bachelet launched Every Woman Every Child Latin America and the Caribbean, the first platform for tailored, regional implementation of the EWEC Global Strategy.

The world will continue to be in need of those leaders who can focus exclusively on a particular cause, and see to the logical conclusion of its achievement. The reason for this is really quite simple. There will always be some human cause or the other to promote or advocate for. There will always be a need for great leaders who will continue to advance LGBTQ rights, the eradication of global hunger, the improvement of healthcare services and the rights of workers. Yet, one of the most compelling of such causes is the question of gender equality and the rights of women and girls, and while it is true that significant advances have been made in that respect, the world still has a long way to go on this terrain.

The world will need more women leaders who are specialized and totally focused on this field. The world will need even greater and more focused energy that is solely directed toward consolidating on the gains of decades of work on gender inequality both at national and international levels. Therein lies the global challenge for more women leaders to rise up to the occasion with greater focus and determination.

How to Gain Access to Your Power of Focus

1. Although the popular refrain is not to remain in a comfort zone, as long as you are focused on an objective, and you are resolutely working toward achieving it, remain in your comfort zone for as long as necessary if that zone supports your efforts.

2. Learn to demonstrate a firm leadership style that radiates nothing but faith and confidence.

3. Consistently subordinate your own needs to those of others.

4. You must be resolute in the fixated pursuit of your objective.

5. Your decisions must remain in correspondence with the needs of your people.

6. In the pursuit of your focused objective, you must engage a combination of pragmatism and intellectual honesty

7. Influence is the power to transform, motivate and inspire others. Therefore, whatever you focus on should raise your followers to higher levels of motivation and inspiration.

8. You will need determination, resilience and perseverance on the steady march toward the actualization of your focused goal.

9. Be prepared to engage your intellect and faculties in as many ways as humanly possible.

10. Learn to be ruthless with your time and energy. Refuse to dissipate them into ventures that are not in alignment with your objective.

CHAPTER 13

THE POWER OF THE INTELLECT

"Investing in women is smart economics,
and investing in girls, catching them upstream,
is even smarter economics."

NGOZI OKONJO-IWEALA

Today's world is a mix of ever-increasing variety, interdependence, connectivity, complexity, change, ambiguity, seamlessness and sustainability. With such a myriad of challenges to contend with, one is left in no doubt that, correspondingly, there is a dire need for more and more leaders with the solid and unassailable intellect to deal with these emerging challenges and demands. Intellect is simply the ability to learn, reason and solve problems – no more, no less.

We are all born with a certain potential, but how far we go in realizing that potential is based on a host of other factors, including health, upbringing, experience and behavior. All things being equal, however, most people of superior intellect who are exposed to environments that genuinely enable their true potential do go ahead to manifest the traits of exceptional leadership.

The world is in need of intellectually versatile leaders, who can easily comprehend challenging problems and then lead the effort to solve those problems and suggest creative solutions, all the while taking challenging and proactive decisions. Two very critical leadership skills fall under the purview of intellect. The first is *mental agility*. Mental agility connotes a leader with a certain fluidity and flexibility of mind that allows for the anticipation or adaptation to uncertain or changing situations. Numerous studies have acknowledged those with a higher cognitive ability as being better able to demonstrate the attributes that contribute to mental agility. For such people, the key approach to evolving leadership skills is to develop the patience to critically and creatively dissect problems and design the more expedient approaches to solve them.

Closely allied to mental agility is *response agility*, which is the ability to respond in an appropriate and controlled manner, regardless of the daunting challenges that a leader is facing. Quite frankly, being agile with response and reaction is key to effective leadership. Agility in response means one is inclined to think before reacting. Effective leaders ask themselves, *"What is needed now?"* It is sound intellect that provides this situational awareness and appropriate reaction. Response agility takes discipline and awareness, and is a core component of leadership intellect. Such women of intellect are also mission-driven leaders who inspire their followers to give their best in the service of a compelling vision, while combining their collective intelligence to achieve overall goals and objectives. To be aware of how others operate and how to inspire them is a core component of intelligent leadership.

The second critical intellectual leadership skill is *sound judgment*. Those who exhibit sound judgment tend to also know they must constantly improve upon their agility of mind. They seem to know when to innovate and where to source the expertise they themselves lack. Finally, they possess an uncanny ability to see and recognize those key moments that require their interpersonal tact in order to achieve collaboration with their principals and partners. When leaders demonstrate sound judgment, usually by their ability to sort through a myriad of information, asking the right questions, and learning from the mistakes of others, they are almost invariably singled out for advancement.

All her working and professional life, Christine Madeleine Odette Lagarde has always been singled out for advancement. Although she was once credited with the profound statement, *"For a woman to get to the top, she needs skin as thick as that of a crocodile."* Christine Lagarde's meteoric rise to the pinnacle of global economic leadership has much more to do with a formidable intellect than the thickness of her skin. Hailed as one of those few leaders with a proven track record in a success founded on genuine intellectual sagacity, Christine Lagarde is seen as a source of inspiration and motivation for women who aspire to break the glass ceiling to reach the pinnacle of their career.

Born in Paris, France, on January 1, 1956, Lagarde holds a law degree from Paris Nanterre University, and a Master's degree from the Political Science Institute of Aix-en-Provence. A confirmed polyglot, she speaks fluent French, English and Spanish. She has several outstanding accomplishments to her name and is seen as a trailblazer for women in global finance and policy making. *Forbes* named her the third most powerful woman and the 22nd most powerful person in the world in 2018.

Lagarde has held top positions in government, in the private sector, and at international and global institutions. She was the first woman to hold the post of Finance Minister of a G-7 country. She was elected the first-ever female Managing Director of the International Monetary Fund (IMF) in 2011, and served for two terms before becoming the first female President of the European Central Bank.

Lagarde started her brilliant career as an associate at the international law firm of Baker & McKenzie, where she specialized in labor, anti-trust, and mergers and acquisitions. She served in several positions, including as partner, managing partner, member of the executive committee and chair of the executive committee. She became a partner at the relatively tender age of 31, and by the age of 43 she had been appointed the international firm's first female chair of the global strategic committee. In public governance and politics, she was first appointed Deputy Minister of Foreign Trade, and later served as Minister of Finance of France.

Succeeding as the leader of a global organization required all of Lagarde's crucial leadership skills, compelling leadership behavior, vision, sense of balance, effective networking and deft management of chaotic international situations. At the time she took over as President of the IMF, the institution was experiencing a very low index of credibility with the global markets and its member countries. Lagarde took over when IMF programs raised more salient questions than catalyzing confidence in investors and member countries. Under her able leadership, the IMF would regain its positive image, once more becoming the much-needed positive catalyst for the global markets and member countries.

Utilizing her managerial and leadership skills to maximum effectiveness, the IMF raised over US$461bn to consolidate and strengthen the institution. IMF member countries found themselves totally inspired by Lagarde's strong presence and authentic, rounded leadership style, approachability, clear thinking and depth of analysis. She was, not unnaturally, rewarded with a well-deserved second term as Managing Director of the IMF. Lagarde fully utilized her managerial skills to embed her anti-corruption stance in the IMF bureaucracy, while the institution expanded its technical assistance to central banks to assist them in curbing money laundering.

As Managing Director of the IMF, Lagarde was ubiquitous on the world stage. Her aura of confidence and competence provided a reassuring calm amidst global crises and economic uncertainty. While the world was veering dangerously toward nationalism and populism, and many were becoming skeptical of the benefits of multilateralism, her leadership stood out as a model of independence, competence and integrity. As the first woman to lead the IMF, she successfully restored the institution's credibility. Her tenure was marked by an enhancement of the role of the IMF, both as a global lender of last resort and as an economic policy leader.

During her term of office, Lagarde accelerated the evolution of the IMF from the perceived rigid orthodox protector of the so-called "Washington Consensus" to the institutional possessor of a nuanced economic approach that took into account new areas of consideration. Among her initiatives was a greater emphasis on the economic benefits of women's empowerment. She also helped explore spillover impacts of a country's decisions on its neighbors, and provided guidance on how to balance the rights of individuals, institutions, countries and private creditors in distressed, overleveraged countries.

As leader of such a global organization, Lagarde personified global leadership at a time when there seemed to be a dearth of such qualities. As a lawyer and not a trained economist, she characterized her tenure with a fine balance between hard-core economics and political reality. Under her leadership, the IMF was no longer under siege by subordinating its policies to political pressure from European partners. Instead, the institution was largely criticized for adhering too closely to those policies, protecting the integrity of its resources, and for not allowing traditional political pressures to influence its decision making.

Her leadership inspired the trust and confidence of member countries around the world. Lagarde's first major test as head of the IMF, after cleaning its Augean stable, was to rescue Greece from its huge debt nightmare, and this involved the IMF partnering with European Union entities, which included the Commission, the Council of Finance Ministers and the European Central Bank. Under her leadership, the IMF also played a critical and constructive role in pulling Ukraine out of virtual bankruptcy by seeking civil society allies and explicitly targeting Ukraine kleptocracy.

Furthermore, the IMF agreed to its largest ever program of US$57bn to rescue a beleaguered Argentina, by centering on advocating sound fiscal and monetary policies and working not only with treasuries but central banks as well. Under Lagarde's leadership, the IMF greatly expanded its technical assistance to central banks to assist them in curbing money laundering. Lagarde was therefore seen as the stabilizing motivator atop a board of all-male executives.

In November 2019, Lagarde's strengths, which include her political acumen, global contacts and networks, and her remarkable ability to build consensus, paved the way for her appointment as the first female President of the European Central Bank, where she would oversee the world's second-biggest currency. Upon taking office as President of the European Central Bank, she expressed her desire to urge the bank to use its fiscal surplus to invest in infrastructure, education and innovation to rebalance the bank's imbalances. She expressed her interest in issues like inequality, female empowerment in finance and the economic impact of climate change, which she considered to be relevant to central bank policies. She continues to prove her mettle in a setting that was hitherto an exclusive preserve of men.

In Muslim societies, women are generally relegated to the looming shadows of men. That is why the rise to pre-eminence of Benazir Bhutto in Pakistan would prove to be a significant milestone in evolutionary trends in such a conservative society. She inherited her father's political mantle to become the world's first-ever Muslim female Prime Minister. She was born in 1953 in Southern Sind Province in Pakistan. Bhutto was an intellectual powerhouse. She studied politics, economics and philosophy at Harvard and Oxford Universities. She was the first-ever Asian student to be elected President of the prestigious Oxford Union, an accolade that was not merely a personal one but one that also rubbed off on her country as well.

Her sights were set on becoming a diplomat. However, on her return to Pakistan, she saw her father, Ali Bhutto, ousted in a coup by the military, who sent him to prison and declared martial law in the country. The execution of her father, two years later, became the defining moment for Bhutto and led her to launch her career in politics.

Bhutto would serve two terms as Prime Minister of Pakistan, from 1988 to 1990 and from 1993 to 1996. She was a strong-willed and intellectually defiant person who never faltered in her belief that she was the best placed person to lead Pakistan to democracy and prosperity. Guided by her determination and confidence, she declared herself the "Life Chairperson" of the Pakistan People's Party.

Bhutto commanded both adulation and contempt during her tenure as Prime Minister. However, she was a charismatic and skillful political player. She made her mark, both in her country and on the global political arena, for her outspoken insistence on the need for Pakistan to evolve into a secular and liberal state. She was committed to the role of women, tolerance, democracy, moderate and centrist values. She was also willing to accommodate good relations with India. Despite being a Muslim country, Bhutto created a new identity for Pakistan, which now became a place where women could aspire to the highest office in the land.

When her father was on his deathbed in prison, she promised him that she would carry on with his work. Upon his death, the Pakistan People's Party was outlawed. For the five years that followed, Bhutto found herself in and out of detention, during which time she was subjected to harrowing and unspeakable prison conditions. At other times, she was placed under house arrest at her home. In 1984, she was allowed to seek medical treatment abroad and she left for London. Once martial law was lifted in December 1985, Bhutto knew it was time for her to go back home to Pakistan and carry on with the work she had promised her father. Her return was celebrated by many people in Pakistan. Her momentous welcome propelled her to undertake a national tour of Pakistan, campaigning for the 1988 elections in which she would claim a decisive victory.

Although she faced a lot of opposition during her tenure, Bhutto was considered an iconic political leader who was looked upon as the hope for development and democracy in Pakistan. As the epitome of great leadership, she fought for democracy for her country, embracing everyone in the process. She was a transformational leader who had a clear vision for her country and committed herself to achieving that vision. Her iconic leadership has been likened to that of Nelson Mandela, Mahatma Gandhi and Martin Luther King. Her charisma, vision and formidable intellect earned her many followers, while at the same time she attracted opposition from many quarters. Her personality drew many people to her, and she used her great interpersonal skills to transform and influence the people. Without doubt, Bhutto's leadership style was based on the four elements of influence, inspiration, intellectualism and individualism.

Her dedication to eliminating dictatorship and to restore democracy in her country never wavered. She also pushed terrorism out of Pakistan and advocated for an equal society. She fought against the discrimination of women, with her election as first female Prime Minister setting the best possible example for women in Pakistan and the rest of the Muslim world. Bhutto was a courageous leader who was not afraid to take risks, and she deployed her immense bravery and courage to fight the formidable odds in a country where men dominated politics. She was also one of the few leaders of Pakistan who advocated for peaceful relations with India. She motivated many women in Pakistan to believe in her and her vision, and the women, in turn, accepted her as their role model.

In the earlier days of her tenure as Prime Minister, Bhutto dedicated herself to helping her people overcome national disillusionment with her ideals of democracy, human rights, peace and prosperity for Pakistan. She was prepared to fight for what was right and never shied away from facing the challenges and personal suffering that came with fighting for the rights of her people. Bhutto believed a strong Pakistan was vital for the prosperity of her country. As such, she committed herself to making Pakistan emerge stronger on the world stage.

Bhutto used her interpersonal skills to inculcate harmonious relationships between state institutions, such as parliament, the judiciary and the armed forces. She ensured that every possible resource was made available to the armed forces to enable them to strengthen their capacity and capability as a defense institution. She accelerated the national nuclear program, while simultaneously launching the national missile technology and other relevant defense programs that were needed to strengthen Pakistan in the sphere of international relevance.

Bhutto was credited for putting an end to media restrictions in Pakistan, and for speaking out in a loud and clear voice for women's rights in her country and around the world. The West saw Bhutto as a charismatic symbol of moderation. To date, Pakistan continues to derive inspiration from Bhutto in all spheres of public welfare and development. She saw her vision and her firm belief in her mission to serve and empower the people of Pakistan as the only way forward for her country. Her high-quality education, solid intellect and international exposure, combined with her charismatic leadership, turned her into a formidable political personality within a short span of time, and she became one of the most charismatic political voices in Pakistan and across the globe.

Despite the travails of the Black race at the hands of the past colonialists and the neo-colonialists, the one fact that the world cannot dispute is that Africa has always been a breeding ground for some of the world's brightest minds in every professional calling, from medicine to engineering, and from law to economics. Africa has produced one of the most brilliant minds in the field of economics in contemporary times. Ngozi Okonjo-Iweala is an eminent economist and international development expert. She made history as the first-ever female finance minister of her country, Nigeria, the world's most populous Black nation, and the largest economy on the African continent.

Born in Ogwashi-Uku in Southern Nigeria, Okonjo-Iweala studied economics at Harvard University, and then went on to obtain a Ph.D. in Regional Economics from the Massachusetts Institute of Technology, after which she was headhunted by the World Bank for recruitment as a development economist. At the conclusion of her first tenure at the World Bank, Okonjo-Iweala returned to Nigeria to assume the office of the country's Minister of Finance. She also later served as Minister of Foreign Affairs. She is the first woman in Nigeria to hold both of these highly sensitive government portfolios. After serving for one term as Minister of Finance, she returned to the World Bank as its Managing Director. Her skill, experience and leadership qualities later made Okonjo-Iweala a highly recommended candidate for the position of President of the World Bank.

As soon as Okonjo-Iweala took over as Nigeria's Minister of Finance, she embarked on a mission to introduce sanity to Nigeria's financial sector, and to clear the country's burden of unsustainable foreign debt. She set about tracking, tackling and preventing corruption that was costing the country over US$15bn per year. Her relentless fight against corruption quickly earned her the sobriquet "Trouble Woman," even as she declared a total and uncompromising war on, and a zero tolerance for, the pervasive culture of bribery and kickbacks. In the process, many corrupt Ministry of Finance officials were ignominiously relieved of their duties. Hundreds of individuals and groups involved in illegal schemes of conning people out of money through notorious internet letters, tricks and scams were sent to jail.

She put her life at risk when she worked to make the energy sector more transparent and targeted military and political leaders who had unscrupulously enriched themselves through corrupt practices, especially the exploitation of the country's massive crude oil potential. Her diligent fight against corruption became a veritable threat to many government officials, and this led to her resignation. At the advent of a new administration in Nigeria, she returned as Minister of Finance for the second time after serving as Managing Director at the World Bank. Having also served as both Coordinating Minister of the Economy and Minister of Foreign Affairs, in many quarters she was considered almost as a sort of de facto Prime Minister without necessarily or officially holding that title.

Okonjo-Iweala has not only been hailed as a brilliant reformer but she has also been credited with the emergence of Nigeria as Africa's strongest economy. Her leadership, competence and passion for Nigeria resulted in the country turning the tide after two decades of reversal in economic growth. During her tenure, Nigeria saw its economy rebound and the country enjoyed strengthened economic growth. Seen as an orthodox economist, she slashed the US$7.5bn fuel subsidy to resuscitate the country's economy and eliminated civil servant ghost positions that were on the government payroll.

In her efforts to drive transparency and good governance, Okonjo-Iweala introduced the practice of the publishing of the monthly financial allocation from the federal government to each state in the popular newspapers. She also helped to build the Government Integrated Financial Management and Information System, an electronic financial management platform that included the Treasury Single Account and Integrated Payroll and Personnel Information System, which helped to curtail corruption. By 2014, the system had eliminated ghost workers from the payroll, saving the Nigerian government approximately US$1.25bn.

Furthermore, Okonjo-Iweala's leadership and pragmatism secured Nigeria a debt cancellation of US$30bn. She led Nigeria in obtaining its first sovereign debt ranking, which strengthened and stabilized the country's public finance systems. During her tenure as Minister of Finance, Nigeria emerged as Africa's largest economy with a GDP of US$481bn in 2015.

Okonjo-Iweala served in several key positions at the World Bank, including as Managing Director. During her tenure as Managing Director, Okonjo-Iweala had the overall responsibility for overseeing the World Bank's operational portfolio for Africa, South Asia, Europe and Central Asia, a portfolio that amounted to US$81bn. She spearheaded several of the initiatives of the World Bank that assisted low-income countries during the food crises and the financial crisis. She served as chair of the IDA Replenishment, which was the World Bank's successful drive to raise US$49.3bn in grants and low-interest credit that was made available to the world's poorest countries. In addition, she was a member of the Commission on Effective Development with Africa.

Okonjo-Iweala's past work and strong experience in governance, economics, finance and development, as well as in the humanitarian sphere, are all indicative of her great leadership skills. Her establishment of the Mortgage Refinance Corporation stimulated the housing market in

Nigeria. She was also involved in various gender and youth empowerment schemes, including the Youth Prize with Innovation, which supports young entrepreneurs and creates jobs for young people. She has been credited for being instrumental in totally reshaping Nigeria's economy by introducing necessary reforms and increasing transparency in governance.

Having served twice as Nigeria's Minister of Finance, having once served as Minister of Foreign Affairs, and having served in the World Bank as Development Economist and Managing Director, Okonjo-Iweala was a highly commendable candidate for the position of President of the World Bank. She serves as Chair of African Risk Capacity, a specialized agency of the African Union that helps member states to prepare for and respond to extreme weather and natural disasters. In addition, she is a senior adviser at Lazard, and serves on the board of the Rockefeller Foundation and the Center for Global Development, among others.

In the wake of the global coronavirus crisis, the Chair of the African Union, President Cyril Ramaphosa of South Africa appointed Ngozi Okonjo-Iweala to a high-powered team of Special Envoys of the African Union that will mobilize international support for Africa's efforts to address the economic challenges African countries will face as a result of the COVID-19 pandemic. The Special Envoys are tasked with soliciting rapid and concrete support as pledged by the G20, the European Union and other international financial institutions. Shortly before this momentous appointment, she had been endorsed for the position of Director General of the World Trade Organization (WTO) by the Economic Community of West African States (ECOWAS).

According to the declaration communique signed by ECOWAS President Mahamadou Issoufou: *"The strong academic and professional background of Dr. Okonjo-Iweala and her large experience in national affairs as Nigeria's Finance Minister (2003-2006 and 2011-2015) and Nigeria's Foreign Affairs Minister briefly in 2006, her long years of managerial experience at the top echelons of multilateral institutions, her established reputation as a fearless reformer, her excellent negotiating and political skills, her experience of over 30 years as a Development Economist with a long standing interest in trade, her excellent academic qualifications, her positions as*

Managing Director World Bank, and currently as Board Chair Gavi, and African Union Special Envoy to Mobilize Financial Resources for the fight against COVID-19, make her the best candidate for the job."

Meanwhile, back in her home country, Nigeria, she received tremendous backing and overwhelming support from Nigerian President Muhammadu Buhari. In October 2020, Okonjo-Iweala was overwhelmingly elected Director General of the World Trade Organization, a position in which she would be tasked with managing the trade war between China and the United States, initiate reforms in the face of rising protectionism, and steer the world to new trade pastures in the face of the novel coronavirus (COVID-19) pandemic. Okonjo-Iweala would become the first woman and first African to hold the position of Director General of the World Trade Organization since it was established in 1995.

Okonjo-Iweala has received various awards, honors and accolades in recognition of her leadership and her outstanding feats as an economist, development expert and humanitarian. She was named by *Fortune* magazine as one of the 50 greatest world leaders in 2015, and by *Forbes* as one of the 100 most powerful women in the world for five consecutive years. In 2014, she was recognized by *TIME* magazine as one of the world's 100 most influential people. Okonjo-Iweala holds various honorary doctorate degrees and she has authored several books, including *Reforming the Unreformable: Lessons from Nigeria*, published in 2012.

There is no denying the fact that leaders in the early 21st century face unprecedented challenges. For instance, they lead three completely different generations of people who view the world through different lenses. The 21st century leader must have a well-honed human awareness acumen that is backed by an unassailable intellect she can draw upon from one challenging moment to the next. These leaders must understand the systemic impacts of their operational environment and be willing to look deeper to understand cultural norms that can impede intellectual agility and innovation.

Leadership intelligence relies on an ability to grow, learn and master new ways to lead people, and in this respect there are three tenets to consider.

These are self-awareness, cognitive function, and response agility. Above all, however, the effective leader must balance her intellect with empathy and always act with integrity. It is the balance of *thinking* and *feeling* that inspires the passion, enthusiasm and commitment that the governments and organizations they lead need to thrive and grow in today's environment.

Intellect is the power of knowing. It is also the capacity for knowledge. It is one of the most prized leadership characteristics, simply because it represents intelligent and rational thought, enabling one to have a direction and a destination to focus on. It is intellect that enables a leader to see the possibilities, or a vision for her followers. Yet, the point must be stressed that intellect merely represents just one wing of leadership. Much as an eagle requires two wings to fly, a leader requires two wings to reach her greatest potential. Indeed, to attain her highest possibilities, the wing of intellect must be combined with the wing of empathic leadership.

HOW TO GAIN ACCESS TO YOUR POWER OF THE INTELLECT

1. You must cultivate the fluidity and flexibility of mind that allows for the anticipation or adaptation to uncertain or changing situations.

2. You must develop the patience to critically and creatively dissect problems, and be able to design expedient approaches to solve those problems.

3. You must be able to respond in an appropriate and controlled manner to challenging situations.

4. You must develop the ability to think before reacting.

5. You will need to be aware of how others operate, and how to inspire them as a core component of intelligent leadership.

6. You will need to consistently demonstrate sound judgment by developing the ability to sort through information, asking the right questions and learning from the mistakes of others.

7. You will need to hone your human awareness acumen, and back it with the unassailable intellect that you can draw upon from one challenging moment to the next.

8. You must be prepared to grow, learn and master new ways to lead your people.

9. You will need to balance your intellect with empathy and integrity.

10. You must develop a vision to see possibilities for yourself and for your followers.

CHAPTER 14

THE POWER OF COURAGE

"Whenever you take a step forward,
you are bound to disturb something."

INDIRA GANDHI

Courage is a character trait that everyone wants. It is the ability to face one's fear despite whatever obstacles may lie in one's path. Throughout the ages, the history of mankind has been culturally decorated with stories of courage and valor that serve as veritable templates for encouraging people to demonstrate bravery in their differing fields of human endeavor. One of the best examples of such courage is seen in the timelessly famous biblical story of David and Goliath, one in which a man defeated a giant whom everyone held in mortal dread. Courage can be physical in connotation, yet it can be moral in expression.

Endurance and innovation are also considered outstanding hallmarks of a courageous person. Although the first thing that occurs to one in any discourse on courage is the act of being brave in life-threatening situations, courage is probably more about making the critical distinction between the two vices of cowardice and recklessness, and acting accordingly. Therefore, courage definitely also compels one to refuse to act carelessly, being more the ability to respond to fear in a proactive manner than a senseless show of misguided bravado. That is why courage is not necessarily the absence of fear but the mastery of fear.

It also connotes the ability to decisively do that which is both proper to do and virtuous, no matter the difficulties one might encounter in that quest. Courage can manifest in many different forms. Some examples of courage in everyday existence include the courage to always do what is right, the courage to accept that some decisions may render one unpopular, and the courage to embark on a course of self-improvement, even if it demands extreme physical or mental discomfort.

Aristotle, the great Greek philosopher, viewed moral virtue as a state of human excellence that leads to honorable actions and genuine fulfillment in living. He believed that being virtuous can lead to nothing but happiness, and that the noble desire to improve one's quality of life can be more easily fulfilled by subscribing to moral rules and creating wholesome habits. Aristotle viewed courage as one of the four main virtues. He regarded courage as the ability to faithfully sustain one's convictions regardless of consequences. Not unnaturally, this valiant inclination itself makes it easier for one to subscribe to other virtues. In an existential context, courage is intimately related to the concept of authenticity, one in which one takes responsibility for the direction of one's life and its meaning. It also means one is able to courageously accept one's fears and anxieties, and being prepared to confront them in a proactively headlong manner.

Having dispensed with the philosophical and intellectual perspectives on courage, we might explore its dictionary definition. The dictionary defines courage as *"The quality of mind or spirit that enables a person to face difficulty, danger and pain without fear."* This suggests that courage is synonymous with bravery, yet if courage is not properly channeled, bravery easily dovetails into acts of recklessness and stupidity.

While the dictionary definition of courage appears adequate, at least on the superficial level, courage actually entails much more than that. In the first instance, three types of courage are recognized. The first is physical courage. Physical courage is what people mostly visualize in any discussion on courage. Physical courage is the quality of spirit that allows an individual to perform the stereotypical act of heroism, such as saving a person from a burning building, or a soldier saving an entire squad in an assault by enemy forces. Any act that physically removes one or many people from danger is an example of physical courage.

Physical courage also manifests itself in the soldier fighting for his country, and the firefighter rushing into the collapsing World Trade Center to save civilians. To have this kind of courage requires one to overcome the fear of a dangerous situation in order to achieve something heroic for the greater good. Physical courage is attained when fear and recklessness balance out, and can be channeled to help others. The second is intellectual courage, and the third is moral courage. In the second instance, there is the moral motivation behind any given courageous act. The final part of a complete definition of courage lies in the cause or purpose toward which a courageous act is performed.

Intellectual courage is the form of courage that iconic political leaders require to hold firmly on to a new idea, totally refusing to buckle under pressure to relinquish that conviction. Charles Darwin and Galileo both possessed this kind of courage. It is human nature to resist change, and both of them were victims of the virulent and caustic criticism that are commonly symptomatic of a resistance to change.

Darwin, an English naturalist, was subjected to ceaseless criticism and unspeakable vilification when he propounded his theories on evolution and natural selection. To this day, his ideas face pockets of disdain and derision, even though they have been accepted and widely recognized as true, principally because his theories contradict certain core Christian beliefs. That Darwin could even endure and survive the unending spate of attacks on his work is nothing short of eloquent testimony to his immense intellectual courage.

Galileo presented a similar case study. His ideas concerning the physical form of the world and the universe contradicted the views of the church of the day. Although Galileo's theories are credited with authenticity and credibility today, in his day Galileo was essentially placed in hell by the pope for publishing his principles on astronomy. Despite the attacks, Galileo published his works, for which reason he is still remembered as a great scientific mind. Without possessing intellectual courage, Galileo would never have been remembered for the great mind that he was.

Like Darwin and Galileo, the world has been blessed with iconic female leaders who have stood firm against all attempt, especially by their male counterparts, to suppress their political voice. One of such women was born into one of India's most prominent political families in 1917.

Indira Priyadarshini Gandhi, hailed to this day as one of the most charismatic leaders in India's political history, was the daughter of India's longest serving Prime Minister, Pandit Jawaharlal Nehru. Gandhi became India's third Prime Minister, and so far has been the only female Prime Minister of that country. Although her political leadership has always invited sharp divisions in opinion, Gandhi was admired for both the strength of character and the iron will that guaranteed India its pride of place in global affairs. To date, she remains an iconic figure in the colorful history of India, having served as Prime Minister twice, from 1966 to 1977 and from 1980 to 1984, totaling 15 years in office, making her the second longest serving Prime Minister of India.

Gandhi was renowned for her courageous leadership and bold decision making. Leading a populous and poverty-stricken nation such as India was not an easy feat, as Gandhi would face near-insurmountable challenges in her bid to combat the extreme levels of poverty and religious divisions that beset India during her tenure. However, her strong willpower would prove a formidable obstacle to anything that stood in the way of her vision for India. She managed to reduce poverty, increase literacy levels and raise food production in the country.

Gandhi's charisma, great communication skills and unyielding pragmatism led to immense changes in India, while also advancing India's role in global affairs. Her ability to cope with the demands of leading one of the world's largest and most populous nations went a long way in consolidating her hold on power. Gandhi had been thrust into politics at an early age in which she became her father's hostess, confidante and advisor after her mother's death. Upon her father's death, she was offered a junior position in government. When the leader of the ruling party died, Gandhi was selected as the compromise choice to lead the party. In the ensuing 11 years, she would unequivocally prove her mettle as a formidable political leader, and embarked upon the process of consolidating her power within the party hierarchy and the country.

Navigating a male-dominated society with uncommon dexterity, Gandhi turned her challenges and controversies into victories to become one of the most inspiring leaders of her time. She employed charisma and great communication skills to walk her talk and emotionally connect with the ordinary people of India. She faced her challenges head-on, converting threats into opportunities, while also overcoming volatility, uncertainty, complexity and ambiguity. Tremendously tenacious and resilient, Gandhi made bold decisions and stood steadfast for principles and philosophies that advocated for the empowerment of women and girls.

Unflinchingly loyal to her country, she expected no less a degree of patriotism from her team and cabinet, who she always consulted prior to taking any important decision. However, once a decision had been reached on any issue, she left no room for a reversal. A consummate strategist and nationalist, Gandhi was a firm and determined leader who deftly matched her policies to the prevailing political, social and economic conditions of the day. She embarked on a nationalization exercise, abolished privy purses, and liberated Bangladesh from Pakistan. She not only succeeded in the Green Revolution, but also built a strong nation, making it possible for India to join other countries that had gone nuclear, making India a powerful South Asian country.

Faced with several constraints and stiff opposition at home and abroad, Gandhi would exhibit an uncommon form of statesmanship that distinguished her as a courageous leader and patriot who worked diligently for India's integrity, unity, prosperity and peace. She received several international awards, honors and accolades, culminating in her being epochally named Woman of The Millennium in a keenly contested BBC online poll. She led India into winning the 1971 war with Pakistan, and saw to the creation of Bangladesh. She left office briefly for three years and triumphantly returned for a second tenure in 1980, and was assassinated in 1984.

Gandhi's leadership style was probably characterized more by pragmatism and the skillful wielding of power than anything else. Certainly, it was more focused on goals than process. She also possessed great managerial acumen, task orientation, information gathering skills and interpersonal relations, all of which she applied in relating with her cabinet, extra-parliamentary party, the opposition, her associates, the media and the public. She advocated strongly for her goals and relied heavily on independent sources of information. Gandhi was also quite accessible and friendly to the media, and demonstrated a consistent pattern of openness and warmth.

Gandhi was more concerned with task implementation than building consensus among her cabinet members, as in fact, she actually oversaw a reduction in the powers of the cabinet. Her approach to cabinet affairs showed that her preferred role was that of an advocate and not a consensus builder. Indisputably, her advocacy was based on both an authoritative and peremptory exercise of power. Also, as an activist Prime Minister, Gandhi was highly involved in the management of information, preferring to research the information herself rather than wait for it to be presented to her by the chain of command.

Despite her seeming bent toward authoritarianism, Gandhi's leadership style and relations with the public was surprisingly quite open. She had a special bond with the masses, who obviously energized her. Her relations with the media alternated between being friendly and accessible to being uninformative, unfriendly and inaccessible. Clearly, her attitude to the media was dictated by prevailing exigencies. She was a highly goal-oriented leader who was tireless in carrying out her duties and obligations to her country. She was also ambitious, dominant and contentious. Yet, her strong interpersonal skills helped her overcome the misgivings of her contemporaries about her, and to create strong personal and effective relationships with the people of India.

In an earlier chapter, this book featured one of the most result-oriented female political leaders in recent world history. Margaret Hilda Thatcher was the word courage defined, in any known or accepted connotation of the word. A key lesson from Thatcher's legacy is that leaders must have the courage to stand firmly by their convictions. Indeed, Thatcher's leadership style was singularly enhanced by courage. It was this courage that gave her the determination to set specific goals and see them through. In fact, if any one particular trait characterized her historic tenure far and above any other, it was this courage, born of supreme confidence in her ideals.

Thatcher's decisive style of governance was so distinctive that her brand of politics was given the sobriquet "Thatcherism." Without doubt, she led her government based on a rare sort of conviction politics that was singularly driven by her own values. Thatcherism actually became a constellation of policies that encompassed, among others, privatization, tax cuts, home ownership and free market economics. In retrospect, Britain was the better for it. After all, it was Thatcher's leadership style and conviction that enabled her to build the strong relationships and to forge the strong political alliances that ensured the United Kingdom remained a force to be reckoned with in global affairs.

Through her strong ideological affinity with American President Ronald Reagan, she re-established a special relationship with the United States. It was this strategic alliance that led to the swift battle victory that won Thatcher, the "Iron Lady of Britain," public support for the 74-day Falklands War in 1982, a defining moment in her political career, and which led to her being re-elected to office in 1983.

Genuine courage is a composite of many traits, and no leader in the contemporary history of governance in the world, whether of the male or the female gender, better exemplifies this truth than the latter-day Baroness Thatcher. Her uncompromising politics and leadership style was considered not only extraordinary but also quite revolutionary. A woman endowed with an unswerving and clear form of moral passion, Thatcher was widely hailed for exhibiting certain remarkable personality traits that included self-confidence, pragmatism, ambition, aggressiveness and a strong moral belief in the way she carried out her duties and obligations. Incontrovertibly, her leadership style was facilitated by an innate ability to strive for power and authority, which in turn allowed her the latitude of having control over decision making. All these traits required uncommon courage.

She was the first woman to become Prime Minister of Britain and the first to lead a major Western power in modern history. Hard-driving and hardheaded, she led her Conservative Party to three straight election wins and held office for 11 straight years, May 1979 to November 1990, longer than any other British politician in the 20th century. The potent economic medicine she administered to a country sick with inflation, budget deficits and industrial unrest occasioned wide and unprecedented swings in popularity that culminated in a revolt among her own cabinet ministers in her final year in office.

Yet, by the time she left office, the principles known as Thatcherism, a composite of the belief that economic freedom and individual liberty are interdependent, that personal responsibility and personal industry are the only guaranteed paths to national prosperity, and that a free-market democracy must stand firm against aggression, had won so many disciples that even her strongest critics were left with no choice than to accord her a grudging respect.

Thatcher's political successes were incontestable and decisive. She broke the power of the labor unions and forced the opposing Labour Party to abandon its commitment to nationalized industry, redefine the role of the welfare state and accept the importance of the free market. Meanwhile, on the international turf, she won renewed esteem for a Britain that had witnessed decline since its costly victory in World War II. Barely 17 months into her first term, in 1980, disaster stared Thatcher in the face. Businesses were failing and unemployment was on the rise. Even her advisers feared that her aggressive push to stem inflation, sell off nationalized industry and deregulate the economy was devastating the poor and undermining the middle class. With electoral defeat looking imminent, cabinet members harangued her for compromise. Thatcher remained adamant. She said, *"I am not a consensus politician. I am a conviction politician."* In the long run, she won the day. She transformed her Conservative Party into the party of reform. Her policies revitalized British business, enhanced industrial growth and buoyed up the middle class.

To her enemies, Thatcher was little more than a woman who railed against the evils of poverty, yet was callous and unsympathetic to the plight of the poor. They considered her policies so cruel and short-sighted as to do nothing but widen the gap between rich and poor, and worsen the plight of the poorest. On the global stage, her relentless hostility to the Soviet Union and her persistent call to modernize Britain's nuclear forces led to fears of nuclear war, worrying moderates in her own party. After a particularly hard-line speech in 1976, the Soviet press gave her the famous sobriquet "The Iron Lady." Yet, for all her seeming intransigence on all matters Soviet, her rapport with new Soviet leader Mikhail S. Gorbachev and her friendship with President Ronald Reagan actually made Thatcher a vital link between the White House and the Kremlin in their tense negotiations to halt the arms race of the 1980s.

Brisk and argumentative, she was rarely willing to concede a point, and she was loath to compromise. Colleagues who were at odds with her were often deluged in a sea of facts and sound intellectual analysis that all but silenced dissension with a devastating finality that brooked no further argument. She had very high standards, and she expected everyone to do their work, because of which she was quite tough on her ministers. Thatcher evoked extreme feelings. To some she could do no right, to others no wrong. Indifference was not an option. Indeed, she managed to stir almost physical hostility in normally rational people, while she inspired fanatical devotion in others.

One of the most defining moments of her leadership arrived on April 2, 1982. Argentina invaded the Falkland Islands. British settlers had lived on the Falklands, long-claimed by Argentina, since the 1820s, and negotiations over their future had been dragging on for ages. Argentina moved to take the Falklands by force, gambling that once the islands were occupied, Argentine forces would never be ousted. In a decisive move that precluded further talks by the United States and other allies on preventing bloodshed, Thatcher ordered a Royal Navy fleet to the South Atlantic. In a ten-week war, the British retook the islands in fighting that left some 250 British servicemen and more than 1,000 Argentines dead. The victory doomed Argentina's military government and cemented Thatcher's reputation as a leader to be reckoned with.

It was accepted as sacrosanct truth in British politics that one never picked a quarrel with the National Union of Mineworkers. Thatcher flouted it. The coal mines, nationalized in 1947, were widely seen as unprofitable, overstaffed and obsolescent, and in 1984 the government announced plans to shut down several mines and to eliminate 20,000 of the industry's 180,000 jobs. A violent strike ensued, in which hundreds of miners battled the police, from one night to the next.

Thatcher believed that the trade unions were harmful to both their members and the public. She became committed to reducing the power of the unions, whose leadership she accused of sabotaging parliamentary democracy and the economy through their strikes. Although many unions embarked on strikes in response to legislation aimed at limiting their power, the resistance eventually collapsed.

According to the BBC in 2004, Thatcher managed to destroy the power of the trade unions for almost a generation. The miners' strike of 1984-85 was the biggest and most devastating confrontation between the unions and Thatcher's government. Thatcher bluntly refused to meet the union's demands. After a year out on strike, in March 1985 the miners' leadership conceded without a deal. Thatcher closed 25 unprofitable coal mines in 1985, and by 1992 a total of 97 mines had been closed, while those that remained were privatized in 1994. The resulting closure of 150 coal mines resulted in the loss of tens of thousands of jobs and had the effect of devastating entire communities.

Strikes had contributed to bring down Edward Heath, Thatcher's predecessor, and Thatcher was determined to succeed where he had failed. Her strategy of preparing fuel stocks, appointing a hardliner as leader of the National Coal Board, and ensuring that the police were adequately trained and equipped with riot gear, contributed to her triumph over the striking miners.

After leaving office, Thatcher traveled widely, drawing huge audiences on the lecture circuit. She sat in the House of Lords as Baroness Thatcher of Kesteven, wrote her memoir and devoted herself to the Margaret Thatcher Foundation, to further her values. Yet, the Iron Lady remained forthright in expressing her opinions. In retirement, she continued to call for firmness in the face of aggression, strongly advocating Western intervention to stop the ethnic bloodshed in the Balkans in the early 1990s. After the September 11 terrorist attacks, she endorsed President George W. Bush's policy of sanctioning pre-emptive strikes against governments that sponsored terrorism. She also backed the war to oust the Iraqi leader, Saddam Hussein. It is a testament to the remarkable life, politics and leadership of Margaret Thatcher that a film titled *Iron Lady*, and starring actress Meryl Streep, was shot in 2011.

At the most basic level, a leader is defined as someone who goes first. A leader forges a path forward and inspires people to follow. This takes courage. The leaders of today are actually writing the rule book of the future because, given the unpredictable times, they are leading in an environment where, more often than not, they can't see the destination. Additionally, there will always be tough decisions to make and sometimes such decisions can impact negatively on people we care about.

Aristotle said, *"Courage is the first of human qualities because it is the quality that guarantees the others."* He was right. Without courage, a leader cannot make a difference. This courage is acting in the face of fear. It means acting in spite of one's imperfections and inadequacies but refusing to be driven by them. Most importantly, in times of change, leaders need the courage to persist. They also need the courage to think differently.

Courage and the comfort zone are not compatible. To remain in a comfort zone is to refuse to learn, grow or forge a new path. That is why, to be an effective leader, one must be prepared to embrace the discomfort of unpopularity and criticism. As soon as we are prepared to embrace discomfort, we are ready to become true leaders. When we become true leaders, we start to live an inspired life, for ourselves and for future generations.

HOW TO GAIN ACCESS TO YOUR POWER OF COURAGE

1. Courage is not synonymous with carelessness. Courage is the ability to respond to fear in a proactive manner rather than a senseless show of misguided bravado.

2. Courage is not necessarily the absence of fear but the mastery of fear.

3. Courage connotes the ability to decisively do that which is proper to do, no matter the difficulties you may encounter.

4. Courage connotes acting in spite of your imperfections and inadequacies, yet refusing to be driven by them.

5. Courage is your ability to faithfully sustain your convictions regardless of the consequences.

6. Courage is the ability to accept your fears and anxieties, and being prepared to confront them in a proactively headlong manner.

7. You must remain tenacious and resilient.

8. You must face your challenges head-on, and be prepared to convert your threats into opportunities.

9. You must develop the courage to stand firmly by your convictions.

10. Courage and the comfort zone are not compatible, and to be an effective leader you must be prepared to embrace the discomfort of unpopularity and criticism.

CHAPTER 15

THE POWER OF THE REFORMER

"I know reform is never easy.
But I know reform is right."

JULIA GILLARD

A reformer is someone who tries to change and improve something such as a law or a social system. Basically, reform refers to changes in the broad fabric of a country's socio-political life, including the function of the government as it relates to the policies that affect the wellbeing of the governed. Such reforms also imply changes in the government's regulatory structures, especially those that are creating bottlenecks in efforts to improve the living standards and conditions of the people. Overall, reforms are always useful in the evolutionary growth of any society, as almost invariably they can only lead to improvements in the human condition.

One reason why those great women leaders who are also reformers eventually acquire the status of heroines is because governments are usually reluctant to pursue fundamental reforms, which tend to be rather difficult and complex processes to undertake. That is why reformers often face stiff opposition. Also, the benefits of far-reaching reforms are usually only seen in the long term, unlike simple monetary policies that can display benefits in the medium term. Ultimately, the only way reformers are able to introduce changes and reforms effectively is if they themselves are at the helm of political and governmental affairs, and that is why the world's greatest reformers are also usually the heads of government of their countries.

The world's most impactful reformers tend to require sufficient time in leadership positions to be able to execute their reform programs. That much was the case with Helen Elizabeth Clark who gained global acclaim when she was elected New Zealand's female Prime Minister in 1999, holding that office for three consecutive terms. Once gracing *Forbes'* list of the World's 100 Most Powerful Women, she was effectively the 37th Prime Minister of New Zealand, serving from 1999 to 2008. After her term as head of government, she served as Administrator at the United Nations Development Program (UNDP) from 2009 to 2017.

Clark is nothing short of a great example of how gender can cut both ways when working toward the highest levels of leadership and success. Although she was considered an unusual candidate for the role, she earned recognition for her strikingly remarkable managerial style of leadership as she worked to reform the long-accustomed bureaucracy and administration of the United Nations Development Program by insisting on greater transparency in the organization.

As a former head of state, the new role at the United Nations Development Program was guaranteed to stretch her leadership skills to their limits, as she was tasked with helping to build the social and economic statuses of nations, especially the disadvantaged and the emerging economies, such that they could withstand crises and achieve sustainable growth. She oversaw an agency with an annual budget of over US$6bn, and which had a staff of over 8,000 people working in 177 countries. Without doubt, as the third highest ranking United Nations official, Clark's ability to navigate the ropes as one of the world's pre-eminent civil servants was tested at the highest level of performance.

Clark served as Prime Minister of New Zealand for three consecutive terms, and it was during those eventful years that she cut her teeth as someone to whom reformation in governance came merely as second nature. It can be safely declared that as a pioneer female head of government in New Zealand, she largely reformed the prevailing male view of female participation in politics and governance. She possessed certain very useful leadership traits. She was self-consciously pragmatic. She was a prudent manager of available resources, who avoided flamboyance and rhetorical bludgeoning.

Clark did, however, have a ruthless streak which reared its head whenever necessary. As one of the few female heads of state in the world, Clark faced the intense media scrutiny that focused more on her personal traits than on her admirable politics and style of governance. She had to engage in a Herculean struggle to establish herself as a credible party leader and potential Prime Minister, all in the face of great opposition and immense political challenge. As a female leader, Clark had to battle intense gender bias to ascend the ladder within a largely male-dominated political culture.

However, an unshakeable self-belief that was grounded on a solid vision, coupled with articulate and consummate research, thorough groundwork, the ability to be able to think ahead and plan feasibly, as well as the constant habit of re-evaluating her plans and resetting her goals, all enabled her to rise to the occasion. During her tenure as Prime Minister of New Zealand, she increased the minimum wage, provided zero-interest rate on student loans, created a carbon emissions trading system and refused to join the United States in the invasion of Iraq. Ultimately threatened with a mass walkout, Clark exerted a refined skill to salvage the Maori caucus and keep them on her side.

It was, however, at the UNDP that Clark demonstrated an unprecedented commitment to reformation. She had always had a long-standing and deep interest in foreign policy and a commitment to the United Nations and its collaborative processes. At the close of her tenure, she adopted a rather proactive approach when she was defeated at the elections of 2008. Instead of heading for the sidelines and settling down to write her memoirs, or like most politicians becoming a fixture on the lecture circuit, she pitched for the job at the United Nations Development Program. Her candidature was considered quite unusual as it would stretch her leadership skills to a different and much more complicated level.

As the number three official in the United Nations hierarchy, Clark ran the UNDP with a quiet effectiveness that tackled global poverty headlong. She would end up leaving behind a track record of reforms, and an inimitable knowledge of the United Nations systems and its flaws. Indeed, she was a formidable reformer. She shook up the United Nations Development Program and focused on taming civil wars and addressing the causes for extremism. Coming from a country that was as much on the front line of climate shifts as most other developed nations, she realized just how imperative it was that the world understood the links between hunger, poverty, conflict, migration, economic cycles and climate change.

At the UNDP, a behemoth long overdue for a more forward-looking way of looking at global economic inequality, Clark offered the kind of leadership style that was needed for the day and for the prevailing circumstances. She oversaw the restructuring and total overhauling of the United Nations Development Program in 2014. Although the decision to restructure was taken by UNDP's executive board, it became Clark's duty to execute the processes incident to that decision. Those processes involved significant staff layoffs and demotions that were considered the largest of any such mass-scale reductions in staff numbers at the United Nations in any one single exercise.

As her United Nations position was not an elected one, Clark did not have to pander to what might be considered acceptable or popular whims or opinions. Yet, her past experience as Prime Minister of New Zealand was painted as a virtue in many quarters. She was universally perceived as a direct, highly competent, cautious and deliberate leader who always weighed issues carefully before reaching a final decision. She also had a ruthless streak and knew how to manipulate power to her advantage. She refused to lose sight of her ultimate objective and focus to run a sustainable and stable government.

Amusingly, she also possessed the charm and sense of humor that appeared to contrast sharply with her ruthless and calculating manner, but which she used effectively and whenever necessary. That charm was used to devastating effect when New Zealand put in a bid to host the 2011 World Cup. Well aware that a woman leader was suitably positioned to attract a disproportionate amount of influence for the simple reason that there were so few of them, Clark became personally involved in the bid and decided to make the presentation to the International Rugby Board in Dublin in person, accompanied by her relevant entourage. She used her leadership skills as Prime Minister to support New Zealand's bid to host the World Cup. Clark was the first-ever head of government to present to the International Rugby Board in person and she utilized her inimitable style to win the day. She also withstood the two-hour grilling at the United Nations General Assembly to articulate New Zealand's bid. The bookies had been betting on Japan and South Africa to host the tournament, but Clark won it for New Zealand.

After achieving ultimate success devoting her life to New Zealand politics, Clark decided to take on yet another high-pressured job at a time when most people would find it appropriate to retire. The clear deduction from her remarkable life of leadership is that to hanker after another tasking and demanding job after three grueling terms in office as head of her country's government must have meant she had something quite remarkable to offer in her new role.

That remarkable mission, which must have strongly motivated her desire for the UNDP top job, was the intention to radically transform that United Nations organ. That she was intent on building a life beyond a career in politics was also an indication that, apart from genuine self-belief, Clark was always aiming at something. She emphasized that as a leader one needs to think ahead, make feasible plans, leave space for oneself, and continually re-evaluate one's plans and reset one's goals accordingly.

One of the world's greatest reformer-leaders was also the world's first female Prime Minister and non-hereditary head of state. Therefore, by this pre-eminent position, one might surmise that her ascension in itself was a reform, the like that the world had never before seen. Indeed, at that time, female heads of government were a definite rarity.

Sirimavo Ratwatte Dias Bandaranaike was born in 1916 in Ratnapura, Ceylon (present day Sri Lanka). She was first elected Prime Minister of Ceylon in 1960 and went on to serve for three terms, from 1960 to 1965, 1970 to 1977 and 1994 to 2000. Bandaranaike started out as a social worker whose focus was on improving the lives of women and girls in the rural areas of Ceylon. She was thrust into politics when she became an informal political advisor to her husband, who was Prime Minister at the time. When her husband was assassinated, Banadaranaike entered politics and was elected Ceylon's and the world's first woman Prime Minister in 1960. In 1972, she created what was probably the first known ministry of women and child affairs, and appointed the first woman to the cabinet, who oversaw that ministry.

Bandaranaike will go down in history as one of the world's greatest and boldest reformers. During her tenure, she advanced a program of socialist economic policies, neutrality in international relations and encouragement of the Sinhalese language and culture, and practice of the Buddhist religion. She totally reformed Ceylon into a socialist republic, and nationalized the banking industry, as well as the education, media and other trade sectors.

Being a former British colony, Ceylonese had always spoken English as the administrative language. Bandaranaike changed this to the local language of Sinhala.

In her first two terms in office, Ceylon experienced high inflation rates, high taxes, high unemployment figures, and a near-total dependence on food imports, all because of her socialist policies. Furthermore, there was heightened polarization between the Sinhalese and Tamil populations. Despite reducing wealth inequalities among the people of Ceylon, Bandaranaike's socialist policies plagued Sri Lanka into economic stagnation, while her support for Buddhism and the Sinhalese language would all but alienate her from the Tamil minority. As a result, Bandaranaike survived two coup d'états in 1962 and 1971. This traumatic development led to Bandaranaike overseeing the drafting of a new constitution that created the position of an Executive President and the creation of the Republic of Sri Lanka.

Bandaranaike's political career thrust her into the limelight as a trailblazer who was burdened with the twin tasks of decolonizing Sri Lanka, then known as Ceylon, and post-colonial state-building. The assassination of her husband created a leadership vacuum at that very crucial period when the country had embarked on decolonization and restructuring of institutions in the political, economic and socio-cultural spheres. Bandaranaike took over the reins of leadership to preserve the political legacy of her husband, and to carry forward the unfinished task of decolonization.

In her first tenure in office, 1960 to 1965, Bandaranaike continued the nationalization program. She introduced a series of initiatives to strengthen the role of the state in the economic affairs of the country. Her government curtailed the influence of external forces on the country's economy and ensured redistributive justice. In her second term in office, 1970 to 1977, she placed emphasis on attending to the three key elements of the post-colonial state-building process. She assigned a foundation ideology for the state; she built an institutional apparatus and developed a physical and human base to this effect. Under her leadership, there was a prioritization of decolonization and distributive justice. She oversaw the promulgation of the first republican constitution in 1972, effectively severing the constitutional umbilical cord, an integral part of the post-colonial institution-building process.

Between 1972 and 1975, Bandaranaike implemented a land reform package that set a ceiling for land ownership. She was able to achieve this by taking over the plantations formerly owned by the British companies. State institutions were established to manage such lands that were acquired by the state. The role of the state was expanded in day-to-day economic affairs in such a manner as to pave the way for the creation of public corporations.

Bandaranaike's leadership mark also gained visibility in foreign policy. She developed and elevated her country's non-aligned foreign policy to earn global fame. Possessing great negotiating and communication skills, Bandaranaike played an integral role in international relations, quickly becoming a negotiator and leader among the non-aligned nations. Under her leadership, Sri Lanka identified with other developing countries to advance their shared interests in global forums. She spearheaded the Indian Ocean Peace Zone proposal at the United Nations. To further the national interests of Sri Lanka, she pursued an effective South Asian policy. She maintained strong and amicable relations with India and China, and also developed strong links with the Arab world.

If in her long political life Bandaranaike had played key political roles in many capacities, her leadership qualities would become even more pronounced once she was out of power. She was greatly admired as a stateswoman who placed humanity as the centerpiece of all she did. It became normal for many people to seek her audience and advice irrespective of their political affiliations, ethnicity, language or religion. Amidst various political cyclones, she held steadfast and resisted being subdued, and remained a staunch democrat throughout her political career.

Her strength of character reflected in the way she handled the political challenges faced by Sri Lanka as a country during her tenure as Prime Minister, starting with the attempted coup d'état of 1962 by top ranking military officers, and the 1971 youth uprising. She did not lose faith in the people of Sri Lanka and believed in the democratic process even under the most repressive political conditions. As a practical political leader, she demonstrated her capacity to win over other political parties by forming political coalitions through compromise and accommodation. Yet, she was also a very pragmatic and sensible leader. Once, she had this to say about her work as Prime Minister: *"I was often asked the question how I functioned with an all-male Cabinet. I must say that I had no problems. They all cooperated and gave me all the support necessary. Well, I appointed my Cabinet of Ministers."*

Women all over the world will continue to see a role model in Bandaranaike, whose steely resolve enabled her to shatter the glass ceiling to become not only the world's first-ever female Prime Minister and non-hereditary head of state, but who also held the office of Prime Minister three times to set a double and still to be surpassed world record.

The opening quote of this chapter is credited to another powerful woman reformer-leader. Born in the Welsh port town of Barry in the United Kingdom, Julia Eileen Gillard is the first-ever female Prime Minister of Australia. She migrated to Australia with her parents at the age of four. As an outstanding student, she was President of the Students Union of Australia while studying at Melbourne University, from where she graduated with a Bachelor of Arts and a Bachelor of Laws. She worked as a solicitor and partner at a law firm that was focused on employment law.

Her entry into politics commenced with her election as a member of parliament in the Labor Party. She was later appointed Chief of Staff to the Victorian leader of the opposition. She would then serve as Deputy Prime Minister from 2007 to 2010, while simultaneously holding the additional portfolios of Minister for Employment and Workplace Relations, Minister for Education and Minister for Social Inclusion. She was elected Prime Minister of Australia in June of 2010.

As soon as she assumed office as Prime Minister, Gillard formed a minority government with the Greens and Independents. She articulated her vision for Australia and formed a climate change panel consisting of Labor,

Greens and Independent members of parliament. The panel announced its backing for a temporary carbon tax, which led to an emissions trading scheme.

In the belief that it is only the development of skills that can lead to high productivity, she placed education at the top of her socio-economic agenda. Focused on her vision to help her people achieve quality education, her government extended tax cuts to help parents to be able to afford to pay for textbooks, stationery and other school equipment under the Education Tax Refund Scheme. Additionally, she revised the original health funding reforms proposed by the previous government and removed the requirement of states to cede a proportion of the GST revenue to the federal government. In Australia, the goods and services tax (GST) is a value-added tax levied on most goods and services sold for domestic consumption.

Gillard's leadership style encompassed discussion, debate and the sharing of ideas. She encouraged people to feel and get involved in decisions that affected them. She was a complete democrat who subscribed to the notion that everyone, by virtue of their human status, should play a part in group decisions. Well known for excellent negotiating skills that dated from her time as a lawyer and a consensus politician in her party, Gillard also had outstanding communication skills that rendered her quite engaging in parliament. Those skills would prove invaluable when she had to defend her position as Prime Minister of a minority government. Constantly involving all factions of parliament in the decision-making process, her remarkable interpersonal skills helped her build an uncommonly strong foundation of trust with her followers, as a result of which her tenure as Prime Minister was essentially a testimony to truly effective and focused leadership.

In the aftermath of the 2008 financial crisis, Gillard managed to maintain Australia's economy on a low inflation rate, low unemployment and low government debt, with high levels of investment, making Australia one out of 33 advanced economies that experienced positive growth during that recession. Under her leadership, Australia took affirmative action on climate change and passed into law the high-profile clean energy bill.

Her government also introduced an emissions trading scheme which included carbon tax and mining tax, the ultimate aim being environmental sustainability, while boosting government revenue.

One of the areas in which Gillard introduced far-reaching reforms was in the health sector. Her government introduced a health reform package that provided increased funding to public hospitals and improved in-patient and emergency treatment services. Extensive reforms in the education sector were announced, and they led to record numbers of students in universities, and in apprenticeships. In a bid to reduce smoking in the country, the government increased control over tobacco branding through legislation.

Her other policy achievements included children's dental care, national broadband network, national disability insurance and the establishment of the royal commission of enquiry into the institutional responses to child sexual abuse. Under Gillard's able leadership, Australia gained a place as a non-permanent member of the United Nations Security Council, and strengthened relations with major partners including China and the United States of America.

As Prime Minister, Gillard ran a disciplined and professional office. A lawyer by profession, her cabinet processes were efficiently and effectively synchronized despite the massive volumes of administrative and policy paperwork that flowed between government departments, the Office of the Prime Minister and her personal desk. Known for her courtesy to her staff, members of parliament, public servants and other stakeholders, she displayed a compassion and empathy that proclaimed that every person is entitled to a viewpoint and had to be given a chance to express their view before any decision could be taken. She respected everyone, was generous with her time and had such a good sense of humor that she always succeeded in lifting the spirits of everyone around her. Uncommonly skilled at remembering people's names and their stories, and being totally empathic toward their situations, she also understood what motivated them most. These traits helped Gillard navigate the numerous negotiations that were a constant feature of her premiership.

As a woman leading the country, Gillard made significant progress in the sphere of the rights of women and girls. She inspired many young women and girls to believe that they could achieve whatever they put their mind to. In fact, her passion for gender issues remains one of Gillard's strongest legacies. In confronting the pressures of being Australia's first female Prime Minster, Gillard spoke out for women and girls against misogyny in parliament, highlighting the injustice, prejudice and the anger and frustration which women in public service face. What was so powerful about Gillard's leadership was that she did not only stand up for herself, but also used her leadership to stand up for all women in her country. She exhibited great strength, grace and dignity in the very difficult circumstances of a premiership that had to contend with leadership of a minority government.

No matter the level of development of a nation, there will always be laws and statutes that need to be reformed so as to serve the interests of the people better. In no singular sphere does the world and its nations continue to need greater fundamental commitments to reforms than on the question of gender inequality and the rights of women and girls.

One significant reason why the world will need more and more women to be inspired to aspire to, and take up positions of, political leadership is the need for those who will continue to drive meaningful change in the fate of women all over the world. Indeed, there is an ever increasing need for the voices of women to be heard along the corridors of power and influence, if only for the vital reason that the best proponents for reformation in the area of women empowerment are women themselves. Thankfully, more and more countries are increasing the position slots for women in their presidential cabinets.

HOW TO GAIN ACCESS TO YOUR POWER OF REFORMATION

1. You must be able to think far ahead of the crowd.

2. You must be able to make very feasible plans, which you will also continually re-evaluate, sometimes at a moment's notice.

3. You must be fully prepared to be a trailblazer.

4. You must be prepared to sever your ties to a past that no longer serves the interests of those whom you lead.

5. Reforms are, more often than not, all about making life better for human beings. Therefore, allow humanity to become the centerpiece of your work.

6. To carry people along with your reforms, remain open to discussion and debate.

7. Remain in a state of total empathy toward the situation of others, so as to be able to understand what motivates them most.

8. Always aim at something and reset your goals whenever necessary.

9. Leave space for yourself.

CHAPTER 16

THE POWER OF ADVOCACY

"You have to make more noise than anybody else. You have to make yourself more obtrusive than anybody else. You have to fill all the papers more than anybody else. In fact you have to be there all the time, and see to it that they do not snow you under, if you are really going to get your reform realized."

EMMELINE PANKHURST

Advocacy is defined as any action that speaks in favor of, recommends, argues for a cause, supports or defends, or pleads on behalf of others. However, the simplest and most well-known definition of advocacy is to defend or promote a cause. This definition clearly shows that advocacy is very active and not passive. Advocacy is also a broad concept that goes far beyond changing or shaping legislation.

Advocacy also seeks to effect change, secure and promote social justice, shape social and political outcomes, systematically influence decision making, and educate the public with the purpose of bringing about change. These actions are not restricted to just legislative efforts. In fact, we know and understand that changes to long-standing systems and protocols often take place at the local, national and international levels.

Most advocates can also be called activists, yet the terms are not strictly interchangeable. Advocates are more people-oriented, and act on behalf of other people and represent the concerns of others. Activists, on the other hand, are more action-oriented. They take concerted steps to influence social or political change.

Advocates can do so as well, but they tend to approach their own actions from the angle of representing others, which is why advocates are often associated with the concept of working within the system and activists are seen as working outside the same system.

Although advocacy is an action that can be defined as being helpful for a particular cause, advocates do not offer specific services. Rather, they work to assist those who are being negatively affected by institutional systems through various means of supporting, pleading, defending or arguing. Some of the world's greatest female political leaders initially cut their teeth as powerful advocates before ascending to the positions of power that enable them to use their positions to implement some of the major social changes they had long clamored for. On the other hand, some advocates do not end up with political power as such, but have acquired so much influence along the corridors of power that their voices have become as powerful as those of the political leaders.

One of such powerful voices was instrumental to women earning the right to vote in Britain. She was the ultimate advocate. In fact, she was the advocate's advocate. To express it even more succinctly, her life and her work totally define the word advocacy, whatever connotation one might choose to credit the term with.

She was born Emmeline Goulden in 1858 in the City of Manchester in the United Kingdom. She founded the Women's Social Political Union (WSPU) and later created the National Union of Women's Suffrage Societies in 1897, an organization whose singular and focused goal was to advocate for women's suffrage by peaceful means. Over the year, Pankhurst would lead members of the Women's Social Political Union in large demonstrations for women's right to vote. Expressed in clearer terms, her name, life and work would become synonymous with the 40-year campaign for women's right to vote in Britain.

In campaigning so ardently for women to achieve the right to vote, she also galvanized women for the fight to gain the same electoral rights as their male counterparts. In successfully leading the militant campaign for women's parliamentary vote in Britain, Pankhurst demonstrated remarkable leadership qualities that included vision, passion, self-belief, charisma, influence, strength and flexibility. She was made aware of the importance of social justice at a very young age, as she was barely 14 when her parents introduced her to the women's suffrage movement.

As a leader of the suffrage movement, she exerted great influence over her followers despite their reservations. In fact, despite those reservations, she was still able to challenge them to rise as one, to further their cause through strength and militant action. This was a feat she was able to achieve because of a combination of self-confidence, self-motivation, passion, empathy, great determination and an incomparable degree of moral rectitude. She would personally motivate her followers, through her own protests and demonstrations, to be ruthless in their endeavor for equal rights for women. Blessed with tremendous foresight, she took care to identify and subscribe to all the required protocols that were needed for her voice to be heard in a male-oriented environment.

In February of 1918, nine months before the end of World War I, the British parliament passed the Representations of the People Act, also known as the Fourth Reform Act, which granted men aged 21 and over the right to vote, regardless of whether they owned property or not, while only women over 30 were granted the right to vote, as long as they met specified property qualifications. Women's right to vote at the age of 21 and above was only granted in 1928, the same year in which Pankhurst passed away.

Today, Emily Pankhurst is remembered in statues, museums and art works all across the United Kingdom. Yet, she remains a controversial figure in British history because of her tactics. She was unrepentantly radical, yet it was her uncommonly bold approach to civil rights that made great change possible for women of all ages and all backgrounds. When the usually peaceful protests for women's enfranchisement by the suffragist movement proved unsuccessful, Pankhurst mobilized the women to adopt more militant protest tactics. What really stood out in terms of her leadership ability was her willingness to persevere, and to do whatever it took to achieve results. Women were astounded at Pankhurst's self-confidence and passion while leading. History remembers her for having the strongly moralistic approach that totally defined her as a genuine and inspirational leader.

Pankhurst's enthusiasm for the suffrage cause was infectious enough to inspire followers whose belief in her determination and commitment to improving the rights of women was total and unequivocal. She suffered incarceration numerous times and on which she embarked on hunger strikes. She deployed her power and influence by working through her committee members. She was, and is still, admired and respected for her unwavering commitment to her cause, and for how she involved women from all classes and backgrounds in the fight for equality.

She undertook militant acts that went far beyond the expectations of most people, in the process inspiring generations of women leaders who joined her to sustain the fight to see the right to vote extended to all women. She used her influence to change not only the prevailing thinking of the time but to also change individual belief patterns. Inspired by such other women's movements in the United States at that time, she organized protests and demonstrations in Britain throughout a career in which she endured humiliation, prison, hunger strikes and repeated frustration. Her bravery in rising to be the guiding light of the suffrage movement, and her ability to stand up for what she believed was right, even if she stood alone, ultimately earned her the hero badge.

Close to the end of her life, during World War I, Pankhurst stopped her militant suffrage activism and redirected her time and energy toward the war effort. She encouraged men to fight and motivated women to help with industrial production in the absence of the men. She was a staunch believer in the war effort and regularly organized rallies, while spurring the British government to encourage women to take up jobs previously held by men. In 1999, *TIME* magazine included Pankhurst in their 100 Most Important People of the 20th century. In 2019, on the 100th anniversary of the commencement of women's right to vote, Pankhurst's achievements were honored with the unveiling of a new bronze statue in Manchester, the city in which she was born. A statue, erected in 1930, already memorialized her in the Victoria Tower Gardens in London. Pankhurst left an enormous legacy for future generations, and she remains venerated as the singularly most significant leader in the struggle for women's rights and equality in Britain.

As might be reasonably expected, powerful voices of advocacy also tend to be pioneers in many more respects than one. Also, their lifetime work tends to defy the tendency to be constrained to one single issue, and is usually much more varied and multi-directional. That is the story of Mary Therese Winifred Robinson's involvement in world affairs, and in the affairs of her country, Ireland.

Robinson was the first-ever female President of Ireland. She is a lawyer who began her political career in 1969 as a senator in the Irish legislature. She also served as the catalytic United Nations High Commissioner for Human Rights. She served as the seventh President of Ireland from December 1990 to September 1997. Born in 1944 into an affluent, elite Catholic family of doctors, her upbringing strongly influenced her sense of righteousness and integrity. Robinson attended boarding school at Trinity College in Dublin, later studied in Paris and broadened her experience at Harvard University in the United States.

Her broad professional experience working as a barrister, professor and a senator was characterized by involvement in many different roles that included lobbying for minority groups, and taking on controversial cases that challenged the Irish constitutional statutes on issues of life, divorce, abortion, contraception and homosexuality. As soon as she embarked on her public career, Robinson established herself as a lifelong advocate for various causes by totally refining her social justice discourse, and began to be identified with her willingness to fight for others.

In 1990, she accepted the nomination as the Labour Party's candidate in the presidential elections, which she won convincingly to become the first-ever female President of the Republic of Ireland. Although her elitist background initially seemed a significant point of social divergence from the people she served, it actually gave her the opportunities and expertise to fight for their rights. The historical, social and cultural contexts of her upbringing would, in effect, act as a catalyst for the development of her own unique and authentic narrative. As senator, she advocated for a range of liberal positions which included the rights of women and girls, especially the need to end the requirement that women resign from public service upon marriage. While in office, she signed two important bills that were high points of her career as a long-standing advocate, the first one being the full legalization of contraception, and the other being the decriminalization of homosexuality.

Both in office as President of Ireland, and as United Nations High Commissioner for Human Rights, Robinson employed the power of charismatic leadership to engender change far beyond the formal authority of those positions. She has been known to use symbols and verbal communication to articulate her vision for the realization of human rights for all. From the outset, Robinson exhibited an intellect that appreciated diversity and valued change for good. She kept her eyes focused on the path that led to greater and more equitably distributed rights for all. As she continued on that path, she crafted a holistic and comprehensive vision that was consistently committed to the singular goal of elevating the status of human rights, both in the practice of governance and as a commitment to social action.

During her tenure as President, she not only stimulated a moral sense of duty in the people of Ireland, but she also inspired them to envision a better future by imagining exciting and ennobling possibilities, thereby changing the perception of the Irish people from seeing themselves as victims of discrimination, economic depression and displacement to that of a people who could enact change for their own ultimate good. Robinson's transformational leadership was a study in a committed leader's ability to empathize and inspire others to follow her own personalized ideals, which she presented with a form of charisma that encouraged others to also see her authentic values as their own moral compass.

Robinson became the United Nations High Commissioner for Human Rights in September 1997, having resigned the presidency of Ireland a few weeks earlier to take up the post. At the time, reports were rife that she had actually been deliberately head-hunted for the post by then United Nations Secretary General, Kofi Annan, for the sole purpose of assuming an effective advocacy as opposed to a purely administrative role.

As it happened, at that point in time, the post of United Nations Human Rights Commissioner appeared to have gradually sunk into a largely bureaucratic one, and Annan probably felt there was a compelling need for a new commissioner who would be a public campaigner outlining principles rather than one who would stick to the old and well-worn implementation and consensus-building model. Robinson's role was clear. She was needed to re-establish a more proactive and principle-based human rights agenda within the organization and internationally, and to decisively refocus its appeal. Robinson was a perfect fit for the job for the very simple reason that she was a born advocate.

Robinson would end up being hailed as a staunch defender of human rights, and she carried her vision of a just world to her position as the United Nations High Commissioner for Human Rights, a post she occupied from 1997 to 2002, and in which she worked successfully to implement sweeping reforms to integrate human rights considerations into all the activities of the United Nations. Upon the completion of her term as United Nations Commissioner for Human Rights, she founded Realizing Rights, an initiative on ethical globalization that advocated for the needs of the world's marginalized through the process of globalization.

She further established the Mary Robinson Foundation for Climate Justice, a center for thought leadership and education advocacy on the struggle to secure global justice for people who are vulnerable to the impact and effects of climate change, and for facilitating action on climate justice for the empowerment of such poor and marginalized people. Her foundation advocates for the achievement of sustainable and people-centered development, calling for a Marshal Plan-styled agreement on climate change to ensure global access to renewable energy and acknowledging its role in tackling poverty.

Throughout her long career, Robinson has demonstrated a unifying thread and a steadfast commitment to bringing coherence and direction to her endeavors through her commitment to improving the human condition using the instrumentality of the principles of human rights. In her working life, she occupied many prominent roles, working on issues as varied as climate change, the rights of women and girls, and poverty alleviation.

Robinson's commitment to improving the human condition through human rights was to continue with her later position as chair of The Elders, a unique leadership model that allows for structured, collaborative guidance from various lifelong advocates and public servants who have personally navigated their own paths through the complexities of large-scale societal transformation. The forum brings together a group of independent global leaders who were originally convened by Nelson Mandela to utilize their independence, influence, collective experience and diverse perspectives to work on peace building, poverty eradication, a sustainable planet, justice and human rights, and the reduction of human suffering worldwide.

Robinson continues to serve in several roles at the United Nations and other international organizations, as well as academic institutions and advisory councils, in addition to speaking at various international conferences. She has been honored for her outstanding leadership qualities with several honorary doctoral degrees from various academic institutions across the globe, in addition to a multitude of other prestigious awards, honors and accolades recognizing her contributions to the global institutionalization of human rights. Robinson can be safely declared to have acquitted herself most creditably in the sphere of contributions to the building of a global order founded on the universal principles of human freedom and dignity.

Far away from the British Isles, across the Atlantic, another powerful advocate arose on the Southern African sub-continent. Joyce Hilda Banda made history when she was sworn in as Malawi's fourth President to become the first-ever woman to serve as President of the Republic of Malawi, following the sudden death of Malawi's incumbent President in 2012. She also became the second female President in the history of the African continent and the first in Southern Africa.

Before becoming President, Banda had served in various roles including being member of parliament, Minister of Gender, Child Welfare and Community Services, Minister of Foreign Affairs and Vice-President of Malawi. Born in 1950 in a village in Malawi, Banda obtained her Bachelor's degree in Gender Studies from the Atlantic International University, an online university based in the United States of America, and a diploma in the management of NGOs from the International Labor Organization Centre in Turin, Italy. She also obtained a Master of Arts degree in Leadership from the Royal Rhodes University in Canada. The university of Jeonju conferred an honorary doctorate degree on her in 2013.

Banda later founded the People's Party, an opposition political party in Malawi. Before venturing into politics, she was already a remarkable and successful businesswoman and philanthropist. She owned and ran various businesses and charitable organizations, including a garment manufacturing concern and a bakery. In addition, she established the Young Women Leaders Network, the Hunger Project, and the Joyce Banda Foundation which addresses rural development and improving the lives of women and children in Malawi.

Banda is a dyed-in-the-wool advocate. An educationist and grassroots women's activist, Banda has been championing women's rights in Malawi and other parts of the world for decades. As Malawi's Minister of Gender, Child Welfare and Community Services, she was the arrowhead of the enactment of the Bill on the Prevention of Domestic Violence and designed the National Platform for Action on Orphans and Vulnerable Children, as well as the Zero Tolerance Campaign Against Child Abuse. As soon as she became President, her government announced the intention to overturn Malawi's ban on homosexuality, with the support of the majority of members of parliament, making Malawi the second country in Africa to legalize same-sex sexual activity. The country suspended laws criminalizing homosexuality.

Banda was also instrumental to the establishment of various international women's organizations, including the African Federation of Women Entrepreneurs, which has operations in over 41 countries in Africa, as well as the Council for the Economic Empowerment of Women in Africa; and the American and African Business Women's Alliance, where she served as the organization's first President. She also served concurrently as a visiting fellow at the Wilson Center and as board member of several other development organizations, including the Executive Advisory Committee of UNIFEM, the Global Leaders Council for Reproductive Health, and the Scientific Advisory Board for the Program in Global Health and Social Change at Harvard Medical School.

Banda has demonstrated consistent commitment to maternal health and reproductive rights through her support of safe motherhood in Malawi. She also supported the Presidential Initiative on Maternal Health and Safe Motherhood, which within two years would record a significant reduction in maternal mortality rates in the country.

As President of Malawi, one of Banda's more compelling challenges was how to restore diplomatic relations with aid donors and neighboring countries like Mozambique and Zambia, and other countries in the Southern African sub-region, including Botswana. In her inaugural speech, she had articulated a vision for Malawi that included moving into the future as a united country, with hope and the spirit of oneness. As soon as she assumed office, her government launched a diplomatic offensive to repair Malawi's international relations with the wider world, rekindling relations with the United Kingdom's Foreign Office and sending a new envoy in the shortest possible time.

She commenced talks with the United States, who promised to resume negotiations on an outstanding energy grant to Malawi. Banda also resumed negotiations with the European Union Foreign Affairs Office and the International Monetary Fund. To attract donor funding, Banda devalued the country's local currency, the Malawian kwacha, against the United States dollar. An empath to the core, she announced her intention to reduce her presidential salary to benefit the Malawi Council for the Handicapped.

Banda will go down as a transformational leader who, within a relatively short period of time, was able to reinvigorate the country's governance. Arguably, she provided Malawi with the sort of leadership that her three male predecessors and many other African heads of state and heads of government in the region had failed to provide in the past. While most of such leaders demonstrated a purely authoritarian and autocratic disposition to leadership, she exhibited the compassionate leadership that was capable of uniting the people of a poor and fragile nation.

Her people-centered policies of good governance and vision of growth for Malawi all served to mobilize the people of Malawi to support her goals. Her key objectives were to provide opportunities for Malawians that would accord them access to better education, better healthcare, economic prosperity and the ability to be able to have a voice to express themselves politically and freely, and in a safe and secure environment. To that end, her policies were focused on strengthening the schools and the education system, improving clinics and hospitals, developing new water and irrigation resources, reducing corruption in the country, and uplifting the people by giving them a real sense of purpose and belonging. While also rapidly repairing and re-instituting relations with donor and neighboring countries in the Southern African sub-region.

Because Banda was able to sever ties to the prevailing political culture of her male predecessors, her tenure in office as President was largely seen as a triumph for democracy. Her leadership qualities earned her various awards, honors and accolades. CNN voted her Leading Woman of the Year in Politics in 2014. She was also recognized as among the most powerful women in the world, and as the most powerful woman in Africa by *Forbes*, while the BBC included her in its list of 100 Most Influential Women.

Advocacy at all levels will always remain an integral part of what can make society better on all fronts. The collaboration of advocate-leaders with political leaders will always bring about more rapid and effective changes. Changes, of course, become much easier to effect when advocates find themselves in positions of political authority.

Fundamentally, however, we will continue to need those who can effectively disseminate accurate information about the issues faced by communities in such a way as to sway both public and governmental opinion and bring about change. In essence, therefore, the world will continue to need more political leaders to rise from the background of very powerful and influential advocacy, and for such leaders to use the instruments of high office to give teeth to their powerful voices.

HOW TO GAIN ACCESS TO YOUR POWER OF ADVOCACY

1. You have to make more noise than anybody else, and you have to make yourself more obtrusive than anybody else.

2. You have to demonstrate remarkable leadership qualities that include vision, passion, self-belief, charisma, influence, strength and flexibility.

3. A strong voice in advocacy demands a very broad mind that a solid educational background can confer on you. Insist on being thoroughly educated.

4. You must be able to inspire others to subscribe to your own personalized ideals.

5. You must be someone who genuinely empathizes with disadvantaged people.

6. You should possess the sort of charisma that encourages others to see your authentic values as their own moral compass.

7. Apart from a sincere belief in a cause, you also need a very strong sense of commitment to that cause.

8. You must be ready to jettison old and prevailing cultures that do nothing to further the interests of the people.

9. You must be there all the time and see to it that you do not get snowed under.

10. You must stand up for what you believe is right, even if it means standing alone.

CHAPTER 17

THE POWER OF MILLENNIALS

"The fact that I'm the third female Prime Minister,
I never grew up believing gender would stand in
my way of doing anything I wanted."

JACINDA ARDERN

From all empirical indicators, this is contemporaneously the age of millennial leadership. The millennial generation defines those born between 1981 and 1996. Studies have shown that what we experience and are taught during our formative years will largely dictate our basic value system for life. Like any other generation, millennials have been influenced by the times in which they have lived, and their major life events have included the 9/11 terrorist attacks and the advent of technology. In fact, they are the first full technology generation.

As a result of these times, and the teachings of those formative years, millennials are generally optimistic about the long-term future, even though they are also uncertain about the short-term future because of the drastic events that have intruded into their otherwise ideal growth experiences. Millennials seem to have a sense of selflessness that leads them to engage in social actions that make a difference. They generally possess a strong core value of teamwork, perhaps because they want to be part of something larger than themselves.

When the members of a generation advance to a new life stage, they almost invariably end up demonstrating changes that are dramatically different from previous lifestyles and patterns. For instance, millennials are already reshaping early adulthood as we used to know it. Certainly, compared to previous generations of young adults, they are postponing marriage, postponing children and sampling a wider variety of jobs, with some having been employed by an average of seven different full-time employers by the age of 30. Significantly, also, many of them are finding it more and more difficult to start careers due to large-scale unemployment occasioned by economic issues, a scenario that is perfectly exemplified by the current coronavirus pandemic.

Of greater significance, millennials are most definitely changing our traditional ways of viewing leadership. It is estimated that in less than two years, millennials will become the largest employee group on Earth. In any case, they have already become the major influence shaping the future of both leadership and work, as the greater majority of baby boomers approach retirement age. Leadership patterns are already undergoing remarkable transformations as this new generation take on the helm of leadership all across the world. For one thing, authoritarian leadership is gradually giving way to inclusive leadership. The emerging trend is a leader who directs, not commands. Long gone are the days when the leader can be a dictator who is disconnected from her followers. In fact, millennials seem to prefer the term *leader* to *boss*.

Millennials also crave direct connections with leadership teams, believing that everyone in the leadership cadre should be accessible, regardless of title or seniority. This more linear method of leadership goes a long way in building trust, loyalty and dedication. As leaders, millennials place a high premium on open government and corporate settings, with less emphasis on hierarchy. They strive to create an inclusiveness in which everyone is given an opportunity to have a voice, regardless of position or title. That is why millennial leadership is also highly collaborative. Millennial leaders consult with peers, mentors and advisors before making crucial decisions. With their networks always at the tips of their fingers, they can quickly consult with their trusted circle of advisors to source the solution to a teething problem.

There are certain reasons why millennials are now, more than ever, prepared to assume leadership roles. Millennials are beginning to come of age and are entering into their 30s, and with a decade or more of experience under their belts, they are getting primed for bigger roles in politics, government and the corporate world. Millennials have officially become the largest generation on Earth, and because there is a growing power vacuum as leaders from older generations retire or climb even higher, millennials present the largest pool of candidates to fill the void. Millennials crave autonomy, and being so confident in their skills they are driven to take charge of more people and more responsibilities.

Overall, millennials are leading in ways that are remarkably different from their older generational counterparts. They value regular feedback. This urge for feedback and their understanding of its importance has been carried into leadership positions. Naturally, as leaders, they will be able to exercise the power to use such feedback to institute powerful changes in the system. Millennials, who tend to be more optimistic and more adaptable when it comes to new technologies, are beginning to institute more advanced platforms, and at a faster rate than their predecessors. They trust the power of technology and know that adopting better systems is the most efficient way to make better decisions.

Millennial leadership generally subscribes to greater flexibility and fewer constraining rules. Yet, millennial leadership may actually demand greater adherence to an ethical culture and core values. Values have always been an important cultural institution for millennials, and it is anticipated that they will continually create and enforce those values within the context of their leadership teams. On an anecdotal note, millennials themselves are beginning to age, and will likely be looking over their shoulder as the next generation, referred to as generation Z, start to rise through the ranks. That means millennials will soon join their generation X and baby boomer counterparts to complain about a new host of youthful characteristics. Until then, millennials are still having their brief period of enjoying the energy of youth alongside the valuable experience necessary to drive true changes in the world, especially in the current perilous and traumatic times.

No leader in the contemporary annals of the world better illustrates the vitality and unique enterprise of the millennial generation than Jacinda Kate Laurell Ardern.

She was born on July 26, 1980, guaranteeing her an indisputable place on the honors roll of leaders born at the incipience of what we now characterize as the millennial generational era. She was elected to office in 2017 to become the third female and youngest Prime Minister of New Zealand at the age of 37 years. She is the second female elected head of government in the history of the world to have given birth to a child while in office, springing to global attention when she took her baby along to attend the United Nations General Assembly.

Ardern has been hailed as an embodiment of the best attributes of the people of New Zealand, which include optimism, common sense, approachability and empathy. She captivated the world with the incomparable courage and exemplary leadership she demonstrated as Prime Minister in the wake of the atrocious terrorist attacks on a mosque in Christchurch in 2018 in which a number of Muslim worshippers were killed, while others were injured.

Her iconic approach to leadership and communication in giving voice to her nation's grief rang throughout the four corners of the globe. She demonstrated that real leadership can be imbued with genuine love, empathy and compassion by giving the people of New Zealand the unique language with which to convey their revulsion at the unprecedented attacks. As a leader, Ardern undoubtedly connected with the emotions that the people of New Zealand were experiencing, turning herself into both comforter and mourner-in-chief in her heroic bid to help the people of New Zealand deal with their collective national grief.

New Zealand is a nation comprising more than 200 ethnicities and 160 languages. In dealing with that tragedy, Ardern deftly bypassed linguistic and ethnic differences to unite the people of New Zealand as one people with shared common values. She exhibited a new style of political leadership that reinforced the idea that leaders must have empathy and compassion for others by consciously choosing their words and actions with scrupulous care, while focusing on kindness, compassion and generosity.

In shifting the focus from the gunman to the victims, Ardern chose the more meaningful path of empathy and inclusivity to deal with the tragedy. For instance, she opted to wear a hijab while visiting those affected by the attacks, and addressed parliament with the Arabic greeting of *As-Salaam Alaikum*. Her linguistic skills helped the country at a time when it would have lost its moorings. She employed inclusive language to send out a message that resonated with all New Zealanders, and which fitted perfectly with her drive to consciously celebrate New Zealand's diverse cultures rather than attempting to homogenize them.

In addressing families, she ensured that she used notable and appropriate words from the indigenous Maori language, and pledged that the Maori language would be taught in all schools in New Zealand by the year 2025. Ardern further announced that her government would cover the funeral costs for the victims and offered financial assistance to the affected families.

There is no doubt that Ardern made her impact as an influential leader with the manner in which she handled the Christchurch terrorist attacks of 2018. Her political response in the face of atrocity was not only progressive but she also deployed courageous leadership and nerves of steel to be able to lead with confidence and compassion in those times of chaos and tragedy. In the immediate aftermath of the shootings, she mobilized politicians to tighten gun laws in the country and announced an immediate ban on assault rifles and military-style semi-automatics.

She also called a national lunchtime prayer which was broadcast live to a worldwide audience. She stood with Islamic leaders and hugged the grieving in a show of respect and compassion. Where the incident could have easily created a resounding social rift, Ardern united the nation through tactful leadership. She single-handedly reduced Islamophobia in her country and other parts of the world. Ardern showed the world what quick and decisive leadership should look like. Indeed, Ardern's leadership qualities were brought to the fore by the quick manner with which she handled the Christchurch tragedy.

Her greatest strengths are empathy and compassion, which she unhesitatingly displayed through her sensitive and feminine side. Ardern's leadership style is filled with love, empathy, care, gentleness – all the skills that are considered to be lacking in the masculine ego-centered world of power. Leading with love rather than hate has always been Ardern's key message. She will be remembered for leading her country with hope amidst intense sadness, and she did it with the swift and decisive action of a confident and constructive leader.

If Ardern can be said to have captivated the world with her sterling leadership in the wake of the Christchurch terrorist attacks, her performance two years later, in the midst of a pandemic that is easily the most devastating in the 5,000 years of recorded human history, would earn her acclaim as possibly the most effective leader on the planet. Simply put, her leadership style, still focused on empathy, didn't just resonate with her people but also placed her country on track for success against the globally ravaging coronavirus. It is said that the coronavirus pandemic may be the biggest test of political leadership the world has ever witnessed. Every leader on the planet was facing the same potential threat.

Expectedly, leaders reacted differently, yet every leader will eventually be judged by the results. Jacinda Ardern forged a path all her own. Her messages remained clear, consistent, sobering and soothing. To quote a predecessor in the same office, Helen Clark, Prime Minister of New Zealand from 1999 to 2008, *"People feel that Ardern doesn't preach at them; she's standing with them. They may even think, 'Well, I don't quite understand why the government did that, but I know she's got our back.' There's a high level of trust and confidence in her because of that empathy."* That is extraordinary endorsement from a former occupant of Ardern's office. Helen Clark added, *"She is a communicator. This is the kind of crisis which will make or break leaders. And this will make Jacinda."*

At the height of the coronavirus pandemic, one of Ardern's innovations was frequent Facebook Live Chats that were both informal and informative. During one such session conducted in late March of 2020, just as New Zealand prepared to go on lockdown, she appeared in a well-worn sweatshirt at her home, just after putting her toddler daughter to bed, for the purpose of offering guidance *"as we all prepare to hunker down,"* as she empathically put it. She sympathized with how alarmed the people must feel by the emergency alert message that essentially informed New Zealanders that life as they knew it was temporarily over. She proffered helpful concepts, such as thinking of *"the people who will be in your life consistently over this period of time as your bubble, and acting as though you already have COVID-19 toward those outside of that bubble."*

She justified government's severe policies with practical examples. For instance, *"You need to stay local, because what if you drove off to some remote destination and your car broke down?"* She announced that she expected the lockdown to last for several weeks, and for cases to rise steeply even as New Zealanders began holing up in their homes. Because of how the coronavirus behaves, *"we won't see the positive benefits of all of the effort you are about to put in for self-isolation for at least 10 days. So don't be disheartened,"* she encouraged.

As early in the pandemic as March 2020, New Zealand was already unique in staking out a national goal of not just flattening the curve of coronavirus cases, as most other countries had aimed to do, but to actually eliminate the virus altogether. COVID-19 testing was widespread and more than adequate. The health system was not overloaded. While new cases peaked in early April, only 12 people had died as at that month. Although, geographically speaking, as a collection of relatively isolated islands at the bottom of the South Pacific, New Zealand was always in a favorable position to eliminate the virus, it is also undeniable that Ardern's government took decisive action right from the onset of the pandemic.

New Zealand imposed a national lockdown much earlier in its outbreak than other countries did in theirs, and banned travelers from China as early as February 2020, before New Zealand had registered a single case of the virus. It closed its borders to all nonresidents in mid-March 2020 when it had only a handful of cases.

In dealing with both the Christchurch terrorist attacks and the coronavirus pandemic, Ardern has been widely acclaimed for naturally empathizing with New Zealanders, while remaining a strong and courageous leader. How she cared and led the country at the same time, and how she did not appear to be preoccupied by her own emotions and reactions, remains a remarkable feat very few leaders are able to achieve.

In October 2020, Jacinda Ardern was elected for a second term as Prime Minister of New Zealand. To commence her new term, she appointed what has been hailed as the most diverse cabinet in New Zealand's history, with indigenous Maori ministers making up a quarter of its 20-strong members and eight posts going to women. Ardern also nominated a gay person as Deputy Prime Minister, and appointed a Maori woman as Foreign Affairs Minister, the first time a woman has held the post in the history of New Zealand. Despite her party winning enough seats to govern, she gave the Green Party two ministerial posts to secure its co-operation in government, this move would give Ardern a commanding parliamentary majority.

While becoming Prime Minister at the age of 37 speaks of great ambition, authority and competition on her part, Ardern never abandoned who she really was as a person, and did not find it necessary to suppress her emotions and natural instincts by adopting the aloofness common to the average politician. For instance, the way Ardern handled her maternity period while in office was innovative, and she never tried to deviate from her personal life but simply showed that it was perfectly permissible to take time to care for oneself without jeopardizing the stability of the work of government. In the final analysis, Jacinda Ardern will probably go down in history as a redoubtable role model for millennial leadership.

Millennial leadership once more took the center stage of global attention when Sanna Mirella Marin, at the age of 34, became the world's youngest serving Prime Minister and the third woman to lead Finland. She entered politics at the age of 27, became a member of parliament at the age of 30, and became Finland's 46th Prime Minister four years later. She had risen through the ranks, having previously been Minister of Transport and Communications. Marin took over as leader of the Social Democratic Party when Finland's former Prime Minister left office. She gained entry into the Guinness World Book of Records when she was sworn into office in December 2019. As a millennial leader, Marin pledged to focus on climate policies at the European Summit in Brussels, just two days after being sworn into office as Prime Minister of Finland.

Marin had a challenging childhood growing up in a same-sex family at a time when this was considered taboo, and her family was not recognized as a true family by many people. She was also the first in her family to go to university. She graduated with a Master's degree in Administrative Sciences from the University of Tampere in 2017. Right from the onset, Marin made her vision clear to make Finland become a better country, and to build a society in which every child could become anything they wanted to be, and in which every human being could live and grow to old age with dignity.

Finland has an epochal history in the realm of women's rights. It was the first country in Europe to grant women the right to vote in 1906. The country is often regarded as something akin to a utopia because it serves as a great example of what a big-spending socially liberal government can achieve. Finland has a well-funded universal education system that is among the most successful in the world. Between 2017 and 2019, Finland ran one of the world's first trials of universal basic income.

Behaving in a most atypical manner for a politician, when Marin became Prime Minister, she talked openly about her upbringing in what was termed a rainbow family in which both her parents were female. Yet, it was both parents that greatly influenced her upbringing, inculcating in her the values that would stand her in good stead as a politician. She also revealed that she grew up in a disadvantaged family. This background allowed Marin to grow into a strong individual who viewed the world through the lens of uncommon empathy.

She strongly defends her country's position as a very generous welfare state from which she has greatly benefited. Her vision and mission for a better Finland, and the building of a better society, include the provision of free day care for all citizens. Free education for all children has since become a reality and mandatory in Finland. Her other priority as leader of Finland is to create jobs, and to cut greenhouse gases and make Finland a carbon neutral country by the year 2035.

At the age of 27, Marin was elected to the city council. She swiftly rose through the ranks to become head of the council of Finland's third largest city, Tampere. Thereafter, she served as Chair of the city council, and was a member of the Assembly of the Council for the Tampere region. In 2014, she was elected deputy chair of the Social Democratic Party, and in 2015 she was elected from the electoral district of Pirkanmaa to Finland's parliament. In June 2019, she was appointed Minister of Transport. In December 2019, she was selected to the leadership of her party when the incumbent left office. Marin's young age is a great advantage within the context of a new generation of millennial leaders who also totally represent a new generation of politicians that are inspiring the world.

As Prime Minister, Marin heads the first-ever coalition government that is run by an all-women coalition of political party leaders. The four other parties in the coalition are headed by women, three of whom are still in their 30s. The all-women's coalition has become significantly symbolic of the rise of a new political dispensation in Finland that is characterized by a high number of women politicians. With 47% women in parliament, this is the first time in decades that Finland has had such a strong female representation in national politics.

With all the leaders in the parties of her coalition being women under the age of 35, Marin heads a new beginning in the world of politics. Marin believes that a joint government program is what effectively glues her coalition together. She took over as Prime Minister in the middle of a three-day wave of strikes that had halted production at some of Finland's largest companies. It was estimated that the strikes would cost a combined total of US$550m in lost revenue.

Marin is representative of just how peculiar millennial leadership can be in many respects. In her own case, she overcame the hurdles of a challenging childhood to become a strong individual with admirable characteristics and leadership qualities. Despite becoming the center of media attention when she was sworn in as Finland's third female and the world's youngest Prime Minister, she continued to exhibit a humility that is infectious. She has made it clear that she did not bask in the media attention she received when she assumed office as much as concentrating on the fact that her new government had a lot of work to do. She also intimated that she has never thought about her age or gender, but has rather been focused on the reasons for her entry into politics and those things for which her government had won the trust of the electorate.

The best way to conclude this chapter will necessarily be how best to help millennials continue to grow as leaders, whether they are in a leadership position already or simply on the path to one. Almost any situation, in politics or any other setting for that matter, can be turned into a learning opportunity. Jacinda Ardern proved this by graduating from effectively managing the aftermath of her country's terrorist attacks of 2018 to even greater competence at managing her country's handling of the coronavirus pandemic in 2020. Millennials should be given the chance to lead. If they start from modest beginnings, and they prove that they can handle the attendant responsibilities, they should be given even greater roles to play, as seen in the case of Sanna Marin of Finland.

Nurturing millennials to positions of leadership is not about giving them the keys to a castle they haven't yet earned. It is about showing them the steps to take to get those keys. Millennials need measurable goals to which they can be held responsible for achieving. Providing millennials with goals to work toward helps them understand how their role fits into the bigger picture.

Millennials can present a bit of a contradiction. They crave both independence and instruction at the same time. The key is finding the balance between them receiving instruction and evolving on their own. One indisputable fact, however, is that the average millennial will always relish a challenge. When they feel trusted and know they have the support of their leadership team, they will often admirably exceed expectations. Indeed, millennials are changing the way we view leadership for the better.

HOW TO GAIN ACCESS TO YOUR POWER OF MILLENNIALS

1. Aim to be a part of something bigger than yourself.

2. Refuse to be disconnected from your leadership team and those whom you lead.

3. Adopt a linear method of leadership that goes a long way in building trust, loyalty, and dedication.

4. Strive for a collaborative and inclusive style of leadership.

5. Seek regular and useful feedback.

6. Aspire to the form of leadership that is imbued with genuine love, empathy and compassion.

7. Habituate yourself into the swift and decisive action of a confident and constructive leader.

8. Insist on turning every experience into a learning opportunity.

9. Be humble enough to start from modest beginnings.

10. You will need measurable goals to which you can be held responsible for achieving.

EPILOGUE

WHAT THE FUTURE HOLDS FOR FEMALE LEADERSHIP

As this book draws to an auspicious close, the one conclusion we can safely arrive at is that future generations of women leaders will need to muster the courage, cultivate the character, and acquire the skills and confidence needed to command respect and authority for effective and influential participation in the global agenda.

The 21st century, more than any other, presents incredible opportunities for women to reassert their position in the gender dynamics, and to be the custodians of legitimate positions of authority that can influence the direction of the global agenda in politics and business. The 21st century woman has the burden of breaking down residual barriers that have held women back for centuries. She will need to have unshakeable self-belief and to unlearn the traditional mindset and social conditioning that have established irrational limits on her full potential.

The heartwarming news is that the future of gender dynamics on the political pedestal is remarkably encouraging. Among some of the initiatives toward gender parity is the allocation of gender electoral quotas aimed at increasing the number of women in political decision-making roles. Quotas have also been introduced in corporate boardrooms to increase the number of women in business decision-making roles. Yet, there is a paradox to all these. Although quotas seemingly pave the way for the increased participation of women in politics and in business, the very notion of quota apportioning implies that women have to seek permission from men to participate at such high levels of influence.

Additionally, because those quotas are decided by those in authority, who almost invariably are men, to express gratitude for such consideration, women appointed to these positions through quotas will, in most cases, be expected only to serve to preserve and protect the interests of the men who put them in those positions rather than the interests of their fellow womenfolk, let alone their own interests. That is why the next generation of women leaders will need to acknowledge that the age of the token woman sitting on the board is over. Women will no longer be needed just to make up the numbers. The next generation of women leaders will be needed to make and influence real decisions in the boardroom, in the senate, in congress, and in parliament.

The 21st century woman will need to utilize all her talents, strengths and wisdom to inspire change, and to lead humanity as a whole to a future of gender equality in order to attain human prosperity and progress for all. To achieve this feat, she will need to lead without necessarily having to seek permission. She will need to be assertive and to believe that it is actually politically correct for her to compete and contribute to social, economic and political activity on an equal footing with her male counterparts, and without feeling that she is overstepping her boundaries to compromise their masculinity.

Democracy is defined by The Economist Intelligence Unit in 2010, as *"a set of practices and principles that institutionalize and thus ultimately protect freedoms... a government based on majority rule and the consent of the governed, the existence of free and fair elections, the protection of minority rights and respect for basic human rights, including equality before the law, due process and political pluralism."* In a nutshell, democracy is the government of the people by the people, and in this age of intensified global democratization, it is widely acknowledged as the preferred form of government due to its emphasis on citizens' equal rights and equal participation in politics.

Also, owing largely to its principle of inclusiveness, democracy is supposed to drive gender parity and subsequently lead to an increase in the number of women in political office. Therefore, it only follows from commonsensical reasoning that a democratic regime as a form of governance should be the vehicle that would drive gender parity in the political decision-making process. The time has come to employ the utility of democracy for renewed and greater effort at encouraging and increasing women's participation in political decision making. Such steps will serve to build on the gains of past initiatives like the Women's Suffrage Movement, the United Nations Convention on the Elimination of All Forms of Discriminations Against Women (CEDAW), the Beijing Platform for Action, as well as the introduction of Electoral Gender Quotas.

Our 21st century world is under an obligation not to willfully squander the opportunity presented by the intensified drive to democratize the world through the globalization of politics. At the risk of sounding repetitive, the quest for democracy is attributed to its principles of inclusiveness, equal participation and equal rights. Globalization promotes democratization, which in itself fuels pressure for the political reforms in which groups and interests can confidently seek a political voice. Therefore, we can assume that with increased democratization, the number of women in political decision making in the world will increase accordingly.

Happily, gender parity in politics has been at the top of the global agenda. Following the United Nations call for gender parity in politics, many countries including Sweden called for 50% women in parliament and other political offices. Addressing the Fifth Global Colloquium of University Presidents in Pennsylvania in the USA, former United Nations Secretary-General Ban Ki-moon reiterated the call, saying, *"Women represent half of the world's population… and should have their fair share in making decisions."* At an event to mark International Women's Day in March 2011, then United States Secretary of State Hillary Clinton echoed the UN's call, saying, *"No government can succeed if it excludes half of its people from important decisions."*

There is no better illustration of what the future might possibly be incubating for female leadership than the emergence of Kamala Harris on the front lines of the very crucial 2020 American presidential race. Born on October 20, 1964, Kamala Devi Harris was elected Vice-President of the United States on a joint ticket with Joseph R. Biden. As at the time of her election as Vice-President, she was serving a first term as the Democratic senator representing California, a seat she had been elected to in 2011, making her the first Indian-American and second African-American woman to serve as a U.S. Senator. Coming from a background of mixed parenthood, with a Jamaican father and an Indian mother, Harris first studied political science and economics to obtain a 1986 B.A. from Howard University. Later, she earned a 1989 law degree from Hastings College. Subsequently, she was Oakland's Deputy District Attorney from 1990 to 1998, a position in which she earned a reputation for uncommon toughness as she prosecuted cases of drug trafficking, sexual abuse and gang violence. Expectedly, she rose through the ranks to become District Attorney in 2004. In 2010, winning by a hairbreadth margin of just one percent, Harris was elected Attorney General of California, making her the first female and the first African-American to hold the post.

She was the first African-American, the first Asian-American, and the third female vice presidential running mate on a major American party ticket after Geraldine Ferraro in 1984, and Sarah Palin in 2008. She is the first Indian-American, and the second African-American woman to serve as a United States senator. She had previously served as California's Attorney General from 2011 to 2017. After a brilliant outing at the 2012 Democratic National Convention, a rising national profile presented her as a very promising politician to her party, and she was encouraged to run for a U.S. Senate seat that she won with relative ease. In the Senate, she has served on both the Select Committee on Intelligence and the Judiciary Committee; committees on which she became famous for her prosecutorial style of questioning witnesses during hearings, a prominent example of which was the attention she drew for her questions to U.S. Attorney General Jeff Sessions who was testifying before the intelligence committee on allegations of Russian interference in the 2016 presidential elections.

Shortly after publishing her memoir, *The Truths We Hold: An American Journey*, she sought the Democratic presidential nomination in 2020. Seen, right from the outset, as a leading contender, she attracted particular attention when, during a primary debate, she engaged fellow candidate Biden in a rather contentious exchange over his opposition to school busing in the 1970s and 1980s, amongst other race-related subject matters. Later in the year, after dropping out of the nomination race, she notably became a front-line advocate for social-justice reforms, close on the heels of the May 2020 death of African-American George Floyd in police custody. Although she later opted out of the nomination race, amidst the call by many democrats for Biden, the party's presumptive presidential nominee, to select an African-American woman as running mate, a demographic strategy that was considered crucial to his election chances, Harris emerged his vice-presidential running mate in August 2020, making her the first Black woman to appear on a major party's national ticket.

As this book was going to press, the world was greeted with the totally wholesome news that, after the narrowly-contested polls of November 2020, Biden received the requisite electoral college votes to become the 46th President of the United States of America. By the same token, Harris emerged on the threshold of history to become America's first-ever female Vice-President, automatically paving the path towards the rare possibility of Harris becoming the first-ever female President of the United States of America. Harris has made history in many remarkable ways. She is the first American female Vice-President. She is also the first Black person, and the first Asian-American person to serve in the office of Vice-President of the United States. Without any semblance of equivocation, the rise of Harris is an enormously significant moment in the eventful trajectory of female participation in the world's largest democracy. Not unnaturally, it is all the more significant that this occurred in the year of the centennial celebration of the 19th Amendment to the American Constitution, which guaranteed American women the right to vote. Naturally, also, it finally lays to rest any lingering myth about the very slim possibility of American women getting elected to the highest offices in the land. Of greater significance, it sends a clear message that the political and leadership fortunes of women and girls are on the ascendancy in the United States.

In conclusion, I am left with no other choice than to unequivocally declare that women need to become increasingly more connected to issues of good governance and best practices in our global community, and in becoming more engaging in definitive initiatives eventually become a force for good by bringing light, inspiring change and creating positive impacts all the way from local neighborhoods to the global stage. This must be the individual dream of each woman. It must be the collective dream of all women.

FURTHER READING

1. African Union. (2010). *Gender Equality and Women's Empowerment: African Women Decade.* African Union.

2. Allen, P. & Cutts, D. (2018). *How Do Gender Quotas Affect Public Support for Women as Political Leaders?* West European Politics.

3. Ara, F. (2019). *Barriers to the Political Participation of Women: A Global Perspective.* Society & Change.

4. Bagilhole, B. (2002). *Four Non-Traditional Occupations for Women: Women in Non-Traditional Occupations.* Palgrave Macmillan, London.

5. Boserup, E. (1970). *Women's Role in Economic Development.* Earth Scan Publishing, UK.

6. Bradberry, T. & Greaves, J. (2009). *Emotional Intelligence 2.0.* Talent Smart, San Diego.

7. Buter, M. (2012). *Prophetess Alice Lenshina, God's African Commander: Her Generational Blessings and Legacy.* Tremendous Wealth Publishers, London.

8. Covey, S. (2004). *The 7 Habits of Highly Effective People: Powerful Lessons in Personal Change.* Simon and Schuster.

9. D'Anna, E. (2020). *The Technology of the Dreamer.* Austin Macauley Publishers Ltd.

10. D'Anna, S.E. (2009). *The School for Gods.* University of Buckingham Press.

11. Dahlrep, D. (2005). *Women, Quotas and Politics.* London, Routledge Publishing.

12. De Geus, R.A., McAndrews, J.R., Loewen, P.J. & Martin, A. (2020). *Do Voters Judge the Performance of Female and Male Politicians Differently? Experimental Evidence from the United States and Australia.* Political Research Quarterly.

13. Eagly, A.H. (2013). *Gender and Work: Challenging Conventional Wisdom.* Harvard Business School.

14. Fedi, A. & Rollero, C. (2016). *If Stigmatized, Self-Esteem Is Not Enough: Effects of Sexism, Self-Esteem and Social Identity on Leadership Aspiration.* European Journal of Psychology.

15. Ferreira, F. & Gyourko, J. (2014). *Does Gender Matter for Political Leadership? The Case of U.S. Mayors.* Journal of Public Economics.

16. Gifford, Z. (2007). *Confessions to a Serial Womaniser: Secrets of the World's Inspirational Women.* Blacker Limited.

17. Goleman, D. (2003). *The New Leaders: Transforming the Art of Leadership into the Science of Results.* The New Edition. Sphere Publishing.

18. Goleman, D. (2007). *Social Intelligence: The New Science of Human Relationships.* Arrow Publishing.

19. Goleman, D. (1996). *Emotional Intelligence: Why It Can Matter More Than IQ.* Bloomsbury Publishing plc.

20. Government of Rwanda. (2010). *National Gender Policy.* Ministry of Gender and Family Promotion, Government of the Republic of Rwanda.

21. Greene, R. (2000). *The 48 Laws of Power.* Profile Books.

22. Haley J. (2006). *NGO Leadership Development: A Review of the Literature.* Praxi Paper 10. INTRAC.

23. Hansen, E.R. & Clark, C.J. (2020). *Diversity in Party Leadership in State Legislatures.* State Politics & Policy Quarterly.

24. Hessami, Z. & da Fonseca, M.L. (2020). *Female Political Representation and Substantive Effects on Policies: A Literature Review.* European Journal of Political Economy.

25. Hinflaar, H. (1994). *The Bemba Speaking Women of Zambia in a Time and a Century of Religious Change (1892-1992)*. Studies of Religion in Africa. E. J. Brill Leiden, The Netherlands.

26. Irwin, T. (2014). *Impact: Great Leadership Changes Everything*. BenBella Books Inc., Dallas, Texas.

27. Jones, J. J. (2016). *Talk 'Like A Man': The Linguistic Styles of Hillary Clinton, 1992-2013*. Perspectives on Politics.

28. Kabeer, N. (2003). *Gender Mainstreaming in Poverty Eradication and the Millennium Development Goals: A Hand Book for Policy Makers and Other Stakeholders*. Commonwealth Secretariat, CIDA, IDRC/2003 -01-10.

29. Karpowitz, C.F. & Mendelberg, T. (2014). *The Silent Sex: Gender, Deliberation, and Institutions*. Princeton University Press.

30. Keenan, L. (2018). *Women in Political Life: The Case of the Republic of Ireland*. Tara Ireland.

31. Kellerman, B., Rhode, D.L., O'Connor, S.D. & Books, I. (2007). *Women and Leadership: The State of Play and Strategies for Change*. J-B Warren Bennis Series.

32. Koch, M.T. & Fulton, S.A. (2011). *In the Defense of Women: Gender, Office Holding, and National Security Policy in Established Democracies*. The Journal of Politics.

33. Krotel, S.M.L., Ashworth, R.E. & Villadsen, A.R. (2019). *Weakening the Glass Ceiling: Does Organizational Growth Reduce Gender Segregation in the Upper Tiers of Danish Local Government?* Public Management Review.

34. Lau, V.W., Bligh, M.C. & Kohles, J.C. (2020). *Leadership as a Reflection of Who We Are: Social Identity, Media Portrayal, and Evaluations of Hillary Clinton in the 2016 U.S. Presidential Election*. Sex Roles.

35. Maxwell, J.C. (1995). *Developing the Leaders Around You*. Thomas Nelson.

36. Maxwell, J.C. (1998). *The 21 Irrefutable Laws of Leadership.* Thomas Nelson.

37. Mbabazi, (2013). *Women's Post-Genocide Success.* Vision News, Rwanda.

38. McDonagh, E. (2009). *The Motherless State: Women's Political Leadership and American Democracy.* The University of Chicago Press, U.S.A.

39. Merkle, O. & Wong, P.H. (2020). *It Is All About Power: Corruption, Patriarchy and the Political Participation of Women.* Springer International Publishing.

40. Morgan, J. & Buice, M. (2013). *Latin American Attitudes Toward Women in Politics: The Influence of Elite Cues, Female Advancement, and Individual Characteristics.* American Political Science Review.

41. Murray, A.F. (2007*). From Outrage to Courage: Women Taking Action for Health and Justice.* Common Courage Press.

42. OECD. (2013). *Gender and Sustainable Development: Maximising the Economic, Social and Environmental Role of Women.* OECD Paris.

43. OECD. (2013). *Social Institutions and Gender Index (SIGI).* OECD Paris.

44. Okonjo-Iweala, N. (2012). *Reforming the Unreformable: Lessons from Nigeria.* MIT Press.

45. Parpart L. J. et al. (2000). *Theoretical Perspectives on Gender and Development.* International Development Research Centre.

46. Peterson, J.B. (2019). *The 12 Rules for Life: An Antidote to Chaos.* Penguin.

47. Philips, A. (1995). *Politics of Presence.* Oxford University Press, U.S.A.

48. Pitkin, H. (1967). *The Concept of Representation.* University of Chicago Press, U.S.A.

49. Potrafke, N. & Ursprung, H.W. (2012). *Globalization and Gender Equality in the Course of Development.* European Journal of Political Economy.

50. Ramose, M. (1999). *African Philosophy through Ubuntu.* Indiana University.

51. Ryan, M.K., Haslam, S.A., Morgenroth, T., Rink, F., Stoker, J. & Peters, K. (2016). *Getting on Top of the Glass Cliff: Reviewing a Decade of Evidence, Explanations, and Impact.* The Leadership Quarterly.

52. Salovey T. & May J.D. 1990. *Emotional Intelligence.* Baywood Publishing Co. Inc., New York.

53. Scholastic. (1996-2011). *History of Women's Suffrage.* Scholastic.

54. Tal, D. & Gordon, A. (2018). *Women as Political Leaders: a Bibliometric Analysis of the Literature.* Society.

55. The Quota Project. (2010). *Global Database of Quotas for Women.* The Quota Project.

56. UN Women. (2019). *Women in Politics: 2019.* United Nations.

57. United Nations. (1995). *The United Nations Fourth World Conference on Women: Platform for Action.* United Nations.

58. United Nations. (2000-2009). *Convention on the Eliminations of All Forms of Discrimination Against Women.* United Nations.

59. United Nations. (2006). *About the Millennium Development Goals. Goals, Targets and Indicators.* United Nations.

60. United Nations. (2009). *African Union Gender Policy.* United Nations.

61. Von Rueden, C., Alami, S., Kaplan, H. & Gurven, M. (2018). *Sex Differences in Political Leadership in an Egalitarian Society.* Evolution and Human Behavior.

62. WHO. (2017). *Country Profiles: MDG Goal 3: Promote Gender Equality and Women's Empowerment.* World Health Organization.

63. World Bank. (2009). *Gender Equality as Smart Economics.* World Bank.

64. Zandberg, J. (2010). *The Philosophy of Ubuntu and the Origins of Democracy.* Lulu.com

ABOUT THE AUTHOR

Justina Mutale has for years consistently advocated for gender equality and the empowerment of women and girls. In 2012, she was named African Woman of the Year. She is Founder and President of the Justina Mutale Foundation, through which she advocates for gender equality and the empowerment of women and girls in political participation and economic empowerment by providing leadership and entrepreneurship training and mentorship.

Justina also advocates for the retention and completion of tertiary education for young women from rural and disadvantaged families in Africa by providing them with scholarships to access tertiary education around the world. Justina previously worked in the gender section of the Commonwealth Secretariat and has been a consistent delegate, speaker and parallel event convener at global forums that address political, economic, social, African and gender issues.

Justina lives in London with her two daughters and a puppy. She leads and serves on various boards of commercial, humanitarian and charitable organizations across the globe, and has been honored with numerous international awards, honors and accolades for her outstanding leadership qualities.